MY FANATICAL, Regrettable TOUR OF MINISTRY

*Memoirs of a Zealous Leader
who Trips Landmines in the Church*

Ron Mahler

MY FANATICAL, REGRETTABLE TOUR OF MINISTRY

Copyright © 2011 by Ron Mahler

All rights reserved. Neither this publication nor any part of this publication may be reproduced or transmitted in any form or by any means, electronic or mechanical, including photocopying, recording or any information storage and retrieval system, without permission in writing from the author.

All Scripture quotations, unless otherwise indicated, are taken from the Holy Bible, New International Version®. Copyright © 1973, 1978, 1984 by Biblica US, Inc.®. Used by permission. Scripture quotations marked KJV are taken from the Holy Bible, King James Version, which is in the public domain.

ISBN:978-1-77069-305-0

Word Alive Press
131 Cordite Road, Winnipeg, MB R3W 1S1
www.wordalivepress.ca

Library and Archives Canada Cataloguing in Publication

Mahler, Ron, 1967-
    My fanatical, regrettable tour of ministry / Ron Mahler.

ISBN 978-1-77069-305-0

    1. Mahler, Ron, 1967-. 2. Clergy--Canada--Biography. I. Title.

BR1725.M335A3 2011   277.1'083092   C2011-903577-4

Dedication

Elaine, you're an amazing woman and you've always been my biggest fan. Your rewards are great. All my love.

Cassidy and Dakota: this is for you.

Table of Contents

Preface 1	Strengthened 133
Great Expectations...................4	The Seeker Bug 137
Bigger! 9	Tire Kicking 142
Epiphany 15	Candidating…Again! 146
Exchanges 19	Saddled Up 151
The Sermon 28	Test Drive 156
Searching 31	Inventory 161
Emulation 37	Bull's-eye 166
Revelations 42	Devil's Manifesto 171
New Groove 47	Stringent Opposition 176
Precious 53	War Rooms 181
Lift-off 56	The Violence of the Lambs 186
Maiden Voyage 60	Exiting 191
The Staff 64	Aftermath 195
Riot Act 69	Grace 200
Nuptials 75	Transition Redux 206
Restless 78	Inquisition 211
Change Awakenings 83	In the Moment 215
Second Thoughts 87	Sparring Partners 219
Divisions 92	Sliding Doors 225
Gathering Storm 95	Difficult Decisions 229
Sick and Tired 98	Blind Acceptance? 233
Overboard 103	Digging Deeper 237
Faulty Wiring 107	Worship 243
Taking the Bait 110	Statements 249
Protests 114	Hello, Goodbye 256
Affronts................................118	Ministry Perspectives 263
Enough 121	Learning Curves 267
Heartaches 125	Future Hope 284
Home Cooking 129	Endnotes 287

"Success is not final. Failure is not fatal.
It is the courage to continue that counts."
—*Winston Churchill*

Preface

Every once in a while, a new book comes along that is dubbed a "must read." I have purchased and read quite a few of these books. The book you hold in your hand, however, at one point held a very different status; it was a "must finish." Though I have spent three years writing this book, it has been in the works for over forty years! That's because it's a book about my life; more to the point, about my time serving God as a pastor in church ministry. Completing it has been a little like nursing an obsessive habit; wherever I went, my laptop and book went with me. I even made sure that the book's document file on my computer, the copy of it on my memory stick, and the updated printed copy were never in the same place for very long—in case of fire.

I know it sounds crazy, but the whole experience makes me feel like I've been sitting on an egg for the last three years, waiting for it to hatch! Far from being an exercise in reliving past hurts and disappointments, working on this project has been a convicting and therapeutic endeavour. Writing it has forced me to reflect upon and further process the many trials I have experienced as a leader in the church. Interestingly enough, I never aspired to be a "writer," per se. Like other pastors who have been preaching for a good number of years, I have written a ton and instinctively know the mechanics involved in putting together a three-point sermon. Writing a book, however, has been an entirely different, and rather arduous, task.

Ron Mahler

Initially, I sensed a personal need to begin putting my thoughts down on paper. My sole intention was to journal through my feelings about how some of the unfortunate events I've encountered in the pastorate have affected me as a child of God. That naturally led me to digress even further back in my life. The result was not only a re-evaluation of the steps that led to my call to the pastorate, but an autopsy on how my life, in B.C. time (before Christ), conditioned and shaped who I am now as a man and leader.

I felt it necessary to write not only for my own emotional and spiritual benefit, but in passing along some of my own hard lessons serving as a pastor it has become a ministry to other leaders in the church.

In the course of my writing, I heard a saying that went like this: "The world will tell you who you are, until you tell world who you are." These words arrested me as I began to relate them to the trials I've experienced as a leader in church ministry. Almost instantly, I felt that my motive in writing this book was affirmed. From that point, the basis for getting this work "out there" was born.

Jesus Christ, as my personal Saviour, continues to change my life; that much I *do* know! However, in terms of some of the struggles and painful failures that mark my years in ministry, God has given me a choice as to how I want them to affect me. I have chosen to believe, therefore, that though trials threaten to deflate our faith and siphon our hope, they don't have to flatten our dreams.

In this book, you'll find that I have covered a vast array of spiritual themes and issues pertaining to the Christian life. At times I speak from the perspective of a Christian leader, where at other points I shoot from the hip simply as a Christian man. This book is not a thesis on how to decipher the vocational call of God upon one's life, though you will surely find traces of how God led me to embrace His will for me. This book is not a manual for formulating church growth, either, even though I do interject some of my own findings on that convoluted subject. Lastly, though the book never claims to reveal the steps one needs to take in order to become a great leader, I do discuss some key learning curves and ministry insights that have been impressed upon me.

So what is this book really about? I begin by presenting a snapshot of my upbringing in a broken home, my personal struggles to come to faith in Christ, and my subsequent call to ministry. I document some of the more dominant trials I endured in the first four churches I ministered in as a pastor. I address, as well, the plethora of challenges I encountered within the cultures of churches, challenges that envelop almost every facet of church leadership.

My Fanatical, Regrettable Tour of Ministry

This is a book that I hope will be beneficial for other leaders, especially those who are feeling alone and stuck in seasons of criticism and conflict. But if you feel called to vocational ministry, this book may also be for you. Finally, it is a book for believers who may feel bogged down in the spiritual quagmire of perceived personal inadequacy and professional failure. If you have blundered greatly in the ministry and wonder whether you could really be trusted by God and used of Him again, I definitely advise you to read on!

Please note, however, that this book raises more questions about the complexities of church leadership than it provides answers. I realize that there's always more that can and should be learned and experienced about church leadership, so take my writings for what they are. I haven't got it all figured out; I simply aim to draw biblical conclusions that directly relate to my own experiences.

Therefore, I invite you to read of my fanatical, regrettable tour in the ministry. It may be a familiar one to some and foreign to others. Yet if my story encourages, ministers to, promotes dialogue in, comforts, or teaches anyone, I'll consider my mission to be accomplished. It is my prayer that you enjoy reading about my tour in the ministry, and will see something of your own life reflected in these pages—whether you are in the ministry, or not.

Though the events described in this book are very real, the names of the individual churches and people I refer to (predominantly pastors) have been altered, to preserve privacy. Indeed, this book is not intended to be an indictment against the character of anyone whom I have been associated with in ministry. I have no illusions of where my proper place is in the Kingdom of Heaven. There is only One Judge who has the right to pronounce a final, perfect verdict on our lives, and I, like you, will face Him one day. We are all flawed servants of God who say and do things we can later regret. Ministry is difficult, and if we could all go back and do things differently, we would. Although it may seem at times that I have some sort of axe to grind, I can unequivocally assure you that I do not. Life is too short, and forgiveness and mercy too rich of spiritual treasures, to waste!

CHAPTER 1
Great Expectations

WHEN I WAS FIVE YEARS OLD, MY FIRST CAREER ASPIRATION WAS TO BE A FIREMAN. It's hard to believe now, considering I can't stand overly warm summer days. At that age, a child believes he can be anything, even President. Such is the whimsical freedom to dream and imagine as a child. I still miss that.

Adulthood, with its broadened horizons and harsh realities, can leave one, well, jaded. I chased a number of dreams as a young boy growing up in small-town Cape Breton, Nova Scotia. I even flirted with becoming an astronaut. There was something mysterious and alluring about looking up at the awesomeness of the vast night-time sky, something about wearing a spacesuit and soaring into the great beyond—at least, some place higher than my treehouse! This dream would not enjoy much longevity. As I got a little older, I discovered that heights and I weren't as compatible as I first thought.

That said, soaring into space continues to fascinate me. I figure I'll experience something like it at the Rapture; for now, I'll settle with watching movies like *Apollo 13* and eating Mars bars. Today I relive much of my childhood quest for space through my son Dakota. I often catch him lying in bed, staring up at the ceiling wishing it was space while manoeuvring his Iron Man doll high up over his head.

In addition to those youthful ambitions, I recall being fascinated with what I referred to as "oilmen." Not the tycoon sort, a la J.R. Ewing, but those who would come around to homes and fill up oil tanks with fuel. Whenever the local oil truck pulled up to our house, I would ask my mother what the man's name was, as well as what colour the oil was. This prompted me to take a stroll around my neighbourhood to examine every oil tank I could find.

What captivated me wasn't the big truck, the distinct smell of fuel, or even the greasy look of the oilman; rather, I was into the details of what I was observing. I have always been a detail person. I can recall, for example, the actual dates of various world events, and even what the weather was like on those days. As well, I could list off at least four significant things I did, or experienced, each year for the last twenty years of my life. It sounds freaky, but I just have that sort of memory.

Paying attention to the broader detail of a given situation is something I seem programmed to be able to do. Most likely, I have spent a large amount of my life preoccupied with the deep recesses of my mind. As a result, a good number of people over the years have described me as being *pensive*. Oxford's Dictionary defines "pensive" as "deep in thought."[1] That word describes me to a T. As a child, I was so preoccupied in my own headspace that it was rather noticeable whenever I came up for air!

My elementary school teachers would say I was quiet and reserved. In reality, however, I found it a chore to articulate what was going on in my mind. It may have looked like I was disengaged, unhappy, or even off on a distant planet, yet my mind was never vacant.

In fact, I've always felt mentally fatigued by ideas and possibilities that often overlap and swim through my mind. To this day, I have difficulty shutting off my brain when I go to bed; though the bedroom light goes off, my mind still seems stuck in the "on" position. Some things never change, for that was me as a child—always thinking, always wondering, always experimenting, always observing. In some ways, I was different from the other kids around me. It didn't take much for me to imagine being like someone else—like a cartoon character, athlete, or movie star.

At the age of six, I would watch a hockey game on a black and white TV in our family living room. That would seem normal enough for any red-blooded Canadian boy. However, instead of getting caught up in the game, I would wonder what colour the players' jerseys were. I remember hoping with all my might that somehow our old Zenith would come to life and magically give birth to living colour.

As a child, I possessed a Daffy Duck transistor radio. I took it with me most places I went, and the music (mostly on the AM dial) provided me with summer anthems for many years back in the late 1970s. I would even plunk the radio on the front doorstep of the house and listen to baseball games. I would hang on every word of the commentator's play-by-play. Before most games were televised, I imagined what the sights and sounds were like, what a "home run swing" looked like, and how fast the ball left the park.

The radio was my own personal connection to the outside world, which many days brought my vast baseball card collection to life. Now and again, this led me to simulate a game of my own. My backyard was converted into a baseball diamond, myself taking on the role of pitcher, hitter, manager, and even the fans. I acted out everything that was stockpiled in my head in terms of sounds, images, and possibilities.

Ask anyone in my family and they'll tell you that I always had a penchant for doing creative things. To a certain extent, I now attribute some of that to not having much in the way of material items. Even so, I did have some cherished possessions to call my own. I was the proud owner of a few G.I. Joes, some army men, a few cars, crayons and colouring books, lots of dirt outside, and an older dog… and whatever I didn't have, I made up for with, you guessed it, *imagination*.

Come to think of it, I was completely and utterly oblivious to what it meant to possess more than what we had as a family. What a simple existence to foster and forge something from practically nothing! Ideally, having little means a person must make the most of what they *do* have. In principle, having little, materially, should motivate one to depend on something else, to compensate for it. For me, that required utilizing my creative capacities in the form of thinking, wondering, experimenting, and observing.

Case in point: when we were quite young, my siblings and I were periodically dragged off to the odd funeral. I can still see it, us children shuffling ever so timidly toward another open coffin, getting just close enough to stare at the latest stiff. We often wondered why we had been brought to the church for such an experience, and what it all meant. All I knew was that the person in the pine box wasn't moving one bit. After each funeral, we would experience interment, another life-shaping event I tried to wrap my mind around.

I think back on my childhood questions and how they were never fully answered. Where was that dead person now? Why do we bury them? My way of processing these observations was through experimentation. I would bury my prized G.I. Joe action figures, as well as some plastic cavemen figurines. I assure you, it didn't lead to any high enlightenment—only tears, when I later couldn't

My Fanatical, Regrettable Tour of Ministry

find where I had buried them in the yard. Yes, in hindsight, the developing, inquisitive mind of a youngster can be a comical thing!

One of the things I have learned as a parent is to sit back and appreciate the moments when I catch my own children doing interesting things, even if they border on the bizarre. Parents can usually spot these priceless moments, such as the time when I stepped on one of my son's Batman action figures, wrapped in wet, red-marker-stained toilet paper. Dakota may not bury his toys, like I did, but apparently he does wound them! I guess I can relate to that, in a sick sort of way!

Both of my children seem to share in my childhood penchant for elaborate artwork. They come by it honestly! I can see myself in them, in terms of how they imaginatively reconstruct what they observe from their environment. When I was seven years old, I became more self-aware of the fact that I could draw better than the average kid in my class. My teachers used to stare idly at my drawings, then glance back at me with "You made this?" looks in their eyes.

My identity as a young boy was being pigeon-holed, if not chiselled down and rounded off; I was a pensive, detail-oriented child who had a natural (God-given) ability to draw. Once while I was still living in Cape Breton, I was asked to illustrate the cover of our elementary school's fall brochure. I chose to draw a picture of a man raking leaves in front of a house. Most people were amazed at the final product.

As a result, my legend grew in the county! I was going to make the Mahler family famous, and all of Cape Breton, for that matter. I couldn't miss! Names like *Da Vinci* and *Rembrandt* were unknown to me at the time, and yet I was told I could be a famous artist one day. In all honesty, I didn't know what the word "famous" really entailed, but I took a shot at it, inquiring, "You mean, like the Beatles?"

So engrossed was I in doing artwork that I used to ask my mom to buy me blank pads at the grocery store so that I could draw continuously. Morning, noon, and night, I would flip a new page and just sketch whatever image came to mind. It came to the point where my mom automatically added blank drawing pads to her shopping list. Then there were the Christmas presents, where lots of drawing utensils annually awaited me under our tree.

All this is to say that my family's projections for my life were predictable. If I was going to be anything in life, chances were I was going to be an artist of some kind.

In 1974, when I was seven years old, our family moved to the city of Toronto. The transition was nothing short of horrific for me. Collectively, we as siblings were all teased to varying degrees. For one thing, I looked different than the average city kid; my hair was not only long and stringy, but being the youngest in my family, I was still wearing my cousins' hand-me-downs. The pants I wore always made me look like I was on stilts, and they invited a steady stream of jokes—according to the other kids, I looked as if I was "waiting for a flood."

I also spoke with a noticeable maritime accent, not to mention I had a stutter. This new shaggy-haired, oddly-dressed import from out of province couldn't help but sorely stick out. These variables led to me being picked on by other kids in school, a pattern that followed me for a few years.

When I was in Grade Six, my art teacher openly praised my artistic prowess in the class. That was a tragic moment for me. No doubt, the teacher intended it to be an encouragement; unfortunately it led to me having to deal with jealous classmates. They let me know this in the schoolyard. I got wrangled into many altercations, even fisticuffs at recess, and then again after school. If it were not for my sister Laurie coming to my aid, let's just say my body might look different today. Whenever she was told that there was someone beating up her brother, Laurie would run to the scrum, whirling her skipping rope like a rancher lassoing a steer. Upon arriving at the scene, she would dare my assailants to keep it up! She had a great way of clearing a crowd. This became a recurring scene. Consequently, she would become my official bodyguard. If we had been in prison, her yard name would have been "The Equalizer!"

As my sister's rescues mounted up, so did my plethora of reputations. The overriding one was that I was the guy who had his sister fight his battles for him. In my dark moments, between the schoolyard conflicts and the persistent unfamiliarity of city life, I would wonder why we as a family couldn't just go back to Cape Breton, back to the simple life. Why couldn't I go back to burying my G.I. Joes, to contemplating the colour of hockey jerseys, to dreaming about space? I missed our home, our spacious property, and that old dog of ours we had to leave behind. Yet we were in the big city now, and my father would always assure us that we could make a better life for ourselves in Toronto.

CHAPTER 2

ONE OF THE FIRST THINGS I NOTICED ABOUT LIFE IN THE CITY WAS HOW everything appeared so much *bigger*. Naturally, the roads were bigger. There were bigger cars (and more of them) than what I was used to! Even city people seemed to be bigger than the people in Cape Breton. I had never seen tall skyscrapers in person before; they appeared to be even bigger than how I had perceived them on television.

As a newly adopted city slicker, I came upon a classic moment in my life. It happened as our overloaded van barrelled down the Gardiner Expressway in downtown Toronto. As rows of sights and sounds whipped past my eyes, I suddenly caught view of the newly constructed CN Tower for the very first time. With my face pressed against the window, I couldn't constrain myself from blurting out, "Wow! Look at that big pen!" I could hardly bring myself to believe that my world, as I had previously known it, included something that big.

I saw more during those poignant moments along the expressway than I ever had in the first seven years of my life. In that instant, G.I. Joes, oilmen, and even astronauts were rendered insignificant. I was certain that the whole wide world was displayed right in front of me, and it was *big!*

After we got more established in our rented Toronto home, my father arranged for the daily delivery of the newspaper. Not a big deal, right? Newspapers today line convenient store shelves. On the internet, we can locate practically any news publication in the world. However, as a born and bred small-town seven year-old, there was something monumental to me about a newspaper subscription. I had never seen newspapers so big, thick, and saturated with information.

I resolved that there must be much more news in Toronto! When I told you I came from a small town, I meant a *really* small town; the kind where if you sneezed, you stood a chance of missing it! The bustling metropolis had so much to offer, contributing to my fascination with images, events, people, and stories. To my young, impressionable mind, all these stimulants only added to my development as an up-and-coming artist. Though my family had already witnessed flashes of my innate flare for experimental creativity, they weren't quite ready for my entrepreneurial side! Everything I found so interesting about the big city was encapsulated in the pages of the newspaper. Being a creature of habit, I began to recreate all that I had observed by combing the pages of each newspaper issue.

In fact, I was so inspired by the legion of images, headlines, and stories that populated my mind that eventually I founded my very own homemade newspaper. My "newspapers" consisted of a vast array of made-up reporters, columnists, photographers, and editors. Every edition included a front page (with headlines), a sports section, reviews, and even classified ads. For the life of me, I cannot recollect a single event I wrote about, or what I found to be so newsworthy at the time. However, I can recall combining fictional people and events with those of a "real life" nature. I literally folded and sectioned each paper.

Thinking back now, most of my family members weren't quite sure how to react to what they were seeing me produce on almost a weekly basis. They would pick up a newspaper, chuckle as they flipped through it, and even stare back at me in a similar way to how my childhood teachers used to, with that "You made this?" look on their face. Actually, it was probably more a "Ronnie, you're a freak!" facial expression.

These homegrown newspapers turned our house into a bit of a museum. Before friends and visitors left our home, my family would almost always comment to them, "Oh, you have to have a look at these papers Ronnie is doing." One thing was for certain, I was the same, pensive, detail-oriented child as ever. Though I was geographically transplanted from my Cape Breton roots, my creativity bridged the distance. I continued to process all that I observed in the world by acting it out in some form or another. However, the innocence and ignorance of my childhood was awakened by an alarm of cold, harsh reality. The grey areas of life—the areas in between the black and white certainties of my childhood mind—gained more clarity with each passing day.

My Fanatical, Regrettable Tour of Ministry

You could say that I was starting to see things in sharp Technicolor. With this change in perception came the painful realization that my parents' marriage of over twenty years was in trouble. Big trouble! Their marital discord led to separation (when I was ten years old), and then to a bitter divorce by the time I was fourteen.

During their four years of separation, as you might imagine, our whole family entered into a lengthy season of struggle, both psychologically and financially. Tucked in the middle of it all were simmering issues incubated in the heat of Broken-Home Syndrome. From low self-esteem to acceptance and identity issues, my older sisters and I encountered them all.

My mother suffered in other ways. Having minimal options for employment, she was forced to take a physically demanding job in a linen factory in order to make ends meet. Unfortunately, because we couldn't afford a nicer place to live, my mother and us lived in a big, bug-infested house for nearly five years.

After six years in the big city, I grew even more restless; not with a desire to go back to Cape Breton, but with a hankering for someone, anyone, to lead our family to something or somewhere better. I didn't know where that place was, or even what it would look like; I just longed for an escape from our circumstances.

There were certainly times when I was oblivious to the realities facing our family. My sisters and I made our own fun and simply tried to be like the other kids in our neighbourhood, despite the fact that we were fairly cognizant that the other families around us seemed to have it "together." However, even in the isolated and blissful moments when my sisters and I manufactured some form of childhood frivolity, challenging circumstances would inevitably arise from our parents' situation.

The resilience of our childhood experiences would often wear thin, only to be replaced with a weighty cloak of hopelessness. As a family, it felt at times like our father had dragged us off to Toronto only to drop us and leave us to our own devices. Thankfully, we knew from our mother's actions that we were loved. This was evident in how she endured laborious employment in order to provide enough money for our pressing needs. She made sure we had a good supper every night. If there is one memory of my mother that I appreciate even more today, it is how selfless she was. Mom often stretched her paycheque to purchase us the odd item we wanted; she did this by sacrificing the things she wanted for herself, things she chose to live without.

Like many women of her era, my mother would stay up late mending our clothes, arranging items in our school lunch boxes, and generally making sure that everything was ready for the next morning's rush out the door. Whenever

Ron Mahler

we needed a sympathetic hug, she was there for us. As a result of our mother's strengths, our father's shortcomings were all the more magnified. Consequently, we couldn't help wondering why we weren't good enough for Dad.

At one time, before my birth, our family was off to a relatively good start. My parents lived in the United States, but they moved the family to Canada after the death of my brother, Richard, in New Hampshire. Prior to his accidental drowning at the age of four, my parents and four older siblings enjoyed some semblance of a normal, even happy life.

My parents' decision to move to Cape Breton was actually a homecoming for my mother, a native of Nova Scotia. It served as a kind of healing reboot for the Mahler family. Even moving to Toronto eight years later was supposed to hold promise for further healing, supplying the impetus we needed to keep moving forward. Although my father was never a demonstratively affectionate man, he did consistently provide for the family, financially, working as an electronic technician. My mom was able to counterbalance the lack of warmth in his demeanour. Mom was the "soft" touch that often pacified my dad's impatience and deeply-engrained moodiness. When my father finally moved out, our family had precious few good friends to draw from; none of them provided us with what we needed most: compassion and emotional support.

Realistically, our mother didn't know many people and was therefore short on options when it came to getting empathy and moral support. Today, being a pastor, I often think in hindsight that we could have benefitted greatly from a good church family, and a minister to call on.

My mother drifted away from the Catholic Church after we moved to Toronto. I attribute that to the fact that she was treading the high waters of low self-esteem. To this day, I don't think any of us children have any inclination of how difficult a season that must have been for her. With the inescapable stigma of being a divorcee hanging over her, socialization and trust could not have come easily. As a result, by the time I was thirteen, we had stopped attending church on a regular basis.

At one point, when we were still in Cape Breton, our family was acclimated to being in and around the church. My sisters and I were all expected to accompany our mother, along with her entire family, to church every Sunday.

To my knowledge, my father never went.

For the first seven years of my life, our family lived in the largely bilingual hamlet of D'Escousse, a tiny town on North Isle Madame, off the southeast tip of Cape Breton. The small Catholic church, not far from our home, was a staple in the community. Going to mass was a regular, even expected practice for many in the town. It was normal to see processions of church-bound people streaming by our house twice a weekend. The attitude was that as long as you were attending the church, you were doing good.

In Toronto, our family no longer seemed to have that spiritual underpinning. At least being in the church had kept our family somewhat preoccupied with the importance of focusing our lives on God. Life in the big city left us disoriented, as if we were drifting along in a vast ocean of uncertainty, without a compass or clue as to where we were headed.

One of the most glaring realities of our home life is that we were a family without vision. Even when my parents were still married, we resembled a ship without a captain or a charted course. I say this because as children we never had the sense that our father, when he was around, could freely communicate his acceptance of us, or his plans for us as a family.

I grew to appreciate my father more in his later years. As his health began to wane, Dad made his peace with all of us children; I'm even confident that he made peace with God. He was amenable to my decision to go into the ministry, and I was able to share my faith with him and pray for him on a few occasions.

My father died in 2006. I have reflected on his life in the years since, having to come to terms with the fact that he was not a leader in our home. Sure, he was capable of making decisions and doing what needed to be done around the house. However, being resourceful (or even resilient) as a parent doesn't always mean that one is a guiding presence. *Leadership* is something entirely different, in that it implies cohabiting and cooperating with a group of people, influencing them towards a common, collective goal.

My father enjoyed his independence far too much to be the leader he should have been. Dad was a very complex person who always seemed to be restless and distant; he preferred to keep some distance between himself and the rest of the family. He liked his space so much that we often mistook him for a foreign object.

Though I was grossly unaware of it at the time, the deficit of a male role model and leader in my life during my formative years had an impact on me as I grew older. It hurt me more than I could possibly have gathered in my adolescent years. To this day, I train myself to dwell on my father's more positive character traits. In many ways, my father had some very admirable qualities—he dreamed dreams, had a great work ethic, took risks, had a survivalist mentality, and even came off as sublimely intelligent at times.

There was a good man locked away within him that every so often was unleashed, to the surprise of many. As well, our father was always waxing eloquent about the merits of getting "a good education," despite the fact that us kids felt like we couldn't live up to his standards.

Other variables greatly factored into our father's personality and behaviour. Not only was he emotionally and psychologically traumatized by growing up in a home with a stern and abusive father, but his participation in the Korean War left him an inward-focused, mysterious, mentally-badgered man. Dad chose to burrow his feelings and memories deep within, so much so that he either wouldn't or couldn't communicate them well. The only thing I know about my father for certain was that he was enigmatic. The truth is that I loved the man. However, I'm not sure, to this day, what it was about him that I loved. I still miss him, or maybe I just miss the thought of him still being around. Maybe I miss the dad I wish he would have been.

After my father moved out of our home, my siblings and I had to muddle through the psychological fallout stemming from the separation and eventual divorce. We had no one to point us in a direction where we could be affirmed and empowered to rise above our circumstances. There's a stark difference between having adversity shape you and having it scar you. As children, we had no concept that we were internally craving leadership, something we badly needed in the wake of our parents' split.

To some extent, my artwork filled that vacuum. Drawing continued to provide an outlet for me to express my inner thoughts in a creative fashion. Nonetheless, I was left to wonder whether that was *all* life had to offer. I wondered that there had to be more to life than merely being happy about what transpired when the lead of my pencil met the blank surface of a piece of paper.

After observing other kids who had both parents at home and enjoyed outings with their dads, I resolved that it was my lot to cultivate my own identity. In an attempt to suppress what I felt was missing in my life, I threw myself deeper into my artwork.

My father seemed to become even more elusive after he left home. As he began to meet other women, we got the sense that if we were to feel even remotely a priority to him, we would have to be the ones to make the effort to see him. Caught between the uncertainties of my relationship with my father and facing a nebulous future, nothing seemed set in stone to me anymore, other than one remaining truth: I would have to find my own meaning and my own way in life. From that, I hoped to one day stumble upon some enduring happiness.

Little did I know at the time that I would be in for some major surprises!

Epiphany

As a pastor, I often have the occasion to sit down with people and listen to their stories. We all have one, don't we? You've read the beginning of my own for the first couple of chapters. Oftentimes, the most powerful and moving stories we hear come from people sharing their testimonies of what God has done in their lives, the events which turned them towards His Son, Jesus Christ.

I have heard many such stories over the years. After a while, though our stories have unique components to them, they can begin to sound similar to each other. I believe that's because there is a connecting principle between each of our salvation stories. The goal of sharing our God-stories is to communicate *how* He ultimately revealed Himself to us. I can tell you quite unabashedly that my testimony is more or less conventional, with a variant of uniqueness tucked away here and there.

The way in which I came to Christ and believed in Him as my Lord and Saviour contains no real shock value. Was I a complete reprobate? Sure I was! But I've heard stories of other individuals whose lives were far worse than mine before they became followers of Christ. The fact of the matter is that I didn't really struggle with any of the more sensational sins or lifestyles before I became a Christian. Did I sell drugs on the street corner? No. Did I spend half my life in the slammer? I assure you, no. Not even one day or night! Did I party hard for many years and then drop out and tune out? No. Was I tempted to? Yes! Was I involved with the Hell's Angels? Nope, and I've never been tempted to join. By my mid-twenties, I was just like many other guys my age; I liked to have a good time, and I really liked girls. I was very guilty of that!

On top of my obvious love for art, I was a closet air-guitarist. I became enthralled with all kinds of music and gained quite a collection of albums, cassette tapes, and eventually CDs. When I wasn't out with the guys, I was drawing, and when I wasn't drawing, I was listening to music. I could listen to music for hours on end, dreaming of becoming a rock star. I dreamed of this almost as much as I pined to become a well-known artist. I am embarrassed to admit that from time to time I would even take to recording my own songs, which were terrible and could be used as blackmail today.

It was such a natural habit for me to don my headphones, lie on my bed, and lose myself in a melodic spiral of tunes. By 1985, I was convinced that the coolest thing in the world was to listen to The Doors, and to look and sound like Jim Morrison, their lead singer. A few years later, I taught myself to play two instruments—drums and guitar—in part by watching and listening to my older brother Rob, who is the real rock star of the family, by the way, and a very fine musician at that.

I can remember asking myself in Grade Eleven what I really wanted to be "when I grew up." I wasn't overly convinced I could make a living by pursuing a career in the arts. After all, what's the age-old saying about artists? They *starve!* In reality, most artists appreciate the value of their works far more than the people who are willing to pay for them. Yet somewhere deep within me, at the age of eighteen—though I couldn't explain it, couldn't understand it, and didn't know who to talk to about it—I knew I was destined to do something entirely different with my life. I had a hunch that I would never be able to shake off, even though I did end up in the commercial art field for seven years, as a graphic designer. Perhaps that was a predictable career move for me.

Finally realizing a career in the arts may have provided me with a steady job, but it was hardly one that I found rewarding, or even satisfying. Anytime a creative person is fed the company line that it's about "quantity, not quality," they have a decision to make. Furthermore, I had a nagging appetite to be part of something that I dared to think could be *greater* than life as an artist. An innocuous, intoxicating thought surfaced in me: *There has to be something more for me in life.* In no way, could I have fully known that my internal convictions were God-forged pathways which would lead me to Him. All I could pinpoint was that my life had gone into soul-searching mode. I was digging for something deeper, but

My Fanatical, Regrettable Tour of Ministry

whatever it was eluded me. It had no name, no phone number, and I couldn't see it in the "help wanted" ads.

Outside my family, I had three major loves: art, music, and girls. I would question why the pursuit of such interests left me feeling so unsatisfied, and why they never seemed to fill the ever-growing void I felt within my heart and life. The more I continued to seek trivial things to fulfill my needs, the more they failed to make the grade. I found them wanting. That's when I realized for the first time that I must have had another set of needs that I either wasn't aware of or couldn't reach.

Then came an epiphany, one of those moments when a door swings open and in flies the future. Leading up to that moment, I had experienced a bevy of hunger pains that pulsated within my soul. I'd felt acute promptings that I was going to end up doing and being something in life, something totally unknown to me.

This epiphany occurred on Christmas Day 1989. I was twenty-two years old.

My mother was making dinner at the apartment I shared with her after my sisters moved out. The morning arose with the familiar sights, smells, and sounds of the holiday season, but this particular Christmas carried with it a promise of another nature. For the first time in many years, my brother and father (who had been estranged from each other for a lengthy period) had the opportunity to meet again that evening to talk. Both of them had warmed to the idea of reconciling. My brother Rob was a bit older and had matured; my father, who had mounting health concerns, wasn't getting any younger and appeared to be softening. However, this day, which held such promise and meaning for the Mahler family, came and went, leaving nothing in its wake but emptiness. My brother did his part by showing up that day, but my father did not. I was crushed.

I wanted so much to wrap my arms around the two of them, in the hopes that after all the wasted years we could be father and sons again. It didn't happen. In fact, it wouldn't be until a much later date that they would come together and talk. However, on that Christmas Day, my world might as well have come to a premature end. To me, having my brother and father united in the same room again, let alone speaking to each other, would have been the greatest gift.

As a result of the failed reconciliation, I became more open than ever before to receiving answers to the questions in my life. As I sat on the edge of my bed later that night and looked at all my new presents, none of them brought me the comfort I thought they would. With head in hands, I slumped over on the end of my bed and began to weep softly until I was reduced to a cathartic mush of a man.

I gushed so many tears, at such a rapid rate, that they pooled on the floor below me like a pond. The disappointment had taken its emotional toll. I clearly remember feeling like I just had to pray and express something to God, who I didn't know very well but believed would be attentive to my words. Despite the fact that I didn't really even know *how* to pray, I sensed that anything I uttered would be on my own behalf, not that of my brother or father. I said something to the effect of, "God, how come I feel like you're telling me something, and that you're going to use me for something?" Even now, some twenty-two years removed, the "Wow!" factor from that moment has never faded. Why did I experience a spiritual inquiry of such a spontaneous and personal nature? How did I even know what to ask for?

None of that matters now, for I have long been convinced that the throne of heaven came crashing into my bedroom that night. The Spirit graced my reality from that moment on, tapping on the back of my desperation. God gave me a question that only He could provide an answer for.

That Christmas night, unbeknownst to me, the Christ-child of Bethlehem visited *me,* and the gift He brought turned out to be one I couldn't possibly refuse.

CHAPTER 4
Exchanges

Perhaps at some point in your life you have participated in a so-called "gift exchange." I'm talking about the company Christmas parties we often attend where we are asked to pick the name of one of our co-workers ahead of time and come to the party with a gift for that person. More often than not, these gifts are actually re-gifts; at best, they're items of a trivial nature, meant to be humorous more than they're meant to touch us.

Perhaps, like me, you too have found yourself on the short end of the gift exchange stick. The weirdest gift I ever received in one of these exchanges was an ugly wooden candleholder that was designed to be hung on a wall. It was the type of object that only the original carpenter's mother could love! Sometimes we can't help but expose the joker by asking, "Okay, who gave me this?" There's always the chance that we will communicate through our facial expressions that we really don't appreciate the gift we've opened.

That's why gift exchanges come with the element of risk. They're intended to be fun, but we often find ourselves wishing that the person who gave us the gift had taken it a bit more seriously. Oftentimes, the gifts we receive at these exchanges just aren't worth keeping. Thankfully, there's at least one gift in life that is offered to everyone. Without a doubt, it's the most worthy of all gifts. It comes to us from the heart of God, and it's also given in the form of an exchange—for eternal life!

Ron Mahler

This is precisely the truth I came to see and believe in when I discovered why Jesus Christ chose to die for sinful humanity. He didn't choose just any mode of death, either; He died nailed to a crossbeam of wood. That wooden cross may have been the ugliest of all carpentry in the history of the world, yet because Jesus hung on it I came to see it, as it were, as a beautiful gift hanging on the wall of my heart. The Bible reveals Jesus' death as being an act of "propitiation."

Propitiation is a big theological word with a simple yet profound spiritual application. It has its roots in the sacrificial system that the priests of Israel carried out in the Old Testament. Essentially, it can be understood in how "God himself takes upon himself in the person of his Son our sin and guilt so that his justice might be executed and our sins might be forgiven."[2] John Calvin, the sixteenth-century reformer and theologian, referred to Jesus' sacrificial death as the "wonderful exchange," in that "becoming Son of man with us, He has made us sons of God with Him."[3]

Jesus knew we needed Him to suffer and submit Himself to the irreverent jaws of death in order for us (sinful humanity) to not only be snatched from the clutches of sin and eternal death, but to gain eternal life. This culminates in our being brought into the Kingdom of God in Heaven. In willingly taking our sin upon Himself and paying the death penalty for it, He gave us the gift of His righteousness, making us right before God (see 2 Corinthians 5:21).

Calvin appropriately dubbed the spiritual efficacy of Jesus' sacrifice the most "wonderful" of exchanges, for in our human, sin-marred state, we could never on our own merit the acceptance of a God so holy. Those who accept Jesus' sacrificial death on their behalf, and trust in Him as their Saviour and Lord, won't come away unhappy with the gift they've received. The central message of the Gospel is this: *"For God so loved the world that he gave his one and only Son..."* (John 3:16)

As a Christian pastor, I meditate quite often on the spiritual implications of that monumental event in history for my own life, and for my sermon writing. I am still amazed at how theologically all-inclusive the substitutional nature of Jesus' death, and the ministry of the cross, is. When Jesus allowed His arms and legs to be pierced to the cross with spikes, He had us on His mind, despite the fact that neither you or I was even born. I had not committed so much as one sin at the time. I wasn't even a zygote! I flat-out nowhere near existed as a human being. In fact, I was centuries upon centuries from being born. However, Jesus knew that I too would need Him to be on that cross.

On Thursday, February 9, 1967, with my infant cries roaring like a babe who came in like a lion, and in the midst of a good old-fashioned snowstorm, I was born. There are days when I most intensely appreciate the redemptive exchange Jesus made for me. There are moments in our lives when it's painfully obvious why we need a Saviour, and why Jesus' vicarious death on our behalf was so wonderful an exchange.

In 1991, when I was twenty-four years old and still working as a graphic artist, I was smitten by a young woman I had met at my sister Linda's home. In meeting her, I would also come face to face with the reality of just how sinful I was, as a man and as a person in general. This international woman of mystery was none other than my sister's nanny. The encounter was a setup. Oh sure, Linda probably had a plan up her sleeve, but the truth is that it was a setup of divine proportions. The very day I walked into my sister's home and introduced myself to this gal, I walked right into the next phase of God's sovereign plan for my life. It's funny to think back on how I unknowingly cooperated with God, and so willingly! In retrospect, there was something keenly magnetic about this young woman, whom I shall refer to solely as the Nanny.

Before too long, however, I innately discovered that the Nanny was someone, and everything, I was not.

What had me so spellbound was how pure and wholesome she appeared. She was unlike the other girls I had known and dated. There was a reason for that, and it had nothing to do with her physical person. As I would come to figure out, it had everything to do with the Person alive in her—Jesus Christ. When I met the Nanny, in a very real sense I met the Son of God. I also believed that I had met someone who could be my future wife. There was a connection from the start. We were both natives of Nova Scotia, and we each enjoyed music and art. We became close and dated for about a year.

During that time, she shared with me her faith in Christ. As a result, we spent hours in numerous conversations about God and what it meant to have faith. I got to hear about the driving force behind her life, and it was opposite to the things I had championed as being indispensible in my own life. Her genuine personality, however, coupled with what I determined was authentic faith, fortified my growing impression of her. At the time, I categorically deemed her a "religious" girl, and with that narrow characterization I saw the Nanny as someone who openly communicated her love for God, without restriction. It was refreshing to me, and also uncomfortable to internalize, personally.

One thing I noted early on in our relationship was that she seemed to be looking for someone in me, looking for a person I wasn't at the time; I was nowhere near being that person. As we spent more time together, I began to wonder if she had a hidden agenda in wanting to hang with me, as if I had missed some conditional fine print that was part of the relationship.

After a few weeks of casually dating, she asked me if I would like to go to church with her. This would be the first time I ever went to a non-Catholic church. The distinction was clear in that she referred to church as a "service" and not a "mass." I agreed to go because she wanted me to, yet not without some trepidation and a pinch of curiosity. Attending her church (a Nazarene church) was an experience, to say the least. There I was, sitting in a rented school gymnasium, listening to a worship team sing songs I had never heard before.

Then something struck me as odd; one of the women singing on the worship team was crying *real* tears. My thoughts automatically flashed to certain religious programs that seemed to define people of faith by their outward, emotional goings-on. I remember also being taken aback by some of the lyrics of the songs—and one in particular, about "the blood of the Lamb."

In a momentary panic, my eyes eagerly panned the room for the nearest exit. Truly, I wondered what I had gotten myself into, and considered that maybe just escaping outside would be enough of a *heavenly* experience for me! But then I turned to look at the Nanny, who I was coming to like even more, looking so happy and smiling back at me. My eyes, which a moment earlier had been busily casing the place, dropped down and looked at our hands clasped together. I resolved, *This can't be so bad!*

The relationship I had with the Nanny provided me with something I knew I needed, but its exact nature remained imperceptible. Our relationship seemed like an extension of the soul-searching road I had started down a few years earlier. I knew it had a destination, but whatever it was, we had not yet arrived. Though it would remain oblivious to me, in hindsight it was actually her love for her Saviour, and her relationship with Him, that was the steering action behind my attraction to her.

However, the one constant in her life—her faith in Jesus Christ, which had once primed my appreciation of her—ultimately turned out to be her guiding measure of me as a man. I was found to be spiritually wanting, for we both knew I could not claim to have faith in God that was uniquely my own. That said, my relationship with the Nanny seemed too right to be so wrong for her. She had a way of stirring a desire in me to personally own the kind of faith she had, one that was real and genuine.

I knew I wanted that same faith for my life, but I knew I couldn't imitate her. After all, an actor can only act so long before forgetting a line! As hard as I tried,

My Fanatical, Regrettable Tour of Ministry

I was a miserable failure at trying to microwave an instant faith. Longing to be the kind of spiritual person the Nanny wanted me to be, I mourned the fact that I was probably going to lose her. She saw right through me, and the last thing she was looking for in a potential mate was a phony. She had already waded through a rolodex of those in her life.

The plain truth was that I constantly struggled to relate to the same assurances she championed about living a life of faith. We got into more than a few conversational tangles over spiritual issues. For instance, we had a discussion about eternal life and if it was possible for someone to be sure they were going to Heaven. In the course of the conversation, I remarked about how John Lennon was a man of "peace," and how that had conditioned my view of the chances of his eternal destiny. Upon hearing that, she shot back, "But did he have peace with God?"

I was silently indignant but didn't respond to her comment. However, I do remember brooding angrily for a day. I wondered how she could just brush aside Lennon's efforts to motivate people to world peace. How could she spiritualize everything?

On another occasion, while we were having a nice lunch (the operative word being "were"), the Nanny excused herself and went off to the restroom. While she was gone, I took a napkin from the table and penned the words "I love you a helluva lot" on it. Well, let's just say that when she returned, it was time for the bill. With a glow of suspense and gratitude on her face, the Nanny began to peel open the napkin I had folded up into little squares. The look on her face that had only seconds before beamed with anticipation in an instant melted into sagging horror as she glared at what I had written on the napkin. Obviously, I had predicted the wrong response. My intentions couldn't nearly make up for my spiritual faux pas. She was mortified and inquired how I could use such a crass saying (which included the word "hell"), in reference to expressing love for someone?

I was confounded at being shot down, my well-intentioned efforts having been dismissed over how I chose to write a love note. After all, I had used the slang "helluva" many times in my life. No one that I was aware of had ever gotten their knickers in a twist over it. My only comeback was insisting that the "helluva" phrase could be salvaged, because the word "helluva" still included the alternative spelling for the word love—"luv."

I thought my retort was brilliant.

She didn't.

Ron Mahler

In fact, my comment made her even more upset. Our relationship was drowning in a deluge of my own making, and the Nanny wasn't about to throw me a lifeline. She may have lacked a sense of humour, yet I just plain *lacked*. The terrible, sinking truth was that I simply didn't measure up—spiritually. She confirmed as much when she revealed the inevitable—"I can't be with you any longer." She validated her decision to break off our relationship by admitting that she had felt that God didn't want us together "all along." Even though I had known that a letdown was probable, I had hoped the day wouldn't arrive. Reality hurt, despite the fact that I should have been well-rehearsed to face it.

The biblical principle that two people can be unequally yoked, spiritually, was both a foreign and confusing one to me (see 2 Corinthians 6:14). I fancied that the one compulsory element of any relationship should be mutual love, not how much each person loved God. I chose to get into a relationship with the Nanny despite her spirituality, not because of it. She could have been an atheist, and that wouldn't have bothered me.

For a time immediately following the breakup, I wrestled with various questions. For one, I wondered what was wrong with the quality of love I'd had for her that couldn't make up for my spiritual deficiencies. I also pondered whether we would have been able to stay together had I "loved" God the way she did. Then, incredibly, an even more insightful thought arose within me: *Why did God allow our relationship to happen in the first place?*

Though I was unsure how I arrived at some of my conclusions concerning the doomed relationship, I resolved to believe that God was, indeed, involved in it, for more reasons than I could see. My brush with God had seemed to be neither a coincidence nor something that would come to nothing. The more I tried to come out from under the shadows of the Nanny's preoccupation with spiritual matters, the larger my memory of her hungering and thirsting to please God loomed, hovering over me and holding me captive.

I couldn't escape the curious thought that if I believed God had whispered to me in my desperate moment of Christmas 1989, it was possible for Him to have some further purpose in speaking into my heart as I processed my regrets over the Nanny. Piecing the spiritual fragments surrounding my 1989 experience with those I was left hanging to in the wake of the breakup felt too vast a task for me to reconcile.

I felt a great angst to resolve how the gentle, caring God I had sensed in my bedroom that Christmas night could be the same God who seemed to have ruthlessly pried the Nanny away from me. Though it didn't appear to be quite the

My Fanatical, Regrettable Tour of Ministry

spiritual eureka it seems like today, I was eventually able to connect the dots in concluding that God had used the Nanny to introduce Himself to me, and that it was His desire for me to have the same relationship with Him that the Nanny had. I could strum up no other satisfying conclusion, for if I could, nothing she had taught me about God would have made any sense. Though the relationship had been spiritually inappropriate, in no way did it abort God's plan for my life.

I credit this discovery to the counsel of a pastor who I'll introduce in more depth in the next chapter. Suffice it to say that God brought this pastor alongside me during the fresh, emotional fallout that resulted from the Nanny and me parting ways. He was instrumental in moving me from thinking of God in terms of the spiritually camouflaged institution of *religion* to the possibility of knowing Him as a person (Jesus Christ), and by the true, biblical ideal of *relationship*.

Some events in our lives can only be explained for their purpose. This was true of my relationship with the Nanny. It was only when we finally got out of the lane we were obstructing, making way for God's oncoming will to unfold, that I was able to grasp why He'd taken her away from me. Although I hadn't fully grasped what "loving" God meant for me, God used the Nanny's departure to continue His overtures upon my life. In her absence, God purposed to reveal the extent of His love for me; in my life He had exchanged the Nanny for Himself. God had never meant for my relationship with her to be about her—or even me, for that matter; it was always to be about His central place in it.

God exchanged my perceived need of the Nanny for a revelation of my spiritual need for Him. God also exchanged the pain of losing her for the gain of beginning to know Him. I would eventually learn to give her up in every facet of my being. I eventually arrived at a point where memories of my time with her no longer had any hold on me.

However, there was still one more thing—one more very personal thing—that I needed to get over. There was so much about myself that didn't honour God, things which I needed to surrender and place into His hands! Though I was never a "bad" guy, by human standards, I was still a sinner in need of becoming a man of God.

The changes God transacted in my life continued. At His perfect pace, God would slowly exchange my ideals for His, my thoughts for His, my questions for His answers, my longings for His provisions. It was a painful and prolonged process, yet God would bring me to that place (post-Nanny), where I could see, with spiritual blinders off, His prized, sovereign plan for me as His child. It was as if my calamitous life resembled a mixed-up Rubik's Cube which God took hold of and began to twist and turn until the colours revealed its ultimate pattern. The resultant life began to make some sense of all my emotional and spiritual displacement and longing. It was St. Augustine, the Catholic theologian and Bishop of Hippo, who said that our hearts are restless until they come to "rest" in God. For certain, nothing could have described my pre-faith life any better: *restless.*

From the very moment I breathed the air of human life, my soul yearned to nestle into an eternally secure, personal relationship with God. When I accepted Jesus Christ as my Saviour and embraced a life reconciled to God, the Creator and lover of my soul, I did so, after spending some twenty-four years in spiritual exile. Therefore, there can be no happier birthday than the one that commemorates when someone was spiritually reborn.

Realizing that being born again is designed to fulfill my deepest, spiritual longings is an experience unlike any other. I will share further about how that all came about in the next chapter. However, no matter who we are, or where we come from, we can come to God in Jesus Christ *as we are,* but we can never remain that way. God has the best plan for our lives, and though segments of that plan may be sovereignly accounted for in the blueprint of our physical birth, it cannot be built to completion without being spiritually reborn.

Christians possess the hope that God can make something out of their lives which was already beautifully thought-out in Heaven before they were born and the world was formed (see Ephesians 1:4). One of the most powerful and moving books I have ever read is Billy Graham's autobiography, *Just as I Am*. I sunk my eyes into its pages and didn't come out until I finished three days later. God plucked a man like Dr. Graham from an obscure town in the Deep South and constructed from him a servant's vessel, a servant He used to reach millions upon millions of people with the Gospel. Billy Graham had it in him from the start; he had the raw materials to do what he accomplished for the Kingdom of God, but it was only after he gave God the reigns of his life that God gave him the supernatural gifting and burden needed to transform him into a dynamic preacher and teacher. He has touched so many lives, a work God had sovereignly prepared for Graham in advance.

When I fully submitted my life to Him, God graciously accepted me just as I was: full of sinful ruts and blemishes. Since that day, He has stretched me and challenged me to keep in step with His Holy Spirit, in not staying in the same condition I was. In fact, God is the greatest interior decorator imaginable! If He was to take up residence in me, He needed to go to work planting and posting

His own desires in the home of my heart. Those desires would hang on its walls like fixtures, giving it a new look and feel, so that God could walk in and see Himself living there.

There are numerous general commands God gives all of His people to obey. Born out of that discipline come other, more specific, spiritual alterations and exchanges that give us internal beauty of eternal consequence. These alterations can only be conceived and crafted by the majestic hands of the Almighty.

In saving me, God implemented a purpose for my life, instilling a desire within my heart that I couldn't possibly have predicted or ever imagined was possible. What eventually resulted was a call to a specialized service, not to serve a country, but to serve the Kingdom—as a pastor.

Absolutely no one on the face of the planet wields the kind of unbridled and transformative power necessary to totally realign our ambitions in life so that they parallel Heaven's eternal purposes for us. Only God Himself can do that! The greatest evidence of spiritual formation at work in the world doesn't come from the empty promises of horoscopes, palm readers, or crystal balls, but rather from the spiritual architecture of ordinary lives, which have been fashioned and framed by the unseen hand of the supreme Architect (Jesus Christ).

Only God could take my love for and devotion to the arts, and my plan and passion to embrace a life as an artist, and change that. Only God could foresee the rendering of a man who at one time was too filled with angst to find meaning in life. Through Him, I ended up leading others to find their meaning, in Christ, just as I did. If we allow Him, God is able to take His divine brush to the canvas of our lives, and with every wise stroke create the masterpiece He conceived in eternity past.

Though many people profess to have plans for our lives, only God has the best one. His is the real deal. As memories of the Nanny dissolved, and a spiritual hunger and thirst gripped my heart, tempered excitement mounted within me in the form of a humbling question: *If I felt so inadequate serving God in ministry, why is He choosing me to do so?* This willing, but hard to convince vessel would need some hefty persuading.

Thankfully, God knew just who to bring along my path to confirm His unlikely call to me. And what better a person to model pastoral ministry than a fellow pastor?

Chapter 5

The Sermon

His name was Pastor Andrews. I formed a bond and mentoring relationship with him after my breakup with the Nanny. The church Pastor Andrews led seemed to come out of nowhere, unexpectedly landing on the doorstep of my needy life. It was the same church the Nanny had attended while we were dating.

Andrews was a very youthful man in his mid-thirties whose preaching I found not only to be very entertaining, but relevant and clear to understand. His pulpit ministry contained all the ingredients necessary to make for a dynamic and effective communicator. On numerous Sundays, I sat before him mesmerized by the knack he possessed to speak as though he had known me all my life. That was true of the very first time I heard Pastor Andrews preach.

I had a decent dose of apprehension that initial Sunday morning when I attended with the Nanny. It was my first experience in a non-Catholic, evangelical church, and it was quite a culture shock. The flow of the service was alien to me; the significance of what I was seeing and hearing all felt somewhat lost in translation until Pastor Andrews got up to speak. Until that moment, everything I had observed was shrouded in mystery. Andrews, however, had a genial personality and was more than capable of drawing in even the most sceptical of visitors, of which I was definitely one.

That morning, I was along for the ride, but I was also more than willing to get off at any time. However, Pastor Andrews held my attention, and consequently my interest. He had a way of getting his point across like no other

My Fanatical, Regrettable Tour of Ministry

religious figure I had previously been exposed to. I had put every priest I'd listened to on a time-limit of one or two minutes. After that, I would shut them out, mentally. Yet one thing that stuck in me as I studied Andrews was that he appeared to be irrefutably genuine.

What is true of sermon content and the art of preaching is true of the arguments we have with people; sometimes, it's all in the way we speak, which is almost as important as what we say. Like so many of my generation, there I was, at age twenty-four, and I had never read the Bible. I was largely unaware of what it really had to say and why I should be reading it. My engrained Catholicism always lead me to believe that the Bible was predominantly for the clergy (priests) to read, and that if I needed to hear something from it, or receive counsel, the best context in which to do that was through participating in confession, or by going to mass. I would have fit right in with most of the lay population in the Middle Ages, who were more or less biblically ignorant. With the Bible out of sight, and consequently out of mind, as I grew up, I had no inclination of its spiritual importance for everyday living; that is, until I heard Pastor Andrews preach from it.

Perhaps the best way to describe my experience that first Sunday morning is to say that it awakened me from years of unconscious slumber towards God's Word. Out of the plethora of topics that could have been preached on that fateful morning, Pastor Andrews announced that his sermon was on the biblical reality of Hell. What an introduction I got to the Bible that Sunday! There's nothing like bypassing the more warm-and-fuzzy content (God loves you, etc.) and getting right to the point. I was a captive audience! The fact that I found myself interested in what Andrews had to say would have made no sense on any other normal day, yet there was nothing familiar or normal about this day in terms of what I was experiencing in my heart. When I came across religious programs on television that smacked of televangelists spouting off about "judgement" and "hellfire," I mockingly heckled the speaker before clicking to another channel with my remote control.

Therefore, it was all the more amazing for someone like me to be so captivated by what Pastor Andrews had to say about the Bible's teaching on the eternal reality of Hell, and why some people land there after their physical death. A topic that had once provoked revulsion in me suddenly caught my undivided attention. At the time, I wasn't even sure if I believed in a literal place called Hell. I remember feeling that if there was such a destiny as Hell, surely it was reserved for sadistic murderers and rapists, who were the only people worthy of going there.

Ron Mahler

Pastor Andrews blew that stereotype apart. He spoke with the depth of spiritual insight and commanding, authoritative conviction that Jesus exhibited. As biblically illiterate as I was, his ability to speak with such conviction was of paramount importance; it made the sermon believable. Even in my own preaching today, I try to remain mindful of the fact that even though someone may not believe what I say is true, nonetheless I must come across as one who believes what he is saying.

The Holy Spirit used Pastor Andrews' delivery, as well as the persuasive content of his sermon, to hit His intended mark: my heart. I recall finding myself becoming more open to consider the possibility that there was a place where *any* person who rejected Jesus Christ went for eternity. The prospects of winding up at such a destination "scared me" (as some would say) into the Kingdom. By the passion he conveyed, it's unmistakable to me now just how burdened Pastor Andrews was to reach those who didn't know God's Son as their personal Saviour.

Prior to that morning, I had never heard that there was a spiritual discrepancy between knowing God cognitively and knowing Him personally. I was confused by one of the biggest misunderstandings people have about the Person and ministry of Jesus Christ: I believed that knowing *about* Jesus was synonymous with knowing Him intimately.

Though many faithful Catholics do grasp and enjoy the spiritual and theological significance of a personal and intimate relationship with Jesus Christ, at that juncture in my life I certainly couldn't claim to. Before I could get to that point, I needed to be convinced that I, too, was Hellbound. God was about to *make my day!* At one point in the sermon, and I will never forget its poignancy, Andrews dropped a life-altering spiritual bomb. It blew away every conceivable notion I had about *who* deserved entrance into Hell at the end of their lives, and who didn't. As clear as yesterday, I remember Pastor Andrews proclaiming, "There are a lot of good, well-intentioned people who will end up in Hell!" No sooner were the words out of his mouth that his statement manifested itself like a verbal javelin spearing my heart. It left me feeling like I had been physically pinned to my chair.

I had no idea of the spiritual magnitude of what had transpired, but that javelin stuck in me for months. The more I tried to forget about it, the more confounding and etched on my mind it became. Though I would continue to attend the church with the Nanny, never once did I mention to her anything about what I had experienced in my seat that first Sunday.

CHAPTER 6
Searching

IN THE WEEKS AND MONTHS THAT FOLLOWED, I COULDN'T BRING MYSELF TO accept that what I experienced during the sermon was mere happenstance. I mentally massaged such probing questions as "What are the chances that I would arbitrarily agree to attend Pastor Andrews' church that morning, only to be affected by it?" and "Why did I seemingly hear the right words, from the right person, at perhaps the most spiritually opportune time?" They were the right questions to ask; but being persuaded of the right answers was even more spiritually vital. I investigated every circumstance that came across the path of my life in those days, just to find suitable interpretations. I was suspicious of God, and of what He would pull on me next.

In a scene from the movie *Fiddler on the Roof*, the story's main character, Tevye, bemoans the fact that he's running out of time to finish his work-related duties before the Jewish Sabbath kicks in. Tevye, in an irreverent tone, remarks that things must have been quiet in Heaven for God to have to strum up some mischief against him. In a similar vein, I was so wary of what God was up to behind the scenes of my life that it felt some days as though He was making things hard for me. It was purely conjecture on my part, of course, but I wasn't far from the truth. I had never felt secure in my relationship with the Nanny, and yet there were times when I thought we were getting closer to being on the same page, spiritually. It got to the point where I wasn't even sure what the status of our relationship was from day to day.

Ron Mahler

I was equally uncertain of where I stood with God, and why I couldn't find it in my heart to come to a place where I could simply surrender to Him. I had a gut feeling dogging me for a week following that initial, revelatory sermon, that God was somehow pursuing me, somehow going ahead of me, somehow reaching out to me… even cornering me.

Jesus said that unless His Heavenly Father draws people to Him (Jesus), they will not be able to see what He (the Father) is doing through His Son (see John 6:44). Some theologians refer to this as "prevenient grace," a teaching stemming from Augustinian theology that was embraced and adapted by the likes of John Wesley. It refers to unmerited, divine grace which precedes a human being's decision about Christ, enabling that individual to receive Him. It wasn't until I eventually accepted Christ that I found out how active the Nanny was in making me an object of prayer to more than a few people, her prayer request being that I would "become a Christian." Behind my back—and even while I was sleeping, no doubt—God was using the prayers of His obedient children to draw me to Him, leading me to say "yes" to His Son.

Before I arrived at that point, all I could grasp from subsequent visits to the Nanny's church was that I needed to make a decision. Was I going to settle for the no-name God of my youth, or was I going to accept Jesus as the leader and Lord of my life? It was as if God volleyed the Gospel truth about Jesus into the court of my consciousness. Would I pick up the ball and whip it as far away from me as possible? Would I hit it back to God in defiance? Or, in humility, would I choose to ask God to teach me to play His way? Either way, God had taken the initiative with me, as He always does, in the pursuit of winning our hearts, capturing our souls, and changing our lives. God would continue accosting me with opportunities to respond to His overtures on my life; each time I would come up with some way to let it pass me by. Even a year after I heard that ground-breaking sermon on Hell and found myself flying solo without the Nanny, God still shadowed me.

No external pressures from anyone I was associated with coaxed me into continuing to go to church. I was free to end any and all experiments and flirtations with Christianity and the Church. Not too long after my breakup with the Nanny, however, I acquired a couple of new relationships to replace her, which delayed the decisions I needed to make about Christ, as well as about my future. The names of these new relationships were *depression* and *isolation*.

If you're familiar with the story of Job in the Old Testament, you can appreciate how innately depression and isolation resemble the "friends" who sought out Job when he found himself at an all-time low. Job had pretty much lost everything in his life; gone were his children, much of his possessions, and most heartbreaking of all, his health (his body broke out in painful boils). Job was not only forced to live with the losses he experienced within his own family, and with the physical pain of his person, but he also had to endure the silence of the God he sought so earnestly for answers.

Job's misguided friends were not much of a help, either. Let's just say they were not the type of people we would want manning the phones of a suicide hotline. They basically concluded that Job was the author of his own misery. Their ill advice could have easily led the poster boy of suffering to a hopeless end. The two buddies hanging off me after the Nanny and I went our separate ways—depression and isolation—advised me in a similar way. They were effective partners in chauffeuring me to their desired destination for my life—a kind of emotional oblivion the likes of which I had never experienced before. Waking up with my eyes swollen from the previous night's tears became a recurring pattern. At one point, I was so fragile and withdrawn that I periodically left my job without announcing that I wasn't returning for the day. The situation deteriorated to such extremes that I didn't even care if I was fired.

If I hadn't had the counsel of the friends I made at Pastor Andrews' church, I don't know what I would have done. It seemed like a co-worker would take me out for lunch every other week just to cheer me up. Even my family members made efforts to sympathize with me, especially my older sister Lisa, who had been through some disappointing relationships herself, and who was always there with a compassionate ear. I was grateful for, and fortunate to have, an understanding supervisor in the particular department where I worked. This caring and sensitive person not only empathized with me, but they believed I was still an asset to the company, despite my troubles.

Though I could have done without the pain, the stone-cold reality was that I still needed my job. I was riding a perpetual tide of anger toward God that eventually left me beached on the shore of bitterness. Though I was learning much about spiritual matters as a result of sitting under Pastor Andrews' teaching, nonetheless it felt like the God I was getting to know was the same God who had brought me to a cliff of despair and left me there. The roots of my disillusionment with God's plan for my life bore deep into my heart.

I got away from Pastor Andrews' church for a time, not long after the Nanny herself stopped attending. Getting away from church for any length of time, as any pastor or mature Christian will tell you, can quickly get you to a place where God would rather you not be. The foolhardy notion that a new Christian (though I couldn't have been branded as such, at that point) can remain spiritually anchored while being dismembered from the very body it's been fused into (the Church) is, to borrow a popular term, "so five minutes ago!" The argument just doesn't wash, biblically. The church community that God provides for us is spiritually formatted for our mutual edification. That's how we grow in our faith! We need fellow believers around us not for only spiritual accountability, but for the reinforcement of our need to belong.

Any Christian, no matter where they are on their journey with Jesus, needs the faith experiences of others in the Body of Christ to put their own experience in perspective. The problem with sin is that it inverts the divine pattern and logic of God's Word. Through the bitterness of my heart, the enemy of my soul, Satan—and, indeed, my own flesh—worked in tandem to turn me away from the spiritual coverage afforded to me in Pastor Andrews' church.

Some of the most harmful and unhealthy vices we have as human beings die a slow death, on par with the greatest drawn-out death scenes that Hollywood has to offer! Even some of Christ's initial followers were prone to returning to their previous lifestyles and activities. Following Jesus wasn't easy for the disciples, by any stretch of the imagination. Whenever they understood a spiritual insight that Jesus taught them, they were enriched and motivated to carry on with the One whom they alone recognized as *"the Christ, the Son of the living God"* (Matthew 16:16).

However, when the Lord's travelling discipleship classes featured a pop quiz, His disciples often failed to get a passing grade. The more they messed up, the more they had to have been tempted to set aside their commitments to Him. Over the long haul, some had enough and simply bid Jesus, "Adios!" (see John 6:66) A disciple had to stay close to Jesus, rolling with the spiritual ups-and-downs that were inherent in befriending a suffering Saviour, in order for their lives to be transformed by Him.

While I was going to church, and remaining velcroed to the knowledge of God's will for my life, I found myself less inclined to live any other way, especially the type of life that attracted me to frequent pool halls and nightclubs with friends. To a certain extent, I would have a hoot hitting Toronto's downtown core on a Saturday evening, taking in the nightlife. Staying out until the early hours of the morning seems to be a habitual rite of bachelorhood; certainly, it was for my friends and myself.

Sometimes we sought to put another notch in the belt of our overgrown, boyish mischievousness, by dancing with girls for the sole reason of getting their phone numbers. A successful night was defined by one of us actually securing one. It rarely happened. As long as I could successfully push aside the occasional prompting within me, telling me that I needed to grow up and get a life, I was fine. This kind of shallow behavior wasn't the worst thing I could do, but it wasn't the best thing, either. For certain, it wasn't God's ideal way for me to conduct myself.

Even though I periodically sensed a spiritual check within my heart, I often chose to ignore it by pressing on and moulding my identity in my own way. I was blinded to the fact that I was traveling down a precarious road, with every passing mile increasing the rate of danger in my life. The spiritual push-and-pull grew more evident with every invitation from my friends. Though I would make the occasional excuse as to why I couldn't go out, choosing to sleep in on a Sunday morning would find me all the more tempted to accompany my buddies on our fruitless, Saturday night carousals.

The reality was that I was steeped in a war of spiritual attrition in which the Spirit was willing, but my flesh was incredibly weak. Quite like putting off that dreaded phone call, or that apology we need to issue, I was putting off what I knew was the inevitable. I simply could not continue dodging interminably in and out of the light of God's grace that had inconveniently exposed a truth about my life. No amount of Saturday night parties could bring me the kind of fulfillment I could only experience from submitting my life to God. I was embodying the witty definition of insanity, by doing the same thing over and over and expecting a different result!

Clearly, I had no semblance of peace. I got too used to living with one foot planted in the carefree zone of life; the other foot was trying the imprint of Jesus' footprint on for size.

An older gentleman I later came to know in my travels as a pastor attended A.A. (Alcoholics Anonymous) meetings to help him control his battle with substance abuse. This man proudly gave me his purple medallion (I still have it) which commemorated nine months of sobriety. He told me that when "the pain of the pain" got to be too much for him, he knew he had reached the juncture where he needed to make a decision.

Well, pursuing the aimless path I was on was hurting me just as much as keeping God at a comfortable, manageable distance. Over time, I became so entrenched in my spiritual wilderness that I awoke most mornings exhausted, agonizing over where I was headed as a person. My bedroom became more than simply a place to sleep; it took on the feeling of an eight-hour prison cell for internal interrogation. I was nearing my own threshold for "the pain of my pain."

I felt remorse over the way I was living, and guilty about the fact that I was struggling to accept a better way—God's way. The manner in which the Devil seemed to be pressing in on my life was urgent and intense. There were intermittent times when I thought of giving up on going to church and turning away from everything I was learning about God's will for me.

A day finally came when I resolved, *What's the use in carrying on with God?* It obviously didn't faze Him, for His Spirit proceeded to impress a warm, peaceful thought within me—that I was forgiven and loved. It was a timely, spiritual deposit from God to keep alive any remaining hunger for Him I had left.

I knew I couldn't find peace until I resolved once and for all where I stood with a God who seemed bent on not leaving me alone. I was twenty-five, and just four years away from my first ministry position. God knew He had to do a serious "reno" job in me in order to get me ready. First, He had to gain internal access to me. I could envision Jesus standing at the door of my heart as I listened to the thumps of his knuckles knocking against its hardened exterior. How wonderful a thought it is, to this very day, to think that God chose to keep knocking until the sound of those raps awakened me from my coma of resistance. I have always been impressed with God's patience!

The fact remained, however, that I preferred to enjoy popularity with my friends, forge my own self-esteem, and galvanize my self-perceptions. God had much to tear down and rebuild in my life. Perhaps because of the vain ventures I pursued as a young adult, I became increasingly lonely, cut adrift from the familiarities of my life. God's advances were like tidal waves of the Holy Spirit crashing in on my weakened and tottering heart. My stubbornness couldn't muscle back any longer. In every fibre of my being, I was burdened to re-evaluate some of the long-held priorities I was nursing. I knew I was like a wanted man, in need of being convinced to give up his running and turn himself in to God once and for all.

Before too long, the phone would ring.

CHAPTER 7
Emulation

PASTOR ANDREWS WAS A SHEPHERD WORTH EMULATING. IF THE DISCIPLES endeavoured to mimic Jesus as they watched Him minister, in Andrews I found someone at least worth emulating. His ministry first showed me what really caring for people looked like. Pastor Andrews was my first glimpse of a person we would say is 'Christ-like.' You could say that he played Jesus to my first-century seeker.

He accomplished this in various ways—through a smile, through conversations I had with him, through a caring handshake, through sermons, and ultimately through... *the phone call.*

On a warm day in May of 1992, I received a call from Pastor Andrews. It was more than welcome. I'd had a rough couple of weeks, and without going into much detail I can assure you that the Devil was in them. Everything from workplace issues, to dating, to friendships; everything that spelled *security* to me was frittering away at the seams.

I faced some potentially devastating turns in my life that were complicated by a series of bad decisions. Never in my wildest dreams had I ever thought I would end up in the place I was—possibly without a friend in the world, without a job, and without a significant other to share it all with. Isn't life like that? We can easily dream up the good stuff we'd like to see happen in our lives, but it's when we try to dream the messing up part that we run into trouble. It doesn't come to us naturally.

However, finding one's self in a life-sized mess can come quite easily when you are as conflicted as I was. Unbeknownst to me, a raging spiritual battle was taking place deep down within the burning embers of my soul. I didn't want to do the wrong things in life. I didn't want to harm anyone, nor did I want to get hurt in the process. My angst was as spiritually-based as the apostle Paul's, as I, too, pondered why I did those things which I really did not want to do, and did them while knowing they were wrong (see Romans 7:14–20).

My folly seemed to accentuate whenever I heard a sermon on sin, or whenever I actually cracked open the inexpensive New Testament I picked up at a bargain bin. Eventually, my heart became pliable enough for God's Word to convince me that I could finally call what was sin in my life, *sin*. Finally, I recall waking up one day keenly aware of the fact that it felt like there was a war going on inside me. The armies consisted of two opposing voices in spiritual stereo, jockeying for supremacy. I could no longer deny the multiple occasions when I felt drawn to God one day, then pulled away from Him the next.

At one time, I dismissed the Devil as pure, religious fanaticism, even extreme and heightened paranoia, but I began to take more seriously the reality that he was a real, active, demonic personality with a plan to wage spiritual war against God's work in people's lives. The more I tried to disregard God's advances on my heart, the more I saw the carnage of my rebelliousness scattered across the battlefield of my life.

The more the Devil sought to slip a noose around my neck, the more I felt my spiritual footing being propped up. However, in being able to resist evil, I still didn't find embracing a life of faith to be all that *irresistible*.

A few chapters ago, I spoke of a time when, as a child, life seemed so much bigger to me, but at the age of twenty-five, my life seemed to be getting smaller. The things I thought I needed for enjoyment and satisfaction were depreciating quicker than I could find new ways to discover *more* enjoyment and satisfaction! Instead of feeling like life was opening up to me, I felt my options closing in.

Standing at the spiritual crossroads, I knew I had to choose between two paths. One of them was a wide path with sufficient space for all the luxuries of hedonism I so desired. It was a tantalizing thought to just stay my own, unhindered course in life, even if that path led me nowhere. The other road was the narrower one, which Jesus says leads to everlasting life. This second path, I learned, was filled to the brim with sacrifice and suffering, a road pock-marked with discipline and selflessness. No wonder it was the path I greatly resisted!

My Fanatical, Regrettable Tour of Ministry

Some of the foolish decisions I made during May of 1992 left me feeling more vulnerably mortal than ever before. It also left me with two all-important thoughts: "Wouldn't it be easier for me to surrender to Jesus?" and "Could it be that simple?" It was!

The call from Pastor Andrews was extremely timely. I picked up the phone, and I honestly can't remember much more after that. The rest was just an emotional vomiting over the sorry situation I'd found myself in at that moment. As we spoke, I wondered how the pastor knew that I needed an ear, and not just any ear, but his. When we are hurting, a call from a pastor is unlike any other. There's something so spiritually medicinal about a shepherd's caring voice. That's why God uses it to treat our earth-bound, sin-prone ailments. At the very least, a pastor's call makes us feel significant, reminding us as sheep that they've got us covered.

In the course of our conversation, Pastor Andrews divulged that he made it a practice of going into his bedroom to pray for all the people in his church. The pastor's revelation was *not* the game-changer in terms of what struck me about his phone call; it was what he said after that sent me reeling. "While I was in prayer," Andrews said, "the Lord wouldn't let me get passed your name. Did something happen? Are you okay?" It was at that precise moment that God proved to me that He had His privileged, divine finger on the pulse of every hidden detail of my life, and loved me enough to let me know it in a practical way—through *a phone call*. I knew that Pastor Andrews could not have had any knowledge of how trying the previous few weeks had been for me. I had stopped attending services and had not communicated with him, or anyone else at the church.

I finally construed, in a moment of complete abandonment, that God was worthy of more than just a few token Sundays; in fact, He was more than worthy of receiving my *whole* life. I had been holding back, slipping in and out of the light of God's truth about my life. I knew I could no longer window shop; I had to receive what He'd already purchased for me in the storeroom of Heaven.

The following Sunday, when Pastor Andrews issued an altar call after the service, I grew springs. Bouncing up from the pew, I came forward with the speed of a Maserati—my past streaking by me in the rear-view mirror, my future offering the promise of a scenic, heavenly view through the windshield ahead. People's heads jerked, ties went flapping, and Bible pages blew open from the wind I stirred up as I sped past rows of people on my way to the front of the church. There was no speed limit that day. I had been stuck in traffic for far too long. The only ticket I could possibly get was the one-way type… to eternal life.

Ron Mahler

As Pastor Andrews put his hands on my head to pray over me, the tears flowed, and Heaven rejoiced.

A few months after I submitted my life to Christ, I began to sense God's reasons for bringing Pastor Andrews into my life. They were far more significant than either of us could have known when we first met each other. Having seen the difference one person, a servant of God (a pastor) can make in a life, like Andrews did for mine, I became certain that I was destined to do the same for others. Though at one time all I wanted to be was a great artist and to be famous for my work, all I was really chasing were the things I thought I was supposed to be. But first, God had others plans. My longings, my pursuits, my spiritual hunger, my very heart… everything had changed. Something about the way Pastor Andrews ministered to me left me wanting to do that for others. If I could be anything, be like any other person, I wanted to be like him, and I wanted to do what he did—pastor! I wanted to make the difference he was making in others' lives.

I was going back to my childhood roots of thinking, wondering, experimenting, and observing things. This time, it wasn't with G.I. Joes, hockey uniforms, or newspapers; it was thinking on, wondering about, experimenting with, and observing *pastoral ministry*. So I began to study Pastor Andrews—his every word, his every move, how he spoke to people, how he handled himself publicly, and how he preached.

One summer night, I walked into the church before Bible study began and, while the others were gathered downstairs, I thought I would pretend to be a preacher. With my Bible tucked beneath my arm, I confidently walked up the firm, clean sanctuary carpet. Cranking my neck, I peered back to see if anyone was around or within earshot. I then grabbed hold of the worn, wooden pulpit with Spurgeon-like authority. Striking a Billy Graham pose, I began to preach. I have no recollection of what I said, but I'm sure it was in no way profound! There probably wasn't much of a spark, let alone fire, and most likely there was little trace of any brimstone… just the feeling of cement in my shoes when I realized how it felt to be up there.

All that mattered to me at the time was getting a feel for it, and yet it felt terrifying, even with all those empty seats facing me! Awe-inspired chills trickled down my spine, weaving down into my fingers and feet. It was like I was a kid hopping in a replica of one of his favourite racing cars at a fair; those kids don't really have to drive the car to feel what it's like to sit in the seat and put their hands on the wheel.

My Fanatical, Regrettable Tour of Ministry

That night before Bible study, I might as well have been Peter in the Book of Acts, and the sanctuary was the masses in Jerusalem to whom he preached his first sermon. However, as that momentary experience faded, I battled some more, spiritually. I continued to wonder how, knowing all my faults and limitations, God could use someone like me. Never mind the King's speech... back then I was convinced that the church wasn't quite ready for the *Pastor's* speech. My speech disfluency was the real deal! Pastors had to preach, and I struggled with a speech-impediment which was most noticeable whenever I was in uncomfortable or pressure-packed situations (a challenge I have since miraculously overcome, by God's grace, though I continue to go through a few hours of speech therapy a week to remain fluent).

I reasoned at the time that although I could probably fool some of the people, some of the time, no amount of wool could be pulled over God's eyes. To say that I felt inadequate and ill-equipped for the public speaking element of ministry would be an understatement. I filled many a day questioning whether my sudden interest in becoming a pastor was purely a product of my admiration of Pastor Andrews' ministry, or if it was actually of God. Besides, I hardly had a leg in the Kingdom, and I was already dreaming up scenarios for the rest of my life, and they resembled tall tales as much as high hopes. At times, I thought I was more cut out to be the unworthy Peter of Luke 5 than the preaching Peter of Acts 2. When confronted with the reality of Jesus' call on his life to be a fisher of men, Peter gave the Lord the cold shoulder in an attempt to send Him away.

Peter probably felt as useless as a hungry tick on a slab of marble when Jesus was handing out job descriptions to His targeted disciples. I, too, was more than willing to shoo Jesus away and decline His invitation to join Him on the harvest field. Sooner than later, however, God would have His way with me. He would not relent until I was served His Kingdom's subpoena to report for pastoral duty. It was a call I knew could be coming my way; I just couldn't accept why it would come to *me*.

CHAPTER 8

Revelations

As I continued to experience God's gentle prodding of my heart towards ministry, I did nothing to inquire about "next steps." In fact, just a year or so after becoming a Christian, I still had not spoken to anyone about my aspirations for pastoral ministry. I was learning to do what every new Christian is supposed to do: I was eating up scripture, trying to develop in every area of the spiritual disciplines. So I joined the worship team in Pastor Andrews' church and volunteered to help with the youth ministry.

However, other distractions soon arose. These diversions aggravated my most pressing need: to do something about the way I felt God leading me in my heart. Firstly, I was still working as a graphic designer in a photography company, a job which offered me the juicy opportunity to climb the proverbial ladder, thereby getting more involved in the photographic industry. Second, in many ways I was still recovering from the Nanny's departure, and became confused when she periodically resurfaced in my life.

Thirdly, another young woman came into the picture. She had "rebound" written all over her; I knew it, and she knew it. We were both trying to create something which I felt from the start wasn't really there at all. Yet it was a relationship I wanted, wise or not, in order to exorcise the ghost of Nanny past.

In the summer of 1992, I was just trying to get back on my happy-go-lucky, pre-Nanny feet. There was a new, spiritual reality about my world. I had a readjusted view of my past, as well as a new outlook on the future. I had new values, new ideals, new goals, and a new direction to blaze. My relationship with Rebound Girl would prove to be an obstacle of my own making. She neither encouraged nor dissuaded me to pray for confirmation as to whether I should have been pursuing pastoral ministry or not.

That was a concern in itself, but even more so were the temptations she brought (not all bad) which I allowed to occupy my heart and grieve my zeal for ministry. Rebound Girl and I attended Pastor Andrews' church together, and even collaborated on some ministry activities with the young people there. Despite that, something did not compute on a spiritual plane, in terms of our compatibility. I saw in her someone who did not have the growing passion for church life that I had. We were dating, but we were not a couple; we were together, but we were together-apart. That is, we were at polar opposites in our spiritual journey.

I was counselled by a good friend to consider ending the relationship before I got too far off course from attracting God's ideal partner for me. I spent the entire summer of 1993, as advised by Pastor Andrews, praying for God's clear guidance about a possible future in ministry, which included asking God for wisdom in choosing a spouse. Summers can seem so short, but when one is waiting on God for answers, even summertime can seem endless.

Morning, noon, and often long nights were spent in prayerful inquiry. Though I was unsure of how exactly I would realize God's answer, the assurance I was seeking finally broke through. No ghost of Nanny past, no Rebound Girl, and no amount of disobedience could keep Heaven silent when God desired to speak into my famished heart. On Monday, July 26, 1993, at approximately 11:48 p.m. (on my digital clock), like that Christmas night in 1989, it was just me and God at my bedside; it was His appointed time for me to hear what He had to say. At the time, I was repenting of something I had said to someone the previous weekend. New believers, it seems, are always much more sensitive of their sin than long-time believers, and they seem to pray about many things that come their way in the course of a day. That was me—late night, on my knees, in the dark, rehashing the day, as well as my failures.

Suddenly, it felt like my words were being cut off, and I became silent.

Then I experienced an unmistakable rush above me, a comet-like movement. In a vision, I saw a purple cloud pattern brush over me, almost like it could have been in the shape of an "M." The Holy Spirit spoke in a voice that seemed to paratroop deep down into my innermost being.

"It is okay to go," He assured.

Just five words, but they were the most welcomed words I'd ever heard. It was all that needed to be said, for I knew what God meant by them. God's oral tap on my eager, receptive ears opened the floodgates of my tears. These were not tears of sadness. Rather, they were a different kind of tears, inciting a different kind of cry—tears of gratitude and love towards God, but also tears signifying my own unworthiness. They were tears of incomprehension that God purposed to choose me for a significant role in ministry. At moments, God's call to me made perfect, biblical sense. "Why *wouldn't* God call me, to serve Him?" I would rationalize. After all, the Bible totes vast evidence of how God tends to choose certain people for His service whom He knows others have already written-off or discarded.

People would remind me that I was saved by a "God of grace" and by the "God of the impossible." I also learned that He's a God who uses others to confirm His calls and assignments for specific ministry. God had been calling me through my friends at church, through what little experience I had in youth work, through my pastor, through my longings, through the void in my life, through all the dissatisfaction and circumstances of my life… calling, calling. On that July evening, I heard Him loud and clear. I took the experience as clear confirmation of another God-encounter I'd had a year or so earlier.

While I was at a favourite park near my apartment, I sensed God speaking to me through a passage I was reading in 1 Corinthians. I was fresh off my breakup with the Nanny and consequently was hurting—bad. As I frequently did in those days, I had gone to the park to be alone, to reflect on my life. Oftentimes, I would sit, dreaming of a day when I could honestly say that I was happy, and that peace and direction were the bosom buddies of my life. I enjoyed the tranquil setting the park provided, which remained largely empty most days.

It was a very spacious park with more than enough benches; and yet there was one bench, in the middle of the park, that I always considered to be my favourite for prayer. The immediate area surrounding the bench (including a small pond framed by flowers) operated as my personal sanctuary and confessional. One day, it became God's microphone; as a result, it turned into a veritable "burning bush" experience. I don't know how Moses felt when God spoke to him through the fiery brush of Midian's desert plain, but when I heard God speak to me that day, it would have been easy to take it as a sign that I was going insane.

I can remember it being a difficult day when I plunked myself on the paint-faded wooden bench. I was already feeling exhausted from searching out God for weeks. I was mired in a deep, dry emotional funk, without a mirage in sight.

My Fanatical, Regrettable Tour of Ministry

Though I hadn't yet committed my life to Christ, I did feel the need to find heavenly solutions for my grievances.

While it seemed as though I had hit rock bottom, I was still willing to not only keep my chin up, but also keep looking up. If God was who the Bible said He was, then He had the corner on any and all inquiries. Interestingly, I decided against leaving my pocket Bible on the passenger seat of my car, taking it with me into the park. I was a man on a mission, and it had everything to do with calling God out to explain why He'd taken the Nanny away from me (unfairly in my eyes), leaving me to wallow barrel deep in feelings of personal inadequacy. I would have settled for a talking frog or a tree with blinking eyes… anything for God to show me *something*, and just lift my barbell of a burden.

I was learning about how I could have new life with Christ, but I wanted to know where God was when the life I did have really needed Him. I had to open my Bible somewhere, so I decided to roll the dice, splitting the pages with my fingers, and opening it to 2 Corinthians 5. I found the passage where Paul exhorts the early church at Corinth to live out their roles as ambassadors for Christ. Unsure as to whether these words told my fortune, I lamented that I hadn't opened to the passage where Jesus promises that if we ask anything in His name, it will be ours! As my eyes roved the words of 2 Corinthians 5, looking for instant answers, they saw a title reading "The Ministry of Reconciliation." I naturally thought, by my lack of biblical knowledge, that God was going to reconcile me to the Nanny. I became moderately excited. As attractive as such a biblical interpretation seemed to me at that moment, I knew it was too easy for me to project my will onto the passage, to make it mean anything I desired.

In impatience, I could have snapped my Bible shut right then and there, but something compelled me to read on, to stay glued to what I was doing. With my head lowered, my eyes busily darting through the same 2 Corinthians passage, I began to hear impressions of thoughts, like panoramic swoops weaving their way in and out of my mind. Though I might have concluded that I was out of my mind, I knew what I heard, and what I heard was not my own voice, nor was it generated by my own will. The still, small voice I received that day left no doubt as to what was whispered to me by the mouth of God's Spirit.

As quick as the experience began, the newsflash was over. In a period lasting about thirty seconds, the Holy Spirit let me in on a few non-negotiables that I couldn't go another day without hearing. The first thing was that God would take care of the Nanny, and I was to leave her to Him. She was no longer to hold my centre of attention, or the reigns of my heartstrings.

I also sensed that any reservations or objections I had about pressing on with God were non-factors. He was willing to put His reputation on the line by taking responsibility for how He was going to lead my life. The Spirit wanted to assure me that I had nothing to worry about. Talk about a field education! I was in God's classroom right there on the grassy knolls of the park, taking Theology 101! I walked away from that encounter comfortably optimistic that God did have a firm grip on my circumstances. For too long I had believed in the lie that I was competent enough to take command of my own life, yet it was my doubts, fears, and anger that I had let take the helm. The Bible says that God is greater than any hopes or schemes, devoid of His blessing and will, we can devise for our lives.

It is not for us to lead our lives; ultimately, it is God alone who is in charge. Proverbs says as much: *"In his heart a man plans his course, but the Lord determines his steps"* (Proverbs 16:9). In similar terms, the prophet Jeremiah prayed, *"I know, O Lord, that a man's life is not his own; it is not for man to direct his steps"* (Jeremiah 10:23). I would come face to face with that truth in a big way when, one year later, God confirmed His call for me to enter pastoral ministry. In hindsight, that's what made the experience in the park that day so meaningful.

To me, this experience acted as a precursor to the time when God would reveal His will for me, in that the "ministry of reconciliation" Paul wrote about in 2 Corinthians 5 was not only to be a role I fulfilled as a believer in general, but as a vocational minister. I can trace back, to the very day I sat on that park bench, the weight I felt on my heart to seek a life of serving God in ministry.

I found myself in a crucible of spiritual evolution. I was a searcher who was coming closer to being a finder; a listener who had become a better hearer. My apprehension of God was giving way to a deeper appreciation for Him. The seed of God's call on my life was planted that afternoon in the summery haze of the park, a call that required the consistent waters of cultivation for it to blossom into the flower of common sense. That night, on July 26, 1993, God had His man (me), and His man had his commission. I was ready, willing, and depending on God to make me able to follow through.

While my family wondered about my decision to go into ministry, it made perfect sense to those in my church. They had been observing my growth for over a year. Many of them saw it coming before I did; God saw it way before they did! Now, I had the humble privilege to begin living out God's perfect plan, a plan I had sensed evolving for a time. The plan for my life was simple: I was to serve the King of Kings and Lord of Lords in pastoral ministry!

Chapter 9

New Groove

By this time, a year had passed since Pastor Andrews' convicting sermon on Hell. Roughly the same amount of time had passed since I first found myself flying solo, without the Nanny on my arm.

The dreaded day came when I sat in my boss's office and explained to him why I had desired to be relegated to part-time status in the company I was working for as a graphic artist. I was in my third year with them and had only been in his office a handful of times. The room was like a principal's office: never extremely comfortable to enter, and it was even worse to sit in "the chair." My boss was a very self-assured kind of guy who came across as a bit intimidating. He always appeared to be in a hurry and never tarried too long in and around the office cubicles. He trusted his workers to do their jobs, and when they didn't he used his good set of lungs to let people know. There were even times when we, in the front of the building, could quite clearly hear him raise his voice all the way back in the warehouse.

What made my visit to his office that day so delicate a venture was that I had just received a memo stipulating that there was a new company policy: there were to be *no more* part-time employees, a rule, I took, that included me.

I had been taking a few basic Bible courses at night, which helped me to confirm how well I was doing academically in my new calling. I had arrived at the point where I was ready to attend those classes on a full-time, full speed ahead basis. The dilemma I faced was that I needed to retain some consistent employment to get me through Bible College while remaining flexible to schedules that required me to take the odd daytime class.

That's what brought me front and centre with my boss. I sat across from him, separated by a giant oak table littered with important looking documents and more than a few pictures of his children. While attending school on a part-time evening basis, I had kept my plans for further theological education a secret. I was overly cautious in trying to figure out how to break the news that I was pursuing another career path.

"Downsizing" was a popular catchphrase back in the 1990s. It captured the business world's desire to function more efficiently and economically. It was a generic, yet cruel term that basically meant someone was about to get the short end of the employment stick. More and more people, some who were at the same job for years, were being handed the pink slips. Fortunately, I was employed by a company that was doing well-enough to keep all its employees, and keep them relatively happy.

However, there I was, locking eyes with my employer, ready to downsize myself! This man, whose signature was on the bottom of my paycheques, had the prerogative to either let me pursue my future the way I'd planned or make things more complicated. Scripture would argue that ultimately God was in control of whether or not my boss was going to grant me my wish. Rightfully so, then, I was justified in believing that it would take a miracle for that to happen.

As a result of my zeal to experience all that I believed God was readying me for, I began to lose my creative flair and competitive hunger for the art field. I was never exactly enthralled with the often thankless and hurried commercial side of it, and I was even less enthusiastic about the cutthroat, rat-race culture surrounding the advertising world. Being in a position to go back to school on a full-time basis couldn't come fast enough for me.

I clearly recall my boss sinking into his shiny, black, leather-bound chair, and asking me, "What do you want to talk about?"

After having prayed intensely for a time, going before my boss that day still felt like a David and Goliath scenario. My boss wasn't a nine-foot giant by any stretch of the imagination, but he still had an imposing, tough exterior.

Then, all of a sudden, as if with the gumption of the shepherd boy David, I blurted out, "I've become a Christian, and I feel God leading me towards the ministry!"

The boss-man had a nanosecond's opportunity to respond before I continued explaining that I required time during the day to take on multiple courses

My Fanatical, Regrettable Tour of Ministry

so that I could graduate before it was time to *retire!* I thought injecting a little humour would soften the blow of my inquiry.

I noticed that as I was talking, my body had slowly lowered down into the chair. It was probably a subconscious defence mechanism, preparing me for a battery of explanations as to why I wouldn't be granted part-time status. As my boss sat quietly, with a stunned look on his face, it occurred to me that my request may actually have shot forth like a stone in a slingshot and hit him right between the eyes. He had the look of a man struck by some foreign object—the furrowed eyebrows, the squinting eyes. His midlife wrinkles were stretched to the max.

It seemed like an eternity before my boss responded. The Lord could have returned to earth, gone back to Heaven, had some lunch, and returned again.

When my boss finally did perk up to respond, his tone was predictably serious. "Ron, did you not hear what I said about not wanting anymore part-time employees in this company?"

I was about to up the ante by offering to shine his shoes, take out the company's trash, wash his spiffy Trans-Am out in the parking lot… anything it took to gain his favour. Then, like the Grinch whose heart grew three times larger in one day, a curled smile formed at the corner of his mouth.

"But for you, Ron, I will make an exception." As if to slay me with further kindness, and as if he really cared, he wished me all the best before inquiring, "What do you plan to take? A divinity degree?"

I felt like someone who had just been told that their terminal disease had been misdiagnosed.

I jumped up from my seat. "Yes! Thank you, sir!" My heart was mega-phoning: *Yes, God! You are good!* The only condition my boss insisted upon was that I was to find extra time to finish my work on deadline.

I remember feeling elated and thankful as I exited my boss's office. I looked forward to the day when I would eventually leave the company, my career in commercial art fading like the setting sun over the horizon of my past. The dreams I had of my art hanging in galleries no longer danced on the heart of my ambitions. It wasn't so much that I didn't think God would ever want me to use that specific talent again—after all, that would be counterintuitive, not only on an intellectual level, but on a spiritual one as well—but I couldn't deny any longer that I'd lost the magnetic and insatiable pull I once had to be characterized as a famous artist.

This sudden and extreme change in career not only puzzled my family, but probably disappointed them. To make matters more confusing, I was closing

Ron Mahler

in on finally capturing a vision for my personal artwork. I had created a series of pencil renderings of famous rock star icons, which I had hoped to patent. In my mind, such an endeavour would have cemented my career as a new breed of pop artist. It honestly had been starting to feel as if all the years I'd spent trying to make it as an artist were finally going to move from fantasy to fruition. I dreamed, like any other artist would, that people would walk into a gallery or store one day, spot my work, and say, "That's a Mahler!" I didn't know whether my dreams were being postponed or being granted a permanent vacation. All I knew for certain was that my heart had done a total 360 in willingly turning towards the possibilities God desired for me in pastoral ministry.

Due to my infant-like faith, I floundered in my attempts to adequately define for my family the spiritual changes I was undergoing. All I would tell them was that I could still draw from time to time. That was never going to change. What would change, I explained, was that I was no longer going to be known first and foremost as an "artist." I could still use the medium of art in some creative capacity, as a ministry, and even paint or draw on occasion for personal, therapeutic purposes. When God revealed Himself to me, He called me away from one thing (an unregenerated life spiritually oriented away from Him) and called me instead towards something else (a life spent in the pursuit of holiness and righteousness). Christ's call for us to follow Him is, first and foremost, a call to Himself.

The pilgrimage of every disciple consists of one ultimate spiritual endgame: *"to be conformed to the likeness of [God's] Son"* (Romans 8:29). That's who we, as Christians, are meant to be as people of God. In His purpose to make me like Christ, God sovereignly willed, in eternity past, that I be a minister of the Gospel. In that way, becoming a pastor was integral to what it meant for me to be conformed, as a child of God, to the likeness of Jesus. Therefore, I felt I couldn't blame those outside the faith who were disappointed in me for putting my art career aside. They didn't have any inkling of just who and what I was meant to be *in Christ*, and what that specifically entailed for me as a servant of God.

By coming to faith in Christ, I put my whole life at the Holy Spirit's disposal. Everything I had once counted as my own became God's for the taking, if He so willed it. With that came the inevitable spiritual challenge of accepting some changes in my life; some were easier to take, while others were downright difficult. For me, saying yes to Jesus meant making a change in vocation, not because I would have failed as an artist, but because God purposed to direct me away from that particular path. My passion for art had to be relegated to a sentimental sidebar in my life; it couldn't be the navigator of my life it had become.

My Fanatical, Regrettable Tour of Ministry

In Christ, God gave me a new set of values and priorities to live by. People would ask me why I couldn't just continue on in my art, why my becoming a Christian meant that my full potential as an artist had to fall by the wayside. I reasoned with those closest to me, many of them non-Christians, that God had long ago placed in me a desire that could only be identified and fulfilled as I came to know Him through a relationship with His Son, Jesus Christ.

I had laboured very hard for many years to fill in the emotional blanks of my life that spoke of the emptiness I often experienced as a young man. I tried to accomplish that by doing what came natural for me—so I drew. I thought that was what I had to do! To me, that was my redemption. However, God knew what He was doing when He turned me away from a life of artistry. I have very little doubt that I am a far greater preacher and teacher today than I could ever have been as an artist.

God never makes mistakes; it is we who sometimes underestimate just how infinite His wisdom really is. After I finally accepted Christ as my Saviour, and *committed* to Him, I could no longer continue to work on the series of rock star drawings I was planning to sell. I can still remember the day back in 1992 when my HB pencil drew the first strokes of a piece of artwork I was working on after my conversion and instead of excitement I felt lukewarm about what I was trying to accomplish. That experience recurred on almost a daily basis. I would stand over my drawing, stare at my pencil container, glance back at the drawing, and feel constricted by indecision. "Maybe another night," I would resolve, and walk away.

On other occasions, even if I did manage to do some work, the pendulum of my interest level would swing to the extremes of indifference. Artists are funny creatures; some are reclusive and eccentric and require seclusion, even unkemptness, in order to do their best work. Other artists have to get "into the spirit" of what they're doing, even if that means surrounding themselves with props and sounds pertaining to their subject. Then there was me, an artist who at one time could draw with felicitous effort, but whose will to keep doing so was suddenly dwarfed by a "new flame" in my life. It became difficult for me to reconcile my faith with what I was doing with my life—drawing images for people to buy and hang in their homes, stores, and offices.

I felt that if I continued with my plan to complete my series of rock star icons, I would be hallowing the fame and acumen of some people whose lifestyles didn't honour God. That decision reflected the extent to which my personal value-system had transformed from where it had been prior to my knowledge of God's will.

Ron Mahler

In July of 1993, I had another burning idea for something I wanted to sell, something else I wanted to make known to people, something that I knew couldn't be found in my chosen vein of artwork. God didn't convict me to stop drawing rock star icons in favour of painting religious symbols and biblical impressions; rather, He endowed me with an overpowering desire to shepherd people in pastoral ministry. As a result, I finally found what I wanted to be "when I grew up."

On the evening of July 26, I experienced a summons from Heaven that was so obvious and irresistible by its encroaching presence that it left me humbled, and certain, that I was *born* to pastor. When God speaks, He does so not only to be understood, but obeyed. As Derek Prime and Alistair Begg express it in their book, *On Being a Pastor*, "God always gives a clear call to those whom He has chosen for the ministry…they can do nothing other than respond to it. They will not be able to say no to it… God does not give uncertain calls."[4]

It may take me a lifetime to appreciate my call to the ministry and the character needed to be a good, faithful spiritual leader and pastor. However, it only took one class, during my first semester as a full-time Bible College student at the age of twenty-six, to be awakened to the precious nature of what it was I was studying and pursuing as a vocation.

CHAPTER 10

Precious

WHILE SITTING IN CLASS ONE SEPTEMBER MORNING, MY PROFESSOR BEGAN HIS lecture by holding up a ratty-looking, taped-up red book. Neither I nor the other students could exactly distinguish what kind of book the teacher was holding in his hand.

In a coy, playful tone, Professor Penrod asked the class, "Do you know what this is? This is precious!"

Only after hearing him say those words did we, as a class, fully realize that the professor was holding up his own well-worn, and certainly well-read, New Testament. Up to that point, I had never heard of the Bible, or any part of the Bible, referred to in those terms. The solemnity of that moment left an incurable imprint upon my memory, so much so that on occasion, while preaching, I still mimic Professor Penrod's example of holding up the New Testament and asking, "Do you know what this is?" Each time I've done this, it has caused me to relive the awe I felt that morning as a student. What a start I received to my full-time studies!

When the professor held up the New Testament, it was like a football coach holding up a football before His team's players and challenging them, "The goal of playing with this ball is not just simply to play football, or even to win a game. The goal of what you do with this ball is to win a championship." Thanks to the professor's moving edict, the goal of my being in Bible College became clearer. I wasn't in school to simply earn a theological degree as a pastor in-training; rather,

Ron Mahler

I was going to be entrusted with the role of leading others (to borrow another football analogy) "down the field" of life, quarterbacking them by the very Words of the God of the universe. In essence, this is an elemental ministry God calls *each* believer to, but especially to those of us in God's family who are shepherds and teachers. We have been given the awesome and noble task, as members of Team Heaven, of carrying God's living Word and the hope that comes from it into every life situation we minister to.

Our game plan needs to be to place the Word atop the greatest challenges and burdens we have in life, like a trophy rewarding the faith of those who are desperate and lonely, those who are seeking, and those who are sick and dying. As a Bible College student, I had many experiences which helped me gain a greater appreciation of the ministry that lay yet ahead. In principle, when a person is preparing or training for ministry, they are, in a sense, already ministering in their sphere. One of the main differences between student ministry and professional ministry is that students do not receive a *salary* for it; yet for me, what I didn't gain monetarily by ministering to others was made up for by the confidence being built in my pastoral abilities. Bible College allowed me the forum to fan into flame the spiritual gifting God had given me, which I would need to use in pastoral ministry (see 2 Timothy 1:6).

The results were immediately affirming. Fellow students in my sphere of influence seemed comfortable around me and communicated their appreciation for my listening ear and pastor's heart. I was the chairman of our student council's Devotional Committee in my last full year of Bible College. One of the responsibilities that position came with was overseeing our school's "prayer box" ministry. When I, along with fellow volunteers, first sifted through the prattle of prayer requests we received, we were startled to discover how many issues even Bible-believing students faced on a daily basis. Even the sheltered bubble of a Christian school, which insulated and buffeted them with accountability, proved penetrable by heightened temptation. I thought to myself that that must have been how Eden was like for Adam and Eve. If that able-not-to-sin environment wasn't entirely safe from the Devil, how much more safe could a Bible College be? Even though we were in school to learn about the application of spiritual wisdom, the reality is that we were still living *in* the world.

In fact, I was instantly overcome with a heavy burden at how much prayer was necessary for students who constantly needed to be brought to the throne of God's grace. Even responding to the people who asked for prayer was a challenge; it seemed easier to give God my words on their behalf than to always have the appropriate words ready to address their problems. Getting to that place, as Christians, where we realize the kind of honour it is to bring another's need, burden, or crisis to the hotlines of Heaven helps us to see how precious the task is.

It's like the advertisement I once came across in a magazine for Christian leaders. The ad showed a professional-looking pastor posing in front of his office library, with a caption that listed the lengthy ministry tasks the pastor had accomplished in one week's time. The main message of the advertisement, however, was found in the wording: "And you consider it all joy." What a portrait that is of the precious nature of God's call to us, as pastors and servants of God! No amount of demand on a pastor's time, or wear and tear on a minister's service, can dull the heavenly afterglow that results from the work God calls His servants to.

Recently, as I was driving home after visiting two very ill people in hospital, I found myself thankful to God for the privilege of being an extension and instrument of His grace. Just having the opportunity to dispense a word of comfort or a touch of compassion seems too sacred to be compensated by a paycheque. No financial reward can equal the matchless spiritual worth of what it's like to minister to the life of someone who's in need. Whether it's reading scripture to the dying, shedding tears with someone who is newly widowed, listening to the concerned, or holding the feeble hand of an Alzheimer's patient, our lives are full of moments that are of precious value.

My Bible College training gave me a preparatory glimpse of the jewel we behold when we experience God working through us to make tangible, spiritual differences in other people's lives. Like a prism being held up to the light, nothing reflects the rays of God's glorious love more than when we serve others as the Saviour Himself did. It didn't take me a day on the job in some church to realize that particular biblical principle, nor will I be able to fully grasp what it means to minister in Jesus' name in my lifetime. Yet the precious nature of pastoral ministry was marvellously captured, for me, in the form of a ratty-looking, taped-up red New Testament, as well as in the contents of a prayer box.

CHAPTER 11
Lift-off

In the early spring of 1996, I was moving ever closer to completing my undergraduate's degree. Though I didn't realize it at the time, I was also nearing my very first paid position in ministry. I hadn't had much in the way of correspondence with any churches that year, despite having applied for several positions. Uncertain as to exactly what position I was supposed to aim for as a student pastor, I tried to remain open to what God had for me as one who was just starting out in ministry.

I prayed fervently for any opportunity to get a solid start in a ministry position, which would hopefully affirm and launch my calling into the pastoral role. A friend pointed out to me how much he thought I was chomping at the bit to get into a church. I was rooming with two other guys whom I'd met in Bible College, just to be able to afford to live off-residence. Money became tight, and my bank account was snug after I left the photography firm I'd worked at for four years.

I was pretty much on my own, financially, and hoped to have my necessities provided for by taking a night job in the warehouse of a Christian bookstore. The only other manual-labour job I ever had was as a teenager, loading trucks and sometimes doubling as an item presenter in my brother-in-law's liquidation and auctioneering business. Therefore, I wasn't afraid of physically demanding work, but at the age of twenty-eight, and having spent the three previous years of my life receiving a theological education, I was ready to put my days of making ends meet with odd jobs behind me.

My Fanatical, Regrettable Tour of Ministry

Little did I realize that a pastor's salary wouldn't exactly catapult me into a more elite financial bracket. Even to this day, as an experienced pastor, I'm still struggling to make ends meet! All I could think about at the time was the life-altering experience of July 1993, as well as the various events confirming and reaffirming God's call to enter into full-time vocational ministry.

Any craving I once had to become an artist seemed like a faded object on the wall of my life's journey which heavenly graffiti, in the form of God's greater plan, had spray-painted over. In my heart, I was ready to break out of the stalls of Bible College and make a pastoral splash in the kingdom of God. Close to possessing my bachelor's degree, and able to truly claim a personal calling upon my life, I was loaded with confidence to begin my ministry.

I felt that I had become an authentic option for God to call upon, at any time, for His service. Though I wasn't certain what ministry role would suit me ideally, I did know that I seemed to click with young people. I had deduced that since I was youthful myself, and had endured many crises in my adolescent years, I could surely be of use to God as a youth pastor, despite the fact that this hadn't been the focus of my program studies. When I sought counsel from the Bible College's personnel, they advised that in order for one to be ready for a senior pastor's position, it was best to work one's way up by starting in either youth ministry or in an associate's role.

I didn't concur with that position back then, and I certainly don't today. I readily accept that there are a limited few twenty-somethings who, by virtue of their spiritual maturity and life experience, are ready for a senior or lead pastoral role when they leave Bible College or seminary. At the same time, however, I don't believe that everyone is cut out for taking on the role of shepherding young people. Youth ministry is difficult in the best and healthiest of churches. It is a unique ministry, in that it requires one to have a specific resonance with a specific culture or group of people, as well as a chameleon-like personality that can balance leadership with friendship. I have seen more than a few willing servants of God get worn-out from the high-ceilinged demands and expectations of youth ministry, myself being one of them. Every town, city, church, and denomination, in my opinion, seems to have its own youth culture, and unique needs to match it.

Given that reality, it is a tricky endeavour to use a one-size-fits-all youth ministry template. Suffice it to say that I have always been baffled as to why some parents think the "youth guy" should be able to turn their teenager around in no time, even though that same young person has had seventeen years or more to get to where they are! Even though I knew I could "hang" with young people, I wasn't quite convinced that I would be able to spiritually lead them along when I myself was still so new in the faith. In hindsight, I probably should have explored more in-depth the expectations that come with a call to youth ministry, and taken further time to prayerfully iron out where I would be best suited to serve. However, I was an idealist, and an impatient one at that. I just wanted to love people, and I despaired waiting any longer to show what I brought to the table for the Kingdom of God.

At times, I struggled with how I could know, for sure, where it was that God willed me to be. I encountered many available positions in parachurch organizations, which came with the challenging stipulation that one had to raise their own support monies. A pastor friend of mine used to tell me I would know when the right church and ministry came along.

In the spring of 1996, I had no prior experience to go on. One church, situated about thirty minutes across the city, was offering a summer internship. I read through the requirements of the job and thought to myself that whoever got the position would be well on their way to being established in the ministry. Then, reality set in. I couldn't see that I would be the one to be so blessed with the job. I counted on there being about as much competition as there might be for a lottery jackpot. However, something about this summer internship caused me not to write it off in novice haste. To this day, I'm glad I didn't. Pastor Goodman, with whom I'm still friends today, was the pastor of First Community Church when they offered that posting for a student intern.

In need of a summer job, I ran up the stairs of my shared basement apartment, on my way to apply at a local Canadian Tire, when suddenly the phone rang. It was the call I had been hoping and praying for. Pastor Goodman was on the other end, extending an invitation for me to interview for the summer pastoral internship.

The interview went well. So well, in fact, that the phone rang once more a few days later, with Pastor Goodman offering me the position. From what I could gauge by my conversations with Goodman, the church was by no means a "happening" place. Even though the church building had an antiquated feel about it, it could have been Willow Creek for all I cared.

All that really mattered to me was that I was wanted. The way I saw it, the same fingers that had once carved out the Ten Commandments were now engraving my call to the ministry, and putting it in stone!

I heard the Lord right, I thought to myself, peacefully, *and God never makes mistakes!*

My Fanatical, Regrettable Tour of Ministry

    Though my new position at First Community Church was hardly a high-profile role, being hired and trusted to fulfill the ministry's requirements of me made me feel needed, important, and all the more set apart (holy) as a believer.

    Bible College had presented, at different intervals, its fair share of challenges, and I had been exposed to varying degrees of politics, even conflict, as I served on Student Council. In many ways, those initial experiences were microcosms of what I would face later in church ministry. However, on that April day of 1996 when I was offered the summer internship, I was lean-dog hungry. I was venturing out to consume all that the noble call to ministry could place at my well-intentioned feet. In no way could I have known what that kind of desire, to serve God, would attract and uncover in the church.

Chapter 12: Maiden Voyage

H.B. London calls pastoral ministry "a way of life...a lofty vocation, a high calling that most people will never experience...The title 'pastor' makes you realize you are special."[5] That's how I would have defined myself, as well as my new occupation in life, back when I shot forth from a galaxy of renowned, godly alumni like a pastoral supernova embarking on the hallowed work of the church.

The lure to perform and perfect one's ministry prowess in a public setting is a very seductive and powerful force to any Bible College or seminary graduate. But for young pastors, landing their first full-time vocational ministry position can be such a blindingly attractive prospect that they are unable to see the long-term costs it may exact from them in terms of energy, wisdom, and time. Though the finely-tuned challenges and realities of ministry that are woven like a helix in spiritual DNA are not the things that immediately jump out at rookie pastors, they nonetheless can function like an ocean's wave coming out of nowhere to knock them off their surfboard of ministry idealism. When I began my time at First Community Church, I ignorantly believed that I was more than ready to take on the onerous demands of church life. For certain, I desired to look and sound the part of a pastor; I wanted to be a man of the cloth.

I can still remember how saintly and ministerial I felt on my very first Sunday morning at First Community Church. As I sat up on the platform with Pastor Goodman, I crossed my legs in authoritative fashion, gripping a thick Bible

My Fanatical, Regrettable Tour of Ministry

on my lap that sported the shiny-new golden tips of its pages. We both had our prim, suit-and-tie looks about us, and it took everything for me to keep myself from smiling, even through some serious prayer requests! There were Sunday mornings when the senior pastor gave me the reigns of the service, to the extent that I felt like I'd comfortably "arrived." The whole pastoral composition, from its look to its voice, to its stride and carriage, was absolutely intoxicating to me. In fact, I found every facet of my pastoral role to be exhilaratingly appealing.

I looked forward to holding court with the formative minds of the youth as much as I looked forward to creating awesome youth events. I also looked forward to that landmark day when I would walk up to the pulpit for the first time and open my large, important-looking Bible to impart the Word of God in sermonic brilliance.

Eventually, I would fulfill all those desires—minus the brilliant preaching—but I was so enamoured with ministry that I was willing to take on all the needy churchgoers. I couldn't wait for someone to come to me with their deep, life-sized problems. Thinking back, I can't fathom what kind of ultra-deceptive hallucinogen I must have been on. You name it, I wanted to experience it. Being able to make the tough decisions as a young pastor? I craved it! Proving that I was able to hold down the fort while the senior pastor was away? Bring it on! Preach a few sermons a month while carrying on my regular youth ministry duties? Priceless! I was looking forward to such prospects, and more. I wanted to be known as a good leader, a powerful man of God, a fun-loving servant, a technically sound theologian, a grand orator, a wise shepherd, a good motivator, and someone who had impeccable ministry sense and solid evangelism tactics.

As my summer internship commenced, I thought I could become that phantom figure in the ministry. I had skyscraper-like expectations in terms of my ability to function in a role I had no prior experience in. Eventually, I would be brought back to humble ground! It's not that I was cocky; I was just confident in how God had gifted me, and in the call He had placed so clearly on my life.

Seminaries really ought to have a course entitled "Great pastors are not recent Bible College graduates." Come to think of it, have you ever noticed how most of the people you and I might associate with "great and respected pastors" either have salt-and-pepper hair, or very little hair at all? In other words, being a great servant of God requires many things, but the most important of these is time. At First Community Church, however, I felt like it was *my* time. I saw myself as some can't-miss, cutting-edge product, fresh out of the training crate, who was already assembled, with no parts missing and a no-money-back guarantee!

Ron Mahler

A buddy I golfed with at the time told my then-fiancée, Elaine, "Ron oozes pastor!" He was getting the pastoral vibe that I intrinsically felt and naturally gave off! I'm not sure whether or not his comment was intended to be taken as a compliment.

However, it only took a few months at First Community Church before I was already questioning my preconceived ideals and notions of what pastoral ministry really looked like. Jesus, I knew, provided the best example, so I resolved that the best way to minister to people was to love as Jesus loved. I would try to bottle that and sell it to the people. My thought was, *If I just love people, they'll love me back.* According to logic, that's an ironclad argument. Like the gospel according to The Beatles says, "All you need is love." Right? Well, that message may have made for a good pop song, but it was an unproven philosophy that's too ultra-utopian for even God's Holy Spirit-powered people to make work in every church situation.

Over the years, I have been more surprised by who has rejected me as a pastor than by who has supported me. Like any bomb diffuser or landmine inspector, one must inevitably anticipate the potential of surprise explosions in the church at any time. Pastoral ministry comes with one guarantee that is good for a lifetime: *there are no guarantees!* Ministry can be just as elating and rewarding to our spiritual life as it can be deeply subversive and injurious. All we have to do is look around. For every church that is seemingly doing well, there is another that's suffering over one or more divisive issues. Look around at the Church today, especially in the western world, and you see a bride of Christ that tends to cover up how undeniably battered and bruised it really is, not so much at the hands of its culture, as one might expect, but via self-inflicted wounds.

From time to time throughout its history, the Church has become front page news, for dubious reasons. Whether it's allegations of sexual abuse amongst the clergy, insensitive and condemning statements made by some of its representatives, or even the regrettably divisive actions taken by some believers, the more we look around at the Church, the more we'd rather close our eyes to it all. The spiritual health and vitality of the North American Church is tenuous at best. Don't get me wrong, I am not saying we're done for, in terms of our witness as the Church. On the contrary, there are countless churches of all sizes that are working hard to maintain a positive testimony for Jesus Christ, and that consistently serve and impact their communities. There are churches that are baptizing, growing, and sending out into the world many believers. Don't you wish we could stop there? But then we hear about all the bad stuff. We hear about all the

My Fanatical, Regrettable Tour of Ministry

factions, about the epidemic of broken Christian marriages, about falling pastors and Christian addicts, about dying congregations and heretical teachings. All we have to do is look around.

At First Community Church, all I wanted was to be used of God to make a difference in the lives of people. That's what I was spiritually gifted for and what I was trained to do. However, I wasn't prepared for the gravity of pain and sin I met in people's lives, or how that darkness would affect me in every manner imaginable. Was I expecting to delve into the terror of people's lives and not come away horrified somehow? Was I expecting to help put the broken pieces of peoples' lives back together and not get cut? It dawned on me one day that if the church is to be the redemption centre God wills it to be, it must also resemble a hospital trauma unit. The reality all around me was that there were people, like myself, who were sinful, problematic, and prone to wander into every conceivable difficulty in life.

I had no idea just how messy I would have to be willing to get in order to minister to people, Christian or not, in the dirt of their lives. Didn't my experiences in Bible College and my education alert me to that reality? Sure it did! Yet like skin cancer, like AIDS, like a sudden tragedy, we never think such realities will come to our front door. Likewise, we seldom think we will have to deal with the worst-case scenarios of our lives—or someone else's. We hope we'll never find those things in the churches we go to as pastors and leaders! Ministry has its bumps in the road; we all know that, yet it sure would be nice to go to a church one day that we'll be able to leave unscathed. That's what we, as pastors, would like. No doubt, it's the best we can hope for.

First Community Church was a nice, friendly flock of believers led by a godly senior pastor who I had the privilege of learning from. The church had a lot of admirable qualities, and yet it was still a sheepfold where sometimes even the most well-intentioned of God's sheep poked at the fences, got away, and wandered headlong into trouble. Months into my internship, I was reminded that the biblical imagery of a shepherd's staff carries with it more than just connotations of sheep being led out to luscious, serene pastures; it also represents a pastor's responsibility over the flock of God. In the Bible, a staff didn't merely *make* someone a shepherd, or even make one *look* the part; staffs were in the hands of the sheep's caretakers to be used. And sometimes, when the shepherd wielded his stick, somebody got a whack.

CHAPTER 13

The Staff

A FEW YEARS AGO, I RECEIVED A GIFT ON THE OCCASION OF MY ORDINATION. It was a nice black handbag with lots of space and compartments to store my laptop and important papers. It was the first time I had ever owned such an item, which in hindsight makes me wonder how I ever got along without one! Now, I am forever toting that bag around. Wherever I go, my black bag goes with me. We are inseparable, and you'd think I had my life's possessions in it! Just to be clear, though, I do not keep it at my bedside while I sleep, and I'm nice enough to let others touch it from time to time. My point is that I find the handbag to be indispensable to my job. I can use it for many purposes pertinent to my duties in the office, and at home. In a physical sense, I carry that handbag gladly.

In a spiritual sense, every pastor carries another indispensable tool—a shepherd's staff. Psalm 23, one of the best-loved passages in the scriptures, gives us a beautiful depiction of how David, the king of Israel, saw the Lord as his shepherd. David was writing from firsthand experience, since as a young boy he had taken care of his father's flocks of sheep. In a profound manner, David, as he wrote the psalm, was inspired to intertwine his own personal work as a shepherd with the character of the God he worshipped. As a result, we have a masterpiece in Psalm 23 which speaks to us of how near our Lord is to us, and how dear we are to Him as His disciples. David's words remind us of that delicate and dependent relationship we have, as sheep, with our Lord and Good

Shepherd, Jesus Christ. Therefore, as "under-shepherds" of Christ, pastors bear their own, unseen shepherd's staff as they minister to their people.

Jesus commissioned Peter to take care of His sheep and to feed His lambs (see John 21:15–16). Well, just like David wrote, pastors are also to lead their people beside the quiet and still waters of reflection and meditation, in administering to them the greenery of God's nourishing Word, which restores their souls. Pastors are to comfort their flock as well, through counsel and through prayer, as if it were a rod or staff. The reassuring presence of a shepherd figure in the lives of God's people is an invaluable guide for sojourners travelling the spiritually treacherous paths of faith.

When my wife Elaine and I used to walk our two small dogs through the neighbourhood, they would instinctively stick close to us. There were times when, as diminutive animals, they would cling to our legs after hearing a loud sound, just to be assured that we, who were bigger, were safely by their side. As God's people, we have that same need, albeit in a spiritual capacity. The remarkable beauty of Psalm 23 shows us that the sheep must know that the shepherd is walking alongside them.

However, it is possible that as a pastor walks with their people, they will also have to use the staff, or rod, for other, less-popular purposes. For instance, sometimes pastors must use their shepherd's staff to put a bit of distance between the faithful sheep and themselves, the primary reason being that they can then make room for scaling the greater field, which Jesus said is ripe with the harvest (see John 4:35). When it comes to the task of personal and corporate evangelism, the souls that can be harvested from the mission field are not always the predominant obstacle. As Christians, we can so easily adopt the spiritually myopic copout that unsaved people either don't want Jesus, or the community doesn't care about church. For some unsaved people, that absolutely may be the case. However, I have come to believe that the mission field is not entirely the problem, precisely because Jesus said there is a harvest to be had within it, and all we have to do is open our eyes (see John 4:35).

Seeking out the spiritually lost is one of the pastor-shepherd's jobs. Jesus said, *"I have other sheep that are not of this sheep pen. I must bring them also"* (John 10:16). The challenge facing pastors—and every Christian, for that matter—is making personal evangelism a priority, and setting aside ample time to be around the unchurched and those people God may be giving to us outside the church. Pastoral ministry that is perceived to be done in the church, for the church, and as part of one's job description is rightly an expected and necessary dimension of the role. Indeed, part of a pastor's responsibility as a shepherd is to lead and feed the sheep that are *already* in his or her pen. Paradoxically, the time and energy devoted towards God's people can very easily take away from the lives of those dying without Jesus.

Pastoral ministry is about many things, yet it *must* be about micromanaging a leader's time, energy, and resources. The pastor's mandate to pursue and connect with people in the immediate context of the church's neighbouring community almost always falls to the wayside. Periodically, I get together with another pastor from my community who recently shared that he felt his church was perhaps expecting too much from its people. He felt that the extent of the commitment his church's leadership was asking of the people—in terms of time spent volunteering in the community, implementing family nights, setting aside time for daily devotions, participating in small groups, making themselves available for ministry training, and serving in various capacities on Sunday mornings—left them with precious little time and energy to scale the mission fields of their lives.

His point was well made. Perhaps some people's biblical priorities are too focussed on living like they're not in this world. They're so preoccupied with "Christian" things, so associated with church culture, that they've forgotten to be in the world, pursuing and forming relationships with the unsaved.

We can see this reality juxtaposed in church on Sunday mornings. Church services often magnify just how ingrown believers can become in the comfortable confines of their own Christian territory. Visitors can sometimes be treated as strangers to be avoided, rather than guests to be embraced. Unintentional as it may be, the general flock can crowd the shepherd from getting to the "other sheep" Jesus spoke of, those who need to be brought into the fold.

I am referring to the natural penchant some of God's people have to flock closely to the shepherd every Sunday. These people either can't wait to tell the pastor what God did in their life that week, are either so encumbered with cares that they must have their weekly prayer requests heard, or just feel they have to critique or affirm every sermon. Whatever the case, most times pastors feel secure in those encounters, often drawing from them professional esteem or personal affirmation. However, there are those Sundays—"on a good day," as some of us in ministry sometimes say—when there happens to be a contingent of new people attending the service. Recently, I decided to change my vocabulary in terms of how I refer to people visiting our church. Instead of saying something old and tired like, "Isn't it great that we have some visitors today?" I challenge our people: "This morning, God has given us the opportunity to visit with people He brought to His house."

Oftentimes, God does bring the mission field to our church's welcome mats. That said, the church building is always a mission field waiting to happen. Pastors, as well as their people, must be mindful of this and compensate for it.

Case and point: I found it odd during my very first Sunday at First Community Church when Pastor Goodman, after the service, stayed up by the front doors, off and away from the lower floor of the front foyer. My best pastoral major's conclusion was that Goodman was being distant with the people. In actual fact, however, Pastor Goodman chose to stand where he did so that he could keep his shepherd's eye peeled to the greater foyer, availing himself to any newcomers who may have been visiting that day.

Sometimes hurting people attend church because they're looking for reasons to still believe in caring Christian leaders. If Pastor Goodman would have made himself available solely to his own flock, who had access to him all week, his eyes and ears may have been diverted from providing some immediate shepherding to any "strays" who might have showed up at his sheep pen. Due to the fact that the regular worshippers at First Community Church habitually gathered on the lower level of the foyer, I was often placed down with them. Initially, I accepted where I was placed after the services as a mark of pastoral honour. After all, that's where Jesus would be: amongst the people! Besides, the number of doting grandmothers moving in and around me each week was heart-warming.

However, things would get really embarrassing for me whenever the elderly ladies complimented me on how I was dressed; even more awkward were those moments when they tried to fix my hair or straighten my tie. My gratification from such experiences, let me tell you, didn't last too long. Before I knew it, I was the weekly treat being served up to the same people, who repeated the same things to me, service after service. I used to think that if I could just escape out the back door before the last hymn was over, that would be a good Sunday!

That said, the older generation at First Community Church were among some of my greatest encouragers during my internship. They politely patted me on the arm whenever I bombed at preaching, just as they led the cheers on those occasions when I did something well. They provided me with some poignant memories, and also, I might add, with some great potlucks along the way! All of God's people are wonderful in their own, unique way: those who fill our bellies, as well as those who drain our patience and break our hearts.

I experienced many firsts at First Community Church, by virtue of it being my maiden voyage in pastoral ministry. These included (but aren't limited to): my first sermon, my first crack at officiating at baptismal and communion services, and my first counselling sessions. The time I spent there was very beneficial. However, when I reminisce about my internship, serving alongside Pastor Goodman, what always comes foremost to mind is the biblical image of a shepherd's staff, an image which jumped off the Bible's pages and came alive for me. Though the whole biblical package of shepherd imagery is often stunningly portrayed on stained glass, there is more to the staff in a shepherd's hand than simply being part of a pretty picture.

The unavoidable and sometimes harsh truth of pastoral ministry is that it has unique seasons which must be weathered. There are times when the sun is shining, people are growing, leaders are coasting, and the blessings of ministry seem lush and enjoyable to behold. Then, there are other periods when the dark clouds of conflict hover over, cool winds move in, and everything that once appeared promising begins to change colour, taking on a bleak outlook. There are times when pastoral ministry isn't very satisfying, when pastors and other church leaders find they are not in their "happy place."

There are pockets of weeks and months when the peaceful image of the shepherd's staff morphs into something else. In my first year of vocational ministry, as an intern at First Community Church, the image of a shepherd's staff also became a symbol for the necessity for church discipline. This was the harshest first of them all; it was also a harbinger of harsher realities yet to come.

Chapter 14

Riot Act

One evening, as I was hanging out with some friends, I received a call from Pastor Goodman, who in a rather serious tone requested that I come to a meeting in his office that Saturday morning. Predictably, my initial thought was, *What did I do wrong?* Pastor Goodman didn't divulge much in the way of what the powwow in his chambers was all about. The only tidbit I was offered was that it had to do with a "serious issue" that pertained to "some people" in the youth ministry. The fact that I was the pastoral overseer of the youth ministry stoked much apprehension in me. It also prevented me from getting a decent night's sleep leading up to the portentous meeting. In fact, I barely went under a few of those nights. The only "under" I experienced the Friday before the big meeting was a desire to hide under the blankets, to keep from facing the unknown the next morning. To my surprise, the sun actually came up and shone bright that inauspicious Saturday morning.

As I prepared to head to the church, I found prayer didn't come easily. Accordingly, I felt very little peace, and more than a teeny amount of anxiety burrowed into me. In driving to the meeting, I sifted through the towering stacks of unnecessary scenarios in my mind.

After arriving at the church, I nervously entered the pastor's office accompanied by one of the main volunteers in the youth ministry. I noticed that a representative board member was also present. This person nodded politely in our direction, but didn't say a word.

Ron Mahler

Then I made eye contact with Pastor Goodman, and from his demeanour I could discern that what he had to tell me and the other youth leader was not going to be easy for him. That's when I noticed another telling factor about the meeting: my other teen volunteer was conspicuous by her absence. Sure enough, Pastor Goodman proceeded to tell us that the missing volunteer was involved in an inappropriate relationship with one of the older teens attending the youth group.

The revelation made the region of my head and neck feel as though it had a thousand-pound bag of cement draped around it. In an instant, the weight of the news caused my eyes to descend to the rug, which I'd never before noticed had an interesting pattern to it. With my head lowered for what seemed like a lengthy period of time, I could have drooled a bowl's worth of saliva. Finally, we got to the consequences of the situation. Both myself and my right-hand volunteer were warned that if any other such allegation came up about us in the future, or if there were any hints of impropriety within our ministry, we were both gone. At the time of the meeting, I felt Pastor Goodman came across a little strong in his admonishments. However, his swift and thorough issuing of the riot act was an understandably justifiable measure, which he took to protect the church's testimony.

Before the meeting adjourned, both the youth volunteer and I had to sign a moral conduct agreement, in which the expectations and standards of spiritual integrity and righteous behaviour for leadership were laid out. I left the office slightly wounded, yet most of all I felt terribly sad for the other youth ministry volunteer, and sadder still for the young person involved in the situation. It took me some time to realize that the whole incident was not primarily about me, or even about my reputation. The silent, selfish struggle I grappled with every time I thought about what had happened was that the whole ordeal had occurred on my watch. Then the self-inquisition commenced, with palpable questions flowing in and through my mind, such as *Why didn't I pursue my observations about the obvious closeness shared between the two people concerned?* and *Why didn't I pray for wisdom about the situation, or consult Pastor Goodman?*

The thought that I could be indirectly culpable for what had happened, even so much as one iota, became all too threatening to my pride. Something that I had only heard of happening to other churches happened in the one I was at—my first one! However, the crisis taught me something invaluable about the leadership of Pastor Goodman. Not only was he dead serious about the spiritual integrity of the leaders in his charge, but he was a shepherd who was unafraid of using his staff to administer a whack of spiritual accountability when needed. Pastor Goodman showed me that though my working relationship with him was great, and even though the youth ministry had made some big strides since I had started, he refused to play favourites. Under the eyes of scripture, I was just as accountable as any other leader, even the senior pastor himself.

Through this experience, I got an eye witness's crash course in the dire and far-reaching spiritual consequences inherent in the moral failures of leaders in the church. There was enough of a ripple-effect at the church after what happened in the youth ministry. Sin in one's life seldom happens in a vacuum. It is a spiritual contagion that lives, breathes, and can easily spread in community. Consequently, sin in the life of an individual Christian, if it goes unabated, inevitably affects the spiritual life of the corporate body he or she is a part of. It may appear to be a private sin to begin with, but sooner or later our sin will expose us (see Numbers 32:23). Usually the result is that people get hurt on account of it.

This heartbreaking incident in the youth ministry was a prime example of how sometimes God's people suffer inadvertently as a result of the sin of others. It may not be the caring pastor, or the faithful committee leader, or even the godly deacon, who personally fall into disobedience; nonetheless, they can still find themselves adversely troubled by it, like anyone else in the Body of Christ. No matter what the context of the organization is, if one fails or falls, morally, everyone feels some form of reverberation.

Within the Church, carnality among Christians always carries with it the possibility of a spiritually-charged domino effect. In his address to the sin-abased church in Corinth, the apostle Paul highlighted this all-too-true principle of church life. *"Don't you know that a little yeast works through the whole batch of dough?"* (1 Corinthians 5:6) If you have ever read up on railroad disasters, you find out that, usually, all it took for a complete derailment was for one rail car to go off the track. The whole line of cars then follow suit.

Sin in the Body of Christ has a kind of speedy, permeating force that can infect even those areas of a church's ministry that are healthy and productive. The challenge exists in controlling the breadth of damage to a ministry while establishing and affirming the appropriate spiritual expectations of those who minister.

As expected, the youth ministry volunteer was asked to step back from her position in order for them to take some time to seek godly counsel and process their indiscretion in prayer. Fortunately, this story has a wonderful ending. God brought about good from the situation, as He often does when we seek to rehabilitate people after they fall. Church discipline requires wisdom, grace, and Christ-like love from its administrators, as well as humility and contrition from the one who is submitting to them. If done properly, a church's disciplining of their fellow Christians can restore, re-enforce, and revalidate them as loved and cherished servants who are called to reflect the glory of God in this world.

Heaven recycles its servants. Too bad for us that we're too quick sometimes to hurl fallen Christians to the no-longer-useful heap. However, we should never give up on people, if for no other reason than God never does. Not one of us can say, "God is finished with me!" To this day, I don't know for certain what became of the young person who was a part of the inappropriate incident that struck the church's youth ministry. However, to my knowledge, that teen volunteer has gone on to a fulfilling and spiritually enriched life.

Although this tribulation was an unforeseen and unwanted baptism of fire, it did sharpen my perspective of how undermining our sinful nature can be, and how seemingly harmless it can appear to us. The truth is that anyone can fall morally, at any time. All it would have taken was a change of circumstances for it to have been another volunteer or pastor—even me! By seeing how easily two other believers can fall into sin, I realized that the spiritually-slick black ice of temptation lies hidden in places we wouldn't expect to find it—in a church.

During my second (and last) summer at First Community Church, Pastor Goodman took a few weeks' holiday, leaving me to supervise a new summer intern for the youth ministry. I found this person to be helpful at the front-end of his stay. In addition to assisting me and the other volunteers during events, he was given various tasks and duties during the Sunday morning service. However, by mid-summer, the intern became quite lackadaisical in his responsibilities and attendance. More problematically, he was suspected of mishandling church funds. Pastor Goodman had already met with him to investigate matters pertaining to his role, and thought that they had an understanding that there would be no further difficulties. In addition, I also spent a few meetings with this person in the hopes of clearing some matters up, but it was to no avail. Questions and disappointments surrounding his attitude towards his employment expectations continued to persist. Pastor Goodman, before he left, gave me the green light to make any further decisions in terms of this intern's employment status, should any more problems crop up.

It was a responsibility I didn't want, yet I wanted to reward the senior pastor's trust, showing him that I was capable of making tough decisions. After seeking

God's will and taking into consideration the various chances this individual had been given, the issue resulted in my drafting a letter to the Board of Deacons, outlining my reasons for terminating his employment at First Community Church. Not only did the intern not take it well, but I didn't feel well for a time afterwards. I liked this person, and I really wanted him to work out. It was the hardest thing I had to do in the year and a half I was at the church. As I sat in my small office at the back of the church building, it hit me like a wayward Frisbee; like Pastor Goodman, I too had a staff in my hand. As hard as it was to break that staff in, by having to let the young intern go, I wasn't doing him any spiritual favours if I didn't use it.

Consequently, I was awakened to nuances of the image of the shepherd's staff that I had missed on past reflections. Not only could pastors use their staffs to put space between themselves and their own flock, a staff could also become the rod of discipline at times, putting space between the sin of God's people and their true spiritual identity to live and be free to choose good and pursue righteousness. When a shepherd's staff is recognized as a tool of responsibility rather than as a weapon of entitlement, God's under-shepherds will be able to administer wise discipline in a Christ-like manner. Being *willing* to serve Jesus, pastor or not, is to be under His accountability.

I eventually moved on from my position at First Community Church a much richer pastor in the making, absorbed with the intention of becoming an effective church leader.

I suppose all of us at First Community Church would have been spiritually impoverished had Pastor Goodman not put his shepherd's staff to godly use. How he did it impacted my young ministry, for it provided me with a timely, ready-or-not crash course on how to do it. Pastor Goodman was an admirable and patient teacher for me during my induction into church ministry. I had nothing but the utmost respect for him, both as a leader and a man, by the time I moved on from the church. Knowing what the specific politics in the church were at the time, it would have been easier for Goodman to choose a path of leniency, to decide not to take the sort of disciplinary actions he did. Certain individuals in the church related to the disciplined intern could have used the incident to cause Pastor Goodman some grief, but fortunately they didn't.

It was abundantly clear that Goodman was a person of principle, something we can't always take for granted with Christians. He feared God, not man, even if that meant his staff had to be firmly whacked on the backs of some of those among his flock in the most decisive of ways. Such an occurrence can leave marks on the hide of a sheep, for a time, and no doubt tufts of wool on the staff of the one who's administering the discipline. However, both are reminders that when one of us falls into sin, especially to a significant degree, *everyone* gets hurt to *some* degree.

Nuptials

IN THE EARLY SPRING OF 1997, I FELT MY ADULTHOOD HAD FINALLY TAKEN OFF. I had been at First Community Church for a year, I was engaged to be married, and I was looking forward to carrying on in ministry by having a "pastor's wife" alongside me. My graduation from Bible College would happen a month before Elaine's and my wedding. That, coupled with my graduation from single life into married life, I hoped would catapult me into a more desired and trusted bracket as a church leadership candidate. A good friend of mine in the ministry concurred and encouraged me by stating that now that I was thirty, and soon to be married, churches would automatically view that as a positive variable in terms of my prospects for pastoral positions.

I recently had a discussion with someone who shared how they felt churches still display an obvious prejudice towards family-oriented pastors, favouring the potential for ministry they bring, with a spouse and children, over single pastors. Unfortunately, the reality is that that observation has more truth to it than it probably should. Pastors who come with a spouse and baby carriages by their side do seem to have a leg up on single pastoral candidates for certain ministry positions.

My life was on the cusp of even further changes. Elaine and I had to face the possibility of leaving the familiarity of family and city in order to pursue another church for me to work at. Elaine was quite happy at her job as an administrative assistant for a surgeon in downtown Toronto. Her income alone would have stabilized our financial situation had I remained at First Community Church after my graduation from Bible College. However, even though they had given me my first break in ministry, I was receiving only a nominal salary… one you wouldn't gain much weight from! As a man and aspiring pastor who would soon have a finished undergraduate education under my belt, my pride took a marginal hit that Elaine was making so much more than I was. I had to make a decision about whether I was going to continue in my role at First Community Church or look elsewhere for another job, even if that job required a major move for us. We were counselled not to let our families dictate our decisions after the wedding, yet not to totally discard their sentiments either, since our families were our support groups and really loved us. Elaine and I were also cautioned against making any significant decisions in our first year of marriage.

We were busy planning a wedding, and if you've ever been involved in such an endeavour, you may agree that it can be one of the most exhausting undertakings imaginable. Ours was, but for more than just the reasons pertaining to the particulars of the ceremony. During our engagement, Elaine and I experienced some challenges within our circle of family and friends which produced unforeseen complications and a few unnecessary trials, which grieved us, somewhat tempering our excitement for the wedding. We were both reasonably content with our employment situations, although I was less so, due to my ongoing inferiority complex as one who might be hard-pressed to contribute my fair share to our marriage—at least, financially.

The status of the youth ministry at First Community Church was evolving at a rapid pace. A year after I had arrived on the scene, the complexion of the group underwent a facelift, a consequence of losing some key young people to university. The social and spiritual dynamic of the Bible studies, drop-ins, and event nights shifted into more challenging gears, due to the fact that we were beginning to attract a motley crew of older teens who brought with them a lot of issues that would disrupt the safe environment that we had prized and promoted. These Jesus-loved yet adolescent mutineers were more interested in drawing attention to themselves than anything else.

Aside from such faith-building hiccups within the youth ministry, I faced another hurdle: the church's board informed me that the resources they required in order to increase my salary, let alone keep me on a long-term basis, were improbable. It was suggested to me by Pastor Goodman that I do some long, hard thinking and praying about Elaine's and my financial situation. If I wanted to continue with the church, perhaps it would be necessary for me to take on a second job.

My Fanatical, Regrettable Tour of Ministry

The pressure I was already under with getting the wedding plans solidified, trying to wrap up my bachelor's degree, and dealing with interpersonal issues pertaining to friends and family members left me feeling like I was about to cave in, both emotionally and spiritually. Thankfully, our circumstances forced Elaine and I to spend prolonged periods of time in God's presence. It was a good test for us and provided some glue for our tattered and seemingly torn expectations of what an engagement was supposed to be like.

Everything seemed to be moving too fast. We didn't have a great deal of time to make quality decisions about our future. It should have been a joyous, expectant time bulging at the seams with wonder and promise for Elaine and me. However, and more importantly, everything within our relationship remained rock solid. We were immovably in love, and no amount of adversity could make even a needle's indentation in the idyllic balloon of what we wanted out of our wedding day.

Not only were we well-insulated by our own times of prayer, but the support and encouragement we received in healthy doses from God's people helped to preserve our engagement as a memorable period in our lives. That's why it was going to be so hard to leave the comfortable confines of the setting in which Elaine and I had met. She had been a worship leader at a church not far from the Bible College I was attending.

The odds of us ever getting together had been long. Really long! She was a golden-haired beauty with a good job; by contrast, I was a tired-looking student with a long way to go before finishing school. In addition to that, I was short on money and much shorter on self-confidence. I often wondered why Elaine wanted anything to do with someone like me, who could barely afford a real date. And if every date is a potential mate, as they say, how could she ever think of herself as the wife of a pastor?

Thankfully, God always takes into account the long and short of things, the improbable and seemingly impossible outcomes, in His sovereign plan for our lives. His permissive hand was in our relationship, and it pleased Him to pave the way for Elaine and me to be together, even if it seemed to go against all the odds.

Not long after we were married, God's hand kept us together. We would eventually say goodbye to friendly surroundings, travel a few hours away, only to step into an unknown future—not to mention, unfriendly territory.

Chapter 16

Restless

If my pastoral internship at First Community Church taught me anything about ministry, it was that the pasture is *not* always greener in another fold. I may not have had it made at Pastor Goodman's church, per se, but I did have it *good* there. My tenure at the church lasted a period of sixteen months, mainly because my mindset was on pursuing a ministry with a future.

I wasn't the first pastor, nor will I be the last, to view their ministry options in such a light. I can tell you, however, that my view has changed over the years. Now, I believe that every ministry setting, no matter where it is or what size it is, holds value and inherently manifests something that God wants taken care of. We may not feel a magnetic, pastoral pull within us to take on smaller ministry opportunities, which we may deem too insignificant for where we are in our ministry life. However, I'm learning that they are still worthy assignments if God's Word and His priorities to seek the lost are honoured. Whether one's ministerial front yard is rural or urban, they are both handed to us via the fingertips of Jesus.

Ministering in perceived geographical obscurity is one of a few fears a pastor has on their Top Ten list of "Things I hope don't happen to me." It's not the worst scenario one could face—losing one's integrity ought to top such a list—but, in speaking to pastors of my own circle, the honest answer is that none of them want to go to a place where no one seemingly knows you're there or remembers you're there. It wasn't necessarily enough knowing that God knows they're there!

Yet when we part the finer hairs of the gospel narratives, we find that the roads Jesus travelled in ministry were often the lonely, obscure, and segregated ones. The Lord's itinerary was always in keeping with the way of the cross, it seems, and who really wanted to go there? *Where* Jesus ministered tells us much about how willing He was to embrace ministry on the outskirts of notoriety. There were times in Jesus' ministry when He did great work while few were looking on.

The church I presently pastor has supported a mission north of where we're situated, on an island that's home to a First Nations reserve. It's an out of the way, out-of-sight ministry which consequently renders it out of the minds of many, and yet there are some miraculous things happening there for the Kingdom of God. Perceived lower profile ministries, though they carry little, if any, prestige, are often amongst the most spiritually fruitful. In order to stay the course, these ministries require much prayer, hours upon hours of work, and a rare willingness to persevere. Such disciplines appear to be missing in action at times in today's Church; they stand in direct defiance of our relished ministerial preferences in that our initiatives yield tangible results almost overnight.

If we're really honest with ourselves, most of us leaders who sweat it out in the gym of strategizing would just like to xerox the most successful and heralded church growth formulas—if only our boards were open to it, our people accepting of it, and our communities responsive to it! It can sometimes be difficult for a pastor filled with biblical ideals and zealous ideas to accept a given ministry for what it is. In general, well-intentioned pastors cannot be too faulted for their natural penchants to want to change things in a church's ministry, things that they perceive are improvements and for the better.

We live in the tension of loving the church as it is, and preferring for it to be the best it can be. The trap to avoid is trying to make any ministry or church like another one we know that's flourishing. In one of my ordination interviews, a pastor on the committee once made the remark, "A lot of guys leave one church, get to another place, and not too long after they're already thinking, 'When can I leave here?'"

Pastors need sage wisdom to know when to "hold 'em" and when to "fold 'em." That is, whether to stay in a particular ministry, or whether to leave. At some point, almost every pastor faces the tension of making sure they don't stay too long, and yet don't leave too soon. That said, I believe there is wisdom in not limiting or minimizing God's potential in any ministry setting. The other extreme is to be avoided as well: letting go of unrealistic and lofty expectations that can lead to frustrations and derail existing areas within a church that really need to be addressed. In any event, God loves His Church and Jesus is the long-suffering designer of it! There's always hope for a church, because its people worship a Saviour. I was in need of some serious throne-of-Heaven guidance in deciding whether to leave First Community Church or stick it out.

I knew I was in desperate straits when I began to feel that if I wasn't employed there, I probably wouldn't *attend* there. That sentiment evoked a vast amount of guilt within me. The slant of the worship services were geared more towards an older crowd. Pastor Goodman was perhaps reluctant to rock the boat on the issue of change; when he eventually hinted at it a few years later, it raised the ire of the more traditionally static people among the membership. The problem at First Community Church, as I saw it, was that there were two distinctive powers in the church vying for two separate visions, and they were polarized. The younger generation was burdened by the fact that growth in the youth ministry was not being transferred into the greater ministry of the church. Practically speaking, they were right. Though the youth group was considered a *part* of the church's overall ministry, the fact that we had a separate facility where we held our meetings and events meant very few of the young people felt it was necessary to take their places in the church's pews on Sunday mornings.

The only time a noticeable contingent of young people graced a service was when I preached; even then, they had a humorous slant, in that they could "heckle" me from the choir bleachers. It was a classic case of people identifying more with a leader than with that leader's church family. It didn't help that First Community Church was home to a cavernous interior, which was, hands-down, no competition for the hipper youth ministry building. In their own space, the young people decorated the rooms with apparel ranging from tie-dye to posters; they even hung beads from every door entrance and decked corners of rooms with retro themes and paraphernalia. The main social room featured a pool table and was wired for some serious sound quality whenever music was played!

However, there was more than a generational "style" barrier that needed to be broached in order for the youth ministry to seem like it was related to the main body of the church. In their own setting, the youth could be who they were—perpetually laid back, relationally clustered, emotionally preoccupied, and spontaneously interactive. Prior to some of our events and meetings, it wasn't uncommon for one of the young people to express a problem they had in which tears, conversation, and intercessory prayer ensued. Such tender moments would set the tone for an evening. They also served as unplanned teaching opportunities. It was even considered the norm during Bible study nights, and even our

Saturday night "gospel" messages, for the teens to cut in to interrupt whatever was discussed by raising on-the-spot, real-life issues that were off-script. God often showed me that I needed to be flexible in allowing the spiritual and emotional untidiness of the young people's lives to interrupt my well-ordered agenda. I had to learn that the issues of their lives could be used of God to point us all in a new direction for a particular evening, if that was what He willed.

These experiences provided some good training ground for me later on. There continue to be times when, as a pastor, I have to take my arm and clear away items on my desk pertaining to the "tyranny of the urgent" in order to deal more immediately with other, unexpected ministry needs. Jesus faced similar realities as He ministered with His disciples. It was during these times that Jesus taught His original disciples some valuable lessons in not only spotting, but meeting out-of-the-blue ministry needs.

One of the best examples of this is when Jesus came up against thousands of hungry people. By all accounts, His disciples hadn't planned on Jesus actually choosing to provide for the physical hunger pains of the masses. They had been with the Lord all day. The day was already a long one when the sudden emergence of multitudes of famished people ended up taking them in a different direction than the one they had hoped for. The disciples' only rebuttal to Jesus' wishes to help the crowd was reasonable enough: *"This is a remote place, and it's already getting late"* (Matthew 14:15). However, Jesus used that occurrence as a priceless teaching tool, with the lesson being: ministry calls for one to be able to adapt to different needs at the drop of a hat, even if they come at the most inconvenient of times.

This was the perfect ministry philosophy for the young people's group at First Community Church. Given the open-ended nature of the ministry, and the pliable philosophy I fostered, many of the young people were unfamiliar with the rigidity of a semi-predictable, traditional church worship setting. Not that there is anything necessarily wrong with structure, but the set way of operating within an ordered church service just seemed too tightly wound, too one-way, for it to be meaningful and relevant to them. The last thing I wanted was to have the young people attend the church's Sunday services for the mere sake of appearances. I came to realize that there was a significant hurdle to overcome if the sheep of the church were to mix and mingle with the sheep of the youth ministry.

We tried all sorts of initiatives: letting the youth sometimes lead worship during the evening services, slotting in various young people to give testimonies in the services, and assigning one young person to an older person (or couple), in which the latter would occasionally send the young person a card and commit to praying for them. Despite our best efforts, however, the generational divide seemed to remain unbridged. Not every older saint, it seemed, enjoyed or was comfortable with the presence of the young people moving in and around them in the pews. Trying to disassociate the aged congregation of its misgivings and hang-ups proved to be a much harder chore than I had originally anticipated. Though the folks at First Community Church hoped to grow their numbers by gaining young families and young people in general, they either didn't want to or were not ready to count its cost, an expense that has nothing to do with dollars or cents, but with *change*.

After I left First Community, I thought I was finished with sorting through such conundrums. Was I ever wrong! Each church ministry has its issues, but anytime the "change" card comes up, it is how a pastor plays it that determines whether they will be successful. This would be a recurring principle issue that would dog my ministry. Far from being reluctant, I would proudly take on the role of a change agent. The difficulty I experienced at First Community Church, in that regard, was a mild taste of the more bitter pills I would have to swallow in a few of the churches I was yet to go to.

Chapter 17
Change Awakenings

I AM OFTEN AMAZED AT THE RATE AT WHICH MY KIDS GROW. IF IT'S NOT THEIR height, it's their feet; if it's not their feet, it's their hair! I often refer to Cassidy and Dakota as weeds that obviously get watered too much! Like other parents, Elaine and I are forever replacing worn-out and undersized clothes. It's the cause and effect principle of parenthood: when my children's feet take a growth spurt, they require bigger shoes. That's life!

Our lives seldom remain static for very long. When families grow, they require a larger home to accommodate that growth; when companies expand operations, they require new facilities and staff; when we finish high school, we seek to gain a higher education. It's a principle that growth, no matter what aspect of life it pertains to, almost always calls for us to make adjustments—or, in other words, change. Oftentimes we view any prospect of change as something to be irrationally resisted instead of faith-swelling opportunities to see God's hand work for our spiritual benefit.

That's why I advocate that unless a church is truly ready to accept the prospects of a particular change, such as to atmosphere and dynamics of the Sunday service (not theological or doctrinal in nature), they are not really ready to grow. Therefore, if a church wants to experience numerical growth, it must be prepared to meet practical challenges head-on, challenges that come via the new personalities, preferences, and prejudices that people bring with them into the existing culture of the church. Making room for more family in the Body of Christ almost always stretches longtime church members who are comfortable with the way things are. It takes spiritual maturity to be consistently selfless. It also takes a lifetime to cultivate. A good question for any believer to ask themselves is this: *What will it require of me in order to see my church's ministry progress?*

In terms of numerical growth, a church must be willing to simultaneously grow spiritually to be able to integrate new people into its congregation (whether they come from transfer growth or the inclusion of new converts). I wasn't convinced that was happening at First Community Church. They hadn't reached the point of being receptive enough to change in order to grow as they desired. I couldn't even take a stab at guessing as to a timeline when the church would, if ever, make this turnaround. That prognosis, coupled with my financial uncertainty, led me to feel a bit "long in the tooth" at First Community, factoring greatly in my decision to resign, even though I had only been there roughly sixteen months. However, by the time I would leave the church, my official internship was over and my undergraduate bachelor's degree was complete.

I felt I had satisfied the conditions and expectations of my original employment contract, that I was no longer obligated to stay, especially since there were adequate and effective volunteers within the youth ministry team that were capable of carrying on where I left off. In a letter I gave to the new leader of the youth ministry (someone who had assisted me since the beginning of my time at FCC), I wrote at the bottom of the page: "Do your best and the Lord will take care of the rest." In some ways, those words piggy-backed my own situation, as I headed off into another ministry I knew very little about. Behind the scenes, and known only to Pastor Goodman, I had opened discussions with another church, some hours away, about a position that I eventually agreed to take on.

With the helping hand of some friends, Elaine and I loaded up the moving van on the last weekend of August 1997. We'd exchanged vows on June 21, just ten days after saying Yes to going to Grace Church. In doing so, we accomplished exactly the opposite of what we were counselled to do. We were diving into considerable changes (a new town, new jobs, a new ministry and church family) just months into our brand new marriage. The ink on the wedding certificate was barely dry when we put our signatures on an agreement to rent a house, located some three hours away from Toronto.

My new ministry position was somewhat more inclusive than the one I'd occupied at First Community Church. It was an enlarged associate's role, in which I was to assist the senior pastor (Pastor Williams) in the overload of his ministry details, on top of leading the Junior High and Senior High youth groups. To say that my desire and confidence was bigger than my ability would be an understatement. However, I was zealous to take my pursuit to the next level and increase in my capacity to lead God's people as a young pastor. Grace Church seemed to be just the ticket, the suitable place in which to do so.

The very first encounter I had with the young people's group sealed the deal for me. Elaine and I sat in a room packed to the hilt with teenagers… as many as they could strum up from out of the woodwork. I can tell you that I never saw many of those faces ever again at a social outing, Bible study, or other youth event. Churches do this kind of thing all the time, to make sure a good first impression sticks. They always try to put their best foot forward in order to woo a pastor, and Grace Church was no different.

As a pastor who has interviewed for many churches, it's not the good foot that should concern us; it's the one you can't see! However, as the meeting wore on, and as more information was shared about the history of the youth ministry and its goals to be a witness to the local high school, I found myself feeling very positive about the situation. The young people were able to articulate their faith very well, and the obvious leaders among them were effective in communicating what they believed were the overriding needs of the youth. I couldn't help but be amazed at how spiritually mature the group of teens came across as being. While I was listening to their input, I genuinely felt that the young people were like sheep without a shepherd.

Tangible compassion worked up within me as they took up the topic of their former youth pastor, a mournful tone overtaking their voices. I could tell they and the previous youth pastor had clearly been attached at the hip. Not only was the previous pastor with them for a solid five years, but he was described in such terms as being "outrageous" and "fun." His leaving Grace Church was considered a "big loss." I wouldn't be honest if I said the former leader's popular standing didn't bother me. It did, to a certain degree. I was thankful that the two youth ministries (Junior and Senior) had some continuity in terms of a singular leadership, yet the prospects of coming on the heels of such a charismatic leader was more than a little intimidating. I wondered from the get-go whether I would be able to measure up, not because I was a morose killjoy, but because, as creatures of habit, we are always looking for personality traits and qualities that are similar to those held by leaders we have been drawn to in times past. Even if they say they want someone different, some churches have a predisposition for desiring an exact duplicate of a particular leader or pastor they formerly favoured.

Ron Mahler

I once interviewed at a church where an older person told me that if I was hired, I would forever be measured against a certain former pastor they'd had many years before. A popular leader, regardless if they were effective *as* a leader, can condition the expectations of any church, which can make it harder for an incoming leader to be accepted for his or her unique assets. Though it's unfair to box in any potential new leader by using the "tale of the tape" to pit them against their predecessor, that's the reality I was facing at Grace Church.

CHAPTER 18
Second Thoughts

IN THE SECOND CHAPTER, I WROTE ABOUT MY EXPERIENCE OF MOVING, AS A child, from a pipsqueak town in Cape Breton to the much larger city of Toronto. When I moved from First Community Church to serve at Grace Church, let's just say that I relived that experience, only this time in a ministry context. As a pastor fresh out of Bible College, going to a much larger congregation held the promise of exciting increases. I was thrilled that my pay was greater (much greater), and that my youth budget was inflated like a blow-up doll containing endless amounts of air. However, that euphoria would eventually be tempered by an uncalculated reality: the expectations upon my ministry, fair or not, were just as big.

I can still see the treasurer walking into my office after I'd only been at Grace Church for two weeks, and handing me my very first paycheque. My eyes couldn't help but catch the amount on it as I politely said "Thank you." I didn't want to look too impressed or surprised by the benefits of my new salary. When the treasurer left the building, I could have done backflips. I had hardly been there a month, had scarcely accomplished anything, and yet I was paid more for that time period than I had been for an entire month's worth of ministry at my previous church.

I can get use to this! I thought to myself. At the start of my tenure at Grace Church, life was very unlike the dormant atmosphere that characterized First Community Church throughout the week. There were a few welcome differences, most notably the fact that the phone rang constantly, and the office bustled with people. I was also thankful to have a more tech-savvy secretary at my disposal.

Then there was Pastor Williams. He was more of a "hands-off" kind of senior pastor in how he related to me, professionally. Williams told me early on, "I don't babysit people. You can come and go as you need to. If I don't see you until next Easter (it was September), then I'll have to wonder about you." I appreciated his laid-back approach. Truth be known, no associate wants their superior, no matter how well-intentioned they are, to act like a mother.

Just months into my position at Grace Church, while I was still in the beginning stages of getting to know people and planning with the main youth leaders, I made a disconcerting observation. Although the youth had their new leader, they were talking and sounding like they were longing for the good old days of the past. The former youth pastor apparently had kept the young people quite busy and more than just a bit entertained. I had been told by the search committee about how my predecessor had often pulled "wild and crazy" stunts with the youth. By all indications, his ministry was highly event-oriented. Spectacle-oriented. Personality wise, I admitted to the search committee that I would be somewhat less adventurous, and even less extraverted. However, they assured me that their reason for choosing me, in particular, was more a case of securing someone they thought could "right the ship."

Any organization that says their ship needs "righting" presupposes that they think they're currently headed in the *wrong* direction. In hindsight, while the committee at Grace Church did make me feel needed, their assessment of the overall youth ministry should have sparked more of a responsible concern in me. I should have checked up on the situation more than I did, jumping on them with questions such as "How do you define a right direction?" or "Would your diagnosis be agreed upon by the former youth pastor?" I was told that from the time the previous youth leader had left, the young people had gotten off-course, were scattered, and in need of a firmer, more disciplined hand. The committee was explicit in their terminology by expressing their desire to see the youth led by someone a little more serious, perhaps someone more "purpose-driven."

As people who had known the teens for years, the search committee's estimation of where the young people's ministry was at was received by me as a thoughtful and honest one. Despite all that I was made aware of, everything smacked of being normative in terms of the challenges most young people face, whether they're Christians or not; because of that, it didn't scare me off. Every ministry is less than ideal, and can always be run better. I wasn't as pastorally astute in

My Fanatical, Regrettable Tour of Ministry

those early days as I am now, so whenever I hear comments about churches and ministries, I am better equipped to read between the lines—or "the lives," shall we say.

From a pastor's perspective, I advocate that it's okay to be more than moderately picky when it comes to searching for a church to serve in. We should never settle for a ministry that we have significant hesitations about. However, with my sophomore's appetite for more pastoral ministry, the pros of Grace Church outshone the cons. So I brushed aside search committee comments like, "We'll need to be praying a lot for you," preferring to cling to statements like, "You're the type of leader and pastor the young people need at this stage." The one that I really liked was, "We need to let you be who you are as a leader."

Since the previous youth pastor seemed to have had that latitude extended to him, I figured that I had already been granted the freedom to be who I was, as a leader, as well. More than anything, it brought me some peace knowing that the search committee had worked through dozens of resumes, only to turn up my name, and deem my personality and strengths the most appropriate for the position.

Initially, I thought that the ministry I inherited at Grace was not dissimilar to that of my last church, albeit in a different town and with a lot more young people and space to hold events. I even dreamed of all the options I would have in terms of volunteers. At First Community Church, I had the responsibility of getting a youth ministry *off the ground*; at Grace Church, the youth were supposedly in *auto-pilot*. Like with a pancake mix, I thought I'd been handed an "instant" youth group, where all the work was done for me; all I had to do was add a little water, stir, and voila! The food would be on the plate in no time and everyone would be fed and satisfied.

I also counted on adjusting well to my new environment, but as is often true in life, naivety acts like a bad pair of glasses, blurring the ugliness of the surface reality. Oftentimes the reality of church life is so camouflaged by the warm fuzzies people get when the pastor first arrives that nothing about the ministry's true, spiritual condition is as it seems. Many ministries and churches that last a good stretch of time without a leader eventually get restless, and unhealthy spiritual habits consequently begin to form in the fold. It's the Proverbs principle: *"Where there is no vision, the people perish"* (Proverbs 29:18, KJV).

This happened, of course, to the Israelites while their leader, Moses, was away receiving the Ten Commandments on Mount Sinai. Moses returned only to find that his own brother, Aaron, had been led down an idolatrous path by

God's people, and had assisted them in casting and then venerating a golden calf (see Exodus 32). It is wholly inherent within us, as sin-committing creatures, to get off-track.

I'm not saying that the youth at Grace Church were erecting any pagan shrines or high places of worship while they were without a pastoral leader! However, to my objective newcomer eyes, idols of different types were present in the attitudes of the senior youth, in the forms of erratic behaviour, unedifying speech, indifference to counsel, brazen disrespect for authority, and Nephilim-sized egos.

You might think this is just run-of-the-mill stuff, the typical adolescent shtick we should come to expect from teenagers. However, for a group largely consisting of "churched" teens who were said to have grown greatly and come from relatively solid, healthy homes, I didn't expect to find such a rebellious spirit. The room of exemplar teens I spoke with the first time I met them became unrecognizable to me in a short period time. I had barely spent any time there before I awoke to the fact that I'd already lost most of the senior youth. I definitely found them to have a Jekyll and Hyde nature. I was never quite sure which was going to show up on any given night: the more cooperative and interested group, or the more "Do I really want to be here?" contingent. Though I appreciated the fact that they were experiencing their own issues and that they were still getting use to me, it appeared as though they had already made up their minds about me. They may also have sensed that I had made up my mind up about them.

By contrast, the junior youth were an absolute pleasure to be around. The majority of them seemed content to head out to various arcades or hold scavenger hunts after a Bible lesson. They didn't even grow tired of the picnics we'd have in the youth room.

On the other hand, there was something peculiar about the spiritual dynamic of the senior youth group. When they were together, something didn't quite feel right. Just as there are mechanical indicators telling us when our vehicles have a problem, there are spiritual sensors built into every ministry setting. It's called having a discerning squint.

Elaine and I recently went out to her brother's farm in order to get a "yard" kitten for our daughter, Cassidy. We were told that the kitten had a couple of fleas, but didn't pose much of a risk to take home. However, once we got the cat in our house, we made a startling discovery. By gliding our fingers through its fur a bit more deeply, much to our chagrin there were more than a "couple" of little critters present. There was a legion of them! We then had the unpopular lot

My Fanatical, Regrettable Tour of Ministry

of telling our kids that we had to return the cat. The cold, hard truth was that we were careless in not making a thorough enough examination *before* bringing it home.

Our experience with the flea-ridden cat mirrored what we discovered at Grace Church just months into our time there. Burrowed deep within the fur of God's sheep was an infestation—a deeply-rooted dissension that threatened to consume every conceivable area and person in the church. A worse reality was the fact that the yeast of this sin had spread to the degree that it would have impressed even the Evil One. A number of young people were taking up their disgruntled parents' offences and beefs. The object of their indignation was surprising, to say the least. Consequently, for the next ten months at Grace, I would enter the school of hard knocks, where I would be introduced to its dreaded headmaster: the dark side of ministry.

CHAPTER 19
Divisions

Just weeks into my tenure at Grace Church, I recall having a conversation with Elaine about the senior pastor. My concern was that Pastor Williams seemed distant, and not very engaging.

"Maybe he doesn't like me," I resolved.

Elaine assured me that my observations were probably inaccurate, but that if I was really concerned, I should talk to him.

One of the fringe benefits of taking the position at Grace was that it afforded me the opportunity to sit under the teaching of the senior pastor. Although there was nothing supremely breathtaking or head-turning about his oratory skills, he was demonstratively deep in his theological application of biblical truths. I could tell Pastor Williams cared about the ability of his audience to receive and apply spiritual truth.

A good teacher knows how to communicate, as well as how to apply profound spiritual truth to his or her students. That was one of Pastor Williams' strengths. He exuded as much respect for the sermonic process as he did the final pulpit product. For that reason alone, Pastor Williams' ministry really attracted me. I was at a place in my young ministry life where I was ready to take my own preaching craft to another level. Not only did I have a general desire to continue growing spiritually, but I wanted that growth to make a discernable difference in how I delivered sermons. Listening to a preacher of substance is to hear the results of how God's Word has tunnelled deep within us. Spiritual shallowness

My Fanatical, Regrettable Tour of Ministry

and homiletic ingenuity cannot be found in the same preacher; neither are they hard to distinguish from one another from the pulpit.

Though every pastor can be profoundly touched by the Spirit as they speak, there are some preachers whose depth of life experiences is palpable enough that you can see it in how they bridge the revealed Word to even the most sceptical of receptors. It's been said that if you meet a Christian who displays a profundity of wisdom and character, they've probably come by it honestly; in other words, they've earned it. Some of the most valuable mentors that the Kingdom of Heaven has to offer are likely disciples who have come through some great trial or spiritual testing. Pastor Williams' character left me with the impression that he fit that bill.

In seminary, I was taught that having integrity in my preaching didn't solely depend on the content of my message; it also depends on the vessel delivering it. All I could gather from Williams' seasoned and spiritually insightful words, not to mention the richness of his sermons, was that his Sunday morning demeanour was neither cosmetic nor superficially acted out. If that had been the case, Williams would have been in the wrong business! I say this, because the man Pastor Williams seemed to be throughout the week was quite different from the person I perceived him to be on Sunday morning. Pastor Williams gave the impression that he was disinterested in really connecting with me beyond the professional duties of the ministry at Grace Church. I would come to apprehend that there was good reason for that.

However, a question would continue to nag at me: "Why does he seem so elusive?"

There were moments when Pastor Williams probably found it tricky to avoid appearing preoccupied and defensive. That was my impression from some of the elders' meetings I attended early in my time there. These often intense and drawn-out bi-weekly sessions were a revelation in and of themselves. One Saturday morning, after my third elders' meeting, I dragged my body home, lamenting, with a gloomy countenance, how many problems the church had.

But it was in the course of one of these elders' gatherings that I detected something even more hazardous going on: a not so subtle rift existed within the personalities and ideologies of the people in the board room. As I observed it, Pastor Williams was on one side, while the elders were on the other, like in the child's game of Red Rover. It was as if Pastor Williams could only try to come over when he was *called* over. This often made me feel like the proverbial monkey in the middle, leaping to grasp the reasons for the demonstrated animosity between the two parties.

There was something discernibly off-kilter with the dynamics of this relationship. For a time, no one overtly admitted to being wrong. It got to a point where I became resolute in my determination to finally confront the senior pastor, alone. I decided to meet with him and communicate my support for him, and to offer prayer as well.

However, two separate incidents beat me to that meeting. The first came by way of a ministry training session, led by Pastor Williams for all the ministry leaders. As I sat there, filling in blanks on the seminar's handout and listening to the various interjections made by the other leaders, Pastor Williams came out with an obtrusive statement, which packed a heavy punch. His words were as ominous, as they were truthful. As if to rabbit trail from his intended text, he said, rather seriously, "No one becomes the leader or gets promoted in ministry by walking over the sprawled body of another leader."

I deciphered his meaning easily. Pastor Williams was sending a clear message that morning, and its intended targets, I assumed, were within earshot. If I had been totally oblivious to the fractious landscape of the church's leadership, Pastor Williams' pointed statement wouldn't have registered so glaringly on my radar. In fact, his straight-shooting words would have probably gone over my head. However, I had discerned my new ministry environment well, and the pastor's not-so mysterious comment served to match the troublesome tone the elders' meetings had taken on.

Pastor Williams' comment may not have been projected at me personally, but it did brush against me and ricochet off the other leaders in the room. The tell-tale statement was disturbing, not because he uttered it in a threatening or sinister kind of way, but because it peeled back the covers of masked unity, showing just how serious the impending crisis was. Pastor Williams was delivering a convicting newsflash, letting his opponents know that he knew what they were up to, and that they needed to be reminded that there was One greater than them who was *actually* in control.

Chapter 20

Gathering Storm

ONE EVENING, I RECEIVED A PHONE CALL FROM A POPULAR FORMER LEADER OF Grace Church. He asked me to pray about a meeting he was having with someone in the church the next day. He was not at liberty to reveal either the source or the object of their concern. All he was willing to offer was that it would hit me hard, because I knew one of the people involved. This cryptic piece of information, of course, only heightened my curiosity. My conversation with the former leader preoccupied my thoughts the rest of that evening.

This was the second incident that beat me to the much-needed chat I planned to have with Pastor Williams.

As I walked into the church offices the next morning, I caught a glimpse out of the corner of my eye of the very former leader I had spoken with. He was sitting with his wife in Pastor Williams' office.

The scene didn't feel or look good at all. From my vantage point, being a stone's throw from Williams' office, I overheard periodic exchanges from the intense tête-à-tête. It was hardly a case of my being a snoop, putting a glass to the wall, as it were, to eavesdrop; rather, it was hard not to be concerned and distracted by the meeting. I'll admit, I should have prayed in that instant rather than inclining my ear. Better still, it would have been a good time to go for coffee!

Pastor Williams, from all I could surmise, was the defendant in what would become a veritable kangaroo court. In the ensuing days and weeks, I witnessed a good, righteous man of character thoroughly torn down, accused of being someone he undoubtedly was not.

Ron Mahler

My suspicions of clandestine meetings and smear campaigns planned against Pastor Williams, led by a misguided camp of people at Grace Church, regrettably proved to be reality. But why? In an attempt to remain objective, I briefly entertained whether or not some of the comments being made by people in the church about Pastor Williams could be justified? Had he, as some had charged, offended pockets of people? Was this a case of a pastor reaping the consequential lumps of an abusive ministry? Or was there something more, something nefarious, perhaps blatantly satanic at the heart of the finger-pointing?

The turning point was an elders' meeting that was doomed to destruction before the seats in the pastor's office were even warm. The elders, with much moxie, admitted to privately giving ear to a person in the church who had brought some potentially damaging and outright slanderous opinions against Pastor Williams. The out-and-out irresponsible nature of these opinions only served to defame Pastor Williams' character. The meeting blew apart when the elders confessed that the party in question had failed to produce any witnesses; nor did they have any proof to corroborate their story. Pastor Williams, before rising up in abject frustration and anger, reminded his elders prior to exiting the room about the biblical protocol for entertaining an accusation against an elder. He said that the matter must be established *"by two or three witnesses"* (1 Timothy 5:19). Pastor Williams then ended his brief admonition by charging the elders not to ever meet without him again in that manner, at least without his permission.

After Williams stormed out of the room, I sensed his time at Grace Church was coming to an all-but-certain close. There are some lines between a pastor and his board that are too thick to come back over once they've been crossed. It's not a matter of whether one can forgive the other, as much as it is whether one can trust and respect the other enough to keep working with them. Though the trust factor between Pastor Williams and his leaders may have been weak to begin with, after that incident it was all but ripped up. However, the most disturbing thing was that not one of the elders seemed to have been willing to come to Pastor Williams' defence.

As I glanced over at the senior pastor's empty chair, still swivelling from the jolt of just being vacated, I couldn't help but imagine what it would have been like if I had been the target of the cannons fired at Pastor Williams. The awkward silence was interrupted by the ill-timed and inappropriate words of one elder, who piped up, "See, Ron, this is what we have to deal with!"

Though I didn't know the senior pastor very well, these poisonous arrows being thrust at him appeared to be grossly unjustified. I felt for the elders, in that some of the events they now had to handle were no doubt new to them. It's easy to make errors in judgment, however, even when one has the best intentions.

I felt physically sick after that meeting; I even felt bad for what Pastor Williams must have thought about me staying behind in the meeting after he had left. Did he think that I, too, would eventually turn on him? The senior pastor's chair would soon be vacant, and I wasn't feeling at all comfortable in my chair, either. As bad as things appeared, it was only the beginning of another sorry chapter at Grace Church, which would lead to a horrible ending for Elaine and I.

My shelf life as a pastor there would officially be less than one year. By the time I celebrated my first wedding anniversary, I had a funny feeling it was only a matter of time before I landed on the unemployment line.

Chapter 21

Sick and Tired

WHEN ELAINE AND I WERE JUST FOUR MONTHS INTO OUR MARRIAGE AND TWO months into the ministry at Grace Church, I contracted a virus that led to a serious bout of pneumonia. This landed me in the hospital for a week. I first noticed the symptoms as we attended a basketball game, which was part of a joint junior and senior youth event. The outing took place in another town, roughly three hours away from the church. As the evening wore on, I began to shake with chills and feel extremely disoriented. It was a damp, cold night, and I could hardly walk from the stadium seats to where our car was parked. During the ride home, I was doubled over with aches and experienced difficulty breathing. Originally, we thought it was just a bad flu, so when we finally got home that night, I immediately crawled into bed in the hopes of sleeping it off.

The following morning (a Sunday), I didn't show up for church. I stayed home for a few days, until I couldn't take the coughing anymore. My head, quite literally, felt like it was splitting in half. When I arrived at the emergency department of the local hospital, I was quickly given an oxygen mask, along with an IV. In a daze, I didn't even notice that I was put in a wheelchair. The nurses on the floor were surprised to see a thirty-year-old with pneumonia being wheeled in. The x-rays taken of my lungs were alarming; only one lung was visible. I was one seriously sick puppy. I had some rough nights and a few pretty long days in hospital, which included lying next to an older man who moaned intermittently in pain; this, while another patient carried on with annoying mutterings of a nonsensical nature.

My Fanatical, Regrettable Tour of Ministry

Then came the moment when I slipped going into the washroom, which caused my IV to get yanked from my hand. A bloody mess ensued. Elaine tried to keep my spirits up by washing my hair (which hadn't been washed for well over a week) and letting me know of everyone who were praying for me. Being the wonderful partner in ministry she is, Elaine also stepped in to help oversee a few of the youth events in my absence. The whole ordeal—the time laid up in the hospital, as well as the time spent in convalescence—actually provided me with a strange satisfaction. I had hoped my illness would incite some compassion among the parents I was in conflict with, causing them to relent. If my wishes were granted, I must have missed it. Some of the more insatiable parents picked up right where they left off before I got sick.

A few of the parents remained covertly active by stirring the pot and refusing to call a truce. My brief period of recovery was the only respite from trials that Elaine or I would know until we ultimately left Grace Church. It wasn't too much of a stretch for me to suspect that, as it seemed to be with Pastor Williams, Satan didn't want me around the church much longer, a sentiment that a very vocal and influential minority agreed with for their own reasons and did the legwork for. Many people within Elaine's and my circle of personal friends, as well as a clump of loyal supporters within the church, wondered whether my illness had been demonically administered. It was hard to disagree with this perspective at times, considering that my bout with pneumonia had exacted a great amount of strength from me, leaving me with lingering fatigue.

It took the better part of three months for me to regain my normal sense of energy; unfortunately, I couldn't seem to regain anything in the way of momentum, or loyalty, with the majority of young people at the senior level. My sickness seemed like just another nail in my ministry's coffin. Only a few token senior youth kept in touch with me while I was convalescing at home, an effort, in hindsight, that I could have made more of. Consequently, when I returned to my youth ministry post, it seemed like the older teens and I were strangers.

At the seven-month mark of my tenure at Grace, the already tumultuous waters of conflict rose to flood-like levels. One morning while I was sitting in my office, someone in the church who I had carefully confided in quite often, flew in, and abruptly asked, "Do you think there is a movement afoot in the church to have you and Pastor Williams removed?"

Conspiracy theorists abounded in the church, and this person was the first to admit theirs. It took me all of two seconds to give him my answer. Looking straight at him, I asserted, "Yes, I do!" It was pretty obvious by that point what was going on; for another, I didn't want to appear as though I was in denial. He stood frozen in front of me, shaking his bowed head, spun around in disgust, and exited my office. I'd had about enough of whispers and murmurings, and of the people who were pecking away at every perceived tear in my ministry and character.

Not long afterwards, I passively entered into a few harrowing encounters with a well-known person in the church, a parent, who was also known for his short temper. He just plain had it in for me. Reading between the lines of his words proved unproductive, for nothing he charged me with could really be substantiated; furthermore, he had a reputation for volatile outbursts, of which I was not the only recipient. The motivating factor behind his adversarial presence in my life was attributed to the fact that a couple of his kids were in my senior youth group; one of them, in particular, made it known that he didn't care for me. His father constantly hounded me with ill-timed and irrational criticisms. I was a stationary target for his carefully plotted, strategically timed rants. Such incidents mostly occurred whenever I was alone in my office or alone in the building.

Being the reluctant, trapped audience of one, I became a verbal punching bag, absorbing this parent's cutting remarks, which were directed at my leadership *and* overall ability in ministry. It came to the point where merely hearing the sheer sound of his voice in the lower office caused my heart to thump in my chest. During one of these encounters, I was nastily accused, among other things, of not caring for the young people—a comparatively tame complaint when put alongside some of the other zingers he threw at me. It was a favourite comment of his, which I tried to automatically dismiss.

This time, I'd had enough. I was long past the advice of Proverbs 15:1; a "gentle answer" was not turning away his wrath!

Instead of attempting to be diplomatic, I piped up, "Why are you treating me like this?" I went on trying to politely but sternly reason with him. It was a colossal waste of my breath. More of his insults followed, until I finally told him to get out of my office, or I would leave so that he could talk to himself.

While I had made the elders' board aware of this parent's unprovoked attacks upon me, they were only willing to console me, to a certain extent. Most times, my concerns solicited only a tepid response; Pastor Williams, on the other hand, was always behind me. The elders not only knew that this person had a propensity for erratic behaviour, they also knew that he held a significant position in the church. My primary concern was not only for myself, but for the precedent the elders would be setting if he was not held accountable for his behaviour. I was also concerned that he had uninhibited and uncensored access to me in my office, whenever he wanted, which was causing me a lot of personal anxiety. To my knowledge, all the elders ever did was to question him lightly, then let the matter go. Their efforts in talking with this abusive parent amounted to a gentle slap on the wrist. I had hoped for a decisive corralling of his privileges and position in the church.

I spent many nights wide awake, pounding my pillow while crying and praying for a breakthrough. It was becoming apparent to me that there was a certain standard in terms of tolerance for this parent. Did that same standard apply to every other leader in the church? I wondered why it was that the elders, who were in a position to put a stop to this man's ridiculous attacks on me, did not. Why were they so reluctant to do so? Why did they seem to soft-peddle the impact that this parent's act was having on the overall situation? The best counsel the elders could offer me was to kill this person with kindness. It was a convenient and safe thing for them to say. I wondered, though, if they would have readily accepted such biblical advice themselves if the shoe had been on the other foot.

It's funny how we think of different ways that we *could* have handled conflicts, when they are relegated to the distant past. For instance, maybe I should have showed up on the overly critical parent's doorstep with a casserole in hand, and just enjoyed the look on his face. In hindsight, I can't say for certain whether any good deed on my part would have heaped enough burning coals on his head to placate his wrath and lead him to repentance. What I do know is that I honestly tried to understand his discontentment with me. Sometimes, pastors simply cannot do enough to satisfy their people. Some parishioners' expectations of their leaders are like the clothes we wear; there comes a time when they need to be *changed*. I suspect that harbouring unrealistic expectations of me had something to do with why this man treated me the way he did.

I had a difficult time relating to his errant son, and a worse time trying to integrate him back into the senior youth group. If that was my fault, I'll take the blame, and yet it didn't seem to matter to the father that I had made efforts with all the older teens. What really mattered was the opinion of his immature seventeen-year-old. He perceived that I was disinterested in the lives of the young people, a subjective perception at best which was simply untrue. However, my decision to side with Pastor Williams may have solidified his impression of me even further, since he was among those who I believed were trying to pull the senior pastor.

Ron Mahler

On all these counts, and others beside, I was viewed in a negative light. It was plain to see that I couldn't win with those who coupled me with Pastor Williams as an object of scorn. Unfortunately, this parent wasn't through with me yet.

Chapter 22

Overboard

ONE OF THE MORE HURTFUL CRITICISMS THAT A PASTOR HAS TO PERSEVERE through are knocks against their ministry that seem to overlap *personally* and *professionally*. Some of the criticisms pastors and ministry leaders receive are no doubt deserved. Many, however, are not. For certain, all of them make some indentation on the hearts of those they are directed at. The office of the pastorate carries with it extremely high expectations, especially in the area of morality. Depending on the type, degree, and frequency of the criticism, it has the potential to devastate those ministers who just long to love people and help them along in their spiritual journeys. Sometimes, the saddest broken heart in the church is the "pastor's heart" of the shepherd. The parent at Grace Church who repeatedly assailed me with his cruel words meant for me to take it personally.

It is unrealistic, if not downright unintelligent, to tell a pastor (or any leader) what you feel about their ministry and then expect them not to take it personally. Some criticisms go beyond superficial "digs." The role of a pastor may be viewed as a profession, yet his or her ministry comes via a specifically-gifted *person*, and thus is *personal*. God uses one's personality in ministry to minister. Just like He uses the personalities of worship leaders to lead a congregation in song and the personalities of Sunday school teachers to teach children, God works with the unique giftedness and subtle nuances of a pastor's personality to minister to His people.

Some criticisms are meant to be taken personally, as well as seriously. The criticism I received at Grace Church from my most vocal opponent could not be rationalized away as being merely a product of their unhappiness. Nothing he dished out to me could have been justified on any spiritual level.

It all came to a head late one evening when he called my home and asked for access to my office, so he could get into a closet behind my desk for some "items" pertaining to his area of ministry. He was borderline polite with me on the phone, but when I declined to do what was asked of me, he went ballistic. I refused to give into his request, because I believed this was another way for him to try intimidating and controlling me. When I asked him what was so important that he needed to get into my office at such a late hour, he wouldn't tell me. However, he did afford himself one final opportunity, while having my ear, to enlighten me.

"You're not a pastor," he growled. "No one in the church accepts you as one."

I tried to ignore what he had just said to me and told him that no matter what he thought of me, I still would not drive to the church and let him into my office at such a late hour.

He then hung up on me and proceeded to phone an elder, whom I heard from later. He also called the maintenance person, requesting that they meet at my office to let him in. The maintenance person called me for my permission first. In response, I instructed him not to allow this parent into my office under any circumstances, and that I was going to arrange to have his "items" removed from there as soon as possible. I thought that was the end of it.

The next morning, I arrived at work only to find my office had been broken into; worse, some of my youth ministry files were missing. You shouldn't have to strain too hard to imagine who I held responsible! It was too coincidental for me to accept that the break-in could have been done by anyone else; I was certain there was a collaborative conspiracy at work against me. When Pastor Williams got to his office that same morning, after observing how huffed and puffed I was, he encouraged me to go home and cool off.

But I needed to get to the bottom of it. I made up my mind as to who I thought should have stepped forward and taken credit for the break-in. The investigation was on. The local police were notified, and they arrived to question several individuals from the ministry; none of them claimed to know who was responsible. Perhaps there was a church-wide "cone of silence" in place, for it was inconceivable to imagine that not one person could shed any light on the unfortunate, law-breaking event.

My Fanatical, Regrettable Tour of Ministry

What really grieved me most of all was the fact that Grace's witness as a community of faith took a beating in town that day. Rumours began to fly about certain people who had apparently taken responsibility for the break-in, yet nothing was ever proven. To this day, I have no knowledge of who actually did the dirty deed, and whether or not they acted alone.

At that point, I put a call into a very close and wise friend of mine, a fellow pastor, who counselled me to consider cutting my losses and getting out of Grace Church as soon as I could. It was incumbent upon me, this mentor reminded me, as the leader of my home, to not only protect my psyche, but my character as well. I was encouraged to do everything necessary to insulate the health and security of my marriage, even if that meant I had to walk away from my ministry position. My good friend's advice echoed what I had been taught in Bible College, yet no one could have convinced me that I would ever have to put those lessons into practice. I was engulfed by feelings of insecurity, and so was Elaine, until our spirits seemed to be totally compressed by the uncertainties we were facing. Personally, I felt humiliated and ashamed at the prospects of my derailed ministry at Grace Church being deemed such a complete and utter failure.

I could hardly recognize in myself the pastor who had only a year and a half earlier effectively guided the young people at First Community Church. After a year at Grace Church, I wasn't that same leader. The trials and tribulations at Grace changed me; the real question was, who would I become in the months ahead? One year after Elaine and I moved to town, we were again hunting for empty boxes, to repack and move once again. There would be no happy one-year anniversary at Grace. I was able to prayerfully wrap my mind around leaving the church, as soon as I could. I just couldn't sense a clear, rational, *God-appointed* burden to muster the will to plan for the forthcoming fall ministry schedule.

Pastor Williams, whom I had grown to respect, had left for another church a few months earlier. There was uncertainty amongst the congregation over his replacement, and what kind of leadership the new pastor would bring.

Making the scenario even murkier was the fact that the remaining elders, along with the combatant father, were still secure in their positions. In addition to that, the senior youth group was still a mess and I lacked the energy to determine how many were with still with me, and how many were not. Another reason for leaving was the sad reality that my wife of just thirteen months could hardly bring herself to attend church anymore. Deep within my conscience, I lamented having been the one to bring this hardship into our marriage. It would take some time before I could rationally process, and eventually shake off, that

Ron Mahler

burden. However, before it came time for me to officially announce my resignation—a predictable but favourable outcome in the eyes of the elders—I had some questions that needed to be answered.

CHAPTER 23
Faulty Wiring

OUR FAMILY ONCE MOVED INTO A NEW HOME. IT WAS A DELIGHTFUL MEDIUM-sized bungalow with a spacious, old-fashioned porch out in front. Everything about the look of the house and the property it sat on was quaint. We coveted the home for the better part of a year.

However, despite its appealing exterior, the *interior* had a problem we overlooked. As it turned out, there were numerous problems with the electrical wiring, but this only came to our attention after we moved in and began to experience trouble with certain wall switches. Until the problem was fixed, Elaine and I had to improvise; for instance, by pulling up a chair in order to unscrew our dining room light bulb, so that it would go off. Then there was our main floor hallway, where only one of the wall switches was capable of turning the lights off.

This is a short list of a very long list of challenges we encountered. With my amateur inspector's hat on, I naturally assumed that either something had short-circuited, or there was a problem with the home's electrical box. However, a professional electrician later enlightened me that it was, in fact, more a case of faulty wiring. I was shown how a simple yet common mix-up, where one wire is improperly crossed over another, can lead to one's switches being unable to open or close a light. It was one of the costliest educations I have ever received! When we were considering the home, Elaine and I weren't able to detect the extent of the electrical deficiencies, because we took for granted that the switches worked. Besides, we only visited the home during the *daytime*.

Ron Mahler

We bought the home as-is after it had been uninhabited for well over a year. It was only once we moved in and did some switch-flicking that we discovered something about the house we hadn't known before. The hard truth about the Church, as an organism, is that it has operational dysfunction on any given level. We can take that to the bank! If pastors are going to accept a call to a certain church, they have to take that church *as it is*. We can only double-date with another ministry for so long before we have to walk down the aisle with *one* of them! We take for granted that the church we're hanging our hats at is in relatively good working order. Once Elaine and I made the transition from shopping for a church ("candidating") to choosing Grace, one alarming reality began to surface: it had a huge spiritual wiring problem.

If outward appearances counted for anything, I was smitten by what I saw the first time I drove up. Farm fields surrounded the building and backstopped the horizon line behind it; the property was pleasing to the eye. It had a fancy sign perched in the middle of the well-manicured lawn adorned by colourful flowerbeds. It was easy to tell that a lot of care was given to the building's inner layout, as well, which was clean, freshly painted, and hosted a tasteful, modern decor. Ambiance aside, the ministry position Grace offered me had all the makings of a can't-pass-up opportunity. It was a place where I could further develop my ministry gifts and pastoral abilities. I had really bought into the bill of goods Grace Church sold me in terms of its spiritual climate and its potential for growth and expansion.

Time and time again, I had been told that Grace was a "good" church. However, all the tantalizing possibilities in the world couldn't cover up the mounting tempest swirling within the church's walls. In retrospect, perhaps instead of concentrating on building up a ministry, the powers that were should have been concentrating on repairing relationships. Church life, it is said, is like family; you love your siblings, but living with them under one roof tests your love for them! And when the light switches of the house are malfunctioning (even if it's God's house), chances are those siblings are going to bump into each other from time to time—and get hurt. The shifting plates of biblical indifference and ignorance left the spiritual terrain at Grace Church diced and choppy, contributing to its unstable and contentious culture.

It's a stretch, even now, for me to recall many, if any, bright moments while I was there. Perhaps there were some dim intervals, but by and large there were many dark moments. Pastor Williams had his own enemies, and to this day I cannot figure out *why* they even existed, although I suspect it boiled down to clashing personalities and politically-energized power wars. The point in all of this is that not every incoming pastor is going to be everyone's "cup of tea." People may have preferred the former blend, the one they consumed prior to the new pastor's advent, but such preferences should never lead the Body of Christ to discard or despise the new, or to crack the cup out of spite. Pastor Williams was following in the footsteps of a very popular and beloved pastor who had been at Grace Church for over thirty years.

Such was the pastoral shadow hanging over Williams from the moment he stepped foot into the town, never mind the church. He continuously struggled against the ghost of pastor past! The church never let him forget who had sat in his office before him, and yet by doing so they set themselves up for their own letdown. Pastor Williams wasn't allowed to be his own man, for he was too busy being told how he was so unlike the one he followed after. A portion of the folk at Grace were so busy craning their prejudicial necks, basking in the blinding light of yesteryear, that it's no wonder they developed a kink.

Was Pastor Williams *really* the problem? Whose business was it to decide? An inconsistent board of elders who weren't in a position to call a spade, a spade? A church who abdicated godliness for the glamour of rumour? Did Pastor Williams really have to wind up wounded simply because he brought a different skillset to the pastoral office of Grace Church? Could any pastor scale the edifice of his predecessor's thirty-something-year reign, and stand on its peak?

The spiritual wires of truth and non-truth were so crossed-up within God's house that it seemed like everyone was left in the dark. This cluster of Christians scurried around in darkness, lunging at different spiritual switches, unaware of whether one would produce more darkness or much-needed *light*, something which should have been provided by its leadership.

Like so many other ministries of that same spiritual temperature, there was something about the feverishly sinful activity at Grace Church that led them to infirm their own. The unfortunate byproduct of that reality was a decent and godly pastor getting undeservedly hurt. Pastor Williams' consolation prize came in the form of embracing the *sufferings* of Jesus Christ, someone who knew what it was like to be unjustly accused and abused by the most unlikeliest of people.

Chapter 24
Taking the Bait

MANY OF THE GREAT SERVANTS OF GOD SCATTERED THROUGHOUT BOTH OLD and New Testaments suffered at the hands of their own people. That's why the trials we face in life always aim to bring us back to the scandalous heartache of Calvary's cross. The casual, non-believing outsider is usually bemused when they hear of Christian infighting. The same, however, cannot be said of God, and His perfect judgement is what we should be most concerned about. God is utterly grieved whenever His children fight with one another, which is why we should be just as grieved. God's own covenant people maniacally feuded with His Son to the extent that it landed the second Person of the Trinity in the middle of two other crossbeams on Golgotha's hill.

God conceded the unthinkable by choosing, in eternity past, to experience death Himself in the form of His righteous Son, so that we (the real, indictable offenders) could be undeservingly forgiven of our sins. It was at that pitiless cross, through the redemption Christ secured for us, where God purposed to rewire us so that the spiritual switches of our lives would return to their intended working order. Being born again means that, as believers, we don't have to choose between light and darkness when it comes to how we are going to treat one another. Scripture exhorts us to live in harmony with our fellow Christians, so we ought not to even debate the issue (see Romans 12:16). We shouldn't have to guess at how we're going to act towards another person, no matter who they are or what the circumstance is.

In that same chapter of Romans, Paul teaches us that the spiritual key to living in harmony with others is predicated upon our being transformed by the renewing of our minds (see Romans 12:2). In other words, we need to use our spiritual brains—actually giving our heads a shake once and a while, wouldn't hurt, either! The fact remains that as lifelong disciples of Jesus, we don't have to choose between the command of God (obedience) and the forbidden fruit of a self-imposed will (disobedience). No amount of our sinful nature can tie our hands, keeping us from being able to follow through with doing God's will. In Christ, we are now free to choose righteousness (see Galatians 5:1).

Therefore, our spiritual switches should always be in the on position. If we are to fully comprehend and experience who Jesus says we are—*"the light of the world"* (Matthew 5:14)—then that light needs to shine at its brightest. The Body of Christ is where we are supposed to be trained to overcome evil with good.

I wish that would have been the prevailing spiritual attitude at Grace Church. Today, conflict in the church is considered a religious anecdote, not the spiritual oxymoron it *ought* to be viewed as. Though strife and discord are not the ways in which we, as Christians, are to show people that we are Jesus' disciples, it does show how much our spiritual wiring, as a human race, became crossed up in the Garden of Eden. The damage done there makes us prone, even as a redeemed people, to keep the fellowship we have with one another polarized and darkened by the overshadowing of our sinful natures. The skies that turned black as Jesus took His last breath attest to that. Everyone who hoped in the Lord, after witnessing the crucifixion, ambled off in confused, spiritual darkness. The supernatural effects visited upon the natural world at Christ's execution scene were a consequence of sin and unbelief.

Sadly, that same darkness comes rolling in at our churches, again and again, like a spiritual eclipse of our senses. Though our struggle is not based on flesh-and-blood encounters between mere human opponents, it can appear to be that way (see Ephesians 6:12). However, every Christian should be willing to admit that Satan can only be blamed for so much. Believers should never advocate extending grace towards the Devil, but we must be realistic about the scope of our own hearts, which have a great capacity for disobedience, even abject wickedness (see Jeremiah 17:9). Satan presented the fruit to Eve, but she *and* Adam did the biting! Judas Iscariot willingly took up the opportunity that Satan afforded him to betray the Lord. *We* mouth the exaggerations about people that Satan merely brings to our mind.

Ron Mahler

God's people also often unfairly hammer His shepherds, because we allow Satan to convince us that they deserve it. While the Devil *is* the evil prime mover who tirelessly looks for chances to squeeze Hell's bellow on the fires of our conflict, *we* are the match-strikers who light our logs of discontent with fellow believers. The Devil is only too happy to oblige by donating his hellish wind, in order to spread the sparks for us. Satan is no respecter of persons in our propensity to be used by him to counterfeit God's work. There are times in the Christian life when we are in conflict with other believers, and in these times we tend to only see flesh and blood fighting against us. Spiritually, however, that's not how things really are. We have an unseen enemy (Satan) lurking behind the curtain of our conflicts, and he is the real producer of discord between Christians.

As people who bear Christ's name on our lives, we cannot underestimate Satan's interest in our weaknesses and foolishness. If we are useful to the Devil, we'll be used by the Devil; if the Devil can use anyone to divide a church and bring its witness into ill repute, be it an elder, a pastor, or a layperson, you can bet your last tithe that he will. Think about it. If God chose not to program us to act as He wills, but created us with freewill, how then can Satan override that freedom and force us to do anything? Therefore, if we aimlessly flick our spiritual switches on and off while our wiring remains crossed up, or attempt to handle spiritual live wires, we will not find the solution to our problems of discord and conflict in the church. So what should we do when faulty wiring in the hearts of God's people leads to the explosive fires of division?

The Bible squarely brings us back to home base: we should immediately seek to call upon our heavenly Electrician, who not only qualified us to be heirs in the kingdom of light, but rescued us from the dominion of darkness (see Colossians 1:12–13). Until we breathe our last worldly breath and have our sin-defaced human natures laid to waste, we will be in need of constant reminders that our true, Christ-like identity is as one of *light-bearers*. From the cradle to the grave, we are in need of His grace to help us keep the peace, containing and dousing the flames of discord in the Body of Christ. Unfortunately, as was the case with Pastor Williams, the ghost of pastor past visited me at Grace Church as well. The ungodly squad of people who ended up setting themselves against Pastor Williams did likewise to me, quite possibly with greater spiritual magnitude and impact.

I counted on facing the comparison with my predecessor in terms of how I lined up as a pastor; I just didn't expect to have it used against me. Never in a million lifetimes could I have foreseen how ugly and off-the-rails my ministry at Grace would get as a result. It was hard enough being separated from family and friends just months after getting married, hard enough getting used to a new town, new church, and two new youth groups. But I also had to deal with a side of ministry I had never fathomed could exist.

The first couple of months on the job were more or less ordinary. I made a concerted effort to balance times of discipleship and prayer with having fun and building relationships with the young people. Most of them, along with my main volunteers, were eager to birth a new era for the youth ministry, a unit which was a bit fragmented owing to the lengthy period between the previous youth pastor's departure and my arrival.

Early on, I sensed that the kids could use a little coming-together time. When I think back, the first four to eight weeks was the "honeymoon," where the group seemed light-hearted and undistracted. A handful of parents kindly expressed their delight in how I was handling the intricacies of the transition. Some of them supported my slightly more serious and purpose-driven approach to leading the youth ministry, and I found their feedback to be quite helpful. They affirmed to me their perceptions that I was on the right track, taking incremental steps towards restructuring and realigning the various aspects of the two youth ministries.

These parents, like other church members, would flash a smile at me on Sunday mornings and even grant me a pat on the back. The odd elder would also acknowledge that they'd heard something positive from the parents. However, like the wind suddenly changing direction, cool drafts began to head my way. Coincidence, or not, it was right around the time when Pastor Williams began to give off vibes that all was not well in senior pastor central.

Chapter 25

Protests

IN ALMOST EVERY CHURCH I HAVE MINISTERED IN, APART FROM FIRST COMMUNITY Church, the people who welcomed me in overly generous and complimentary ways turned out to be camouflaging a hidden agenda. It may sound like a cynical remark, but I've come by that deduction honestly. At Grace Church, these not-so-well-intentioned people existed in good number.

An occasion arose when I happened to have need of new tires for my car. I was told to call the garage associated with a certain church member. One morning while I was at the office, this person quietly had my car removed from the driveway of my home and proceeded to have all the tires changed, at no cost. On top of that, they had the vehicle returned by the time I got back from the church later that day. I was thrilled and touched by the thoughtful gesture; it was the first time anyone had ever done such a thing for me.

The person responsible for the charitable act also became an occasional occupant of the token visitor's chair in my office. Now and again, on his way to work, he would walk into my office and wax spiritual. He would often offer a prayer before leaving, voicing support of my leadership. It was all positive stuff... until you get to the rest of the story. This man and his spouse had two teenagers who were officially counted as a part of Grace's youth ministry, though neither teenager made much effort to attend. These two young people were kind of like strays; every once and while they would show up on the doorstep of a youth event. Very rarely would they seem motivated enough to actually come out to an evening of group Bible study. To further complicate matters, they, along with some of their peers, had issues with other kids in the group. As a result, they chose not to be around much.

Before too long, I gained a reputation amongst certain negative teens for leading long and boring Bible studies. Whether their assertions had much stock or not, after I considered their criticisms, I fought more than a few times to resist the onset of offence, in my spirit. In general, I think it is difficult for pastors to ingest observations or criticisms (even if they are said to be constructive) about their ministry techniques, especially when they come from those who treat the pastoral duty as something to be consumed with a drive-thru, give-it-to-me-quick mentality. My thoughts were that if a young person could endure, on average, a two-hour movie and a two-hour drive, both ways, to get to that movie, then surely they could find it in them to scrape together thirty or forty minutes out of their week to study God's Word.

Interestingly, the same teens who hid behind their distaste for my leadership were the ones who had a history of not contributing much to the community of the young people's ministry. Everyone has an opinion about a pastor, but not every complaint has to, or should, be aired. I felt I was more than understanding and gracious towards the dissenters who thought they had the lowdown on me; their parents, on the other hand, I found hard to comply with when they refused to even be slightly objective about the fruit of their kids' attitudes and actions.

It's unfortunate in life when one ends up hearing complaints that people have about you from everybody except the very person who's actually *doing the complaining*. I began to hear complaints, shared by a small segment of young people, about my personality, approach, and priorities. These complaints also came from the parents and other influential leaders the dissenters had in their back pocket. Many of these adults, I felt, couldn't argue with me objectively. They seemed to be more interested in running with the complaints than hearing me out. In the end, when all was said and done, I felt uncomfortable when parents who had initially been with me when I'd started out suddenly turned their back on me.

Consequently, the same person who put the new tires on my car for free, and who had regularly showed up in my office to offer me a word of praise and encouragement, eventually revoked his prior support of my ministry and joined the ranks of other disgruntled parents. Even if parents do know about what's going on in their kid's lives, they can't possibly know or see all sides of them. Guess who gets to see some of that other side? The inconvenient youth pastor!

Ron Mahler

Oftentimes, it's not a case of parents being blind to the rebelliousness of their teens; it's that they don't want to see certain things. In life, some people will set their first impressions of us in stone if we look at them the wrong way.

Youth ministry is no different. Young hearts and lives are influenced quite easily. Some teens will only give you one chance to impress them. This was the case with a certain young person who was clearly not a fan of mine, right from the get-go. He played in the church's youth band and was considered a pretty cool customer; he also had "watch out" written all over him. I'm lost for words as to why exactly I wasn't able to connect well with this cat. Today, things would probably be different; I'm older (hopefully a bit wiser, too), and I'm a parent myself, which might have helped me relate better. When I shared my concerns about this particular young person with Pastor Williams, his encouragement to me was refreshingly welcome. He refrained from criticizing any of the young people on his way to acknowledging that sometimes pastors and leaders struggle to speak into people's lives, but that God only expects us to be faithful, not necessarily successful.

The young person in question, to my knowledge, had a good relationship with the prior youth pastor, a reality that made my job that much more of an uphill climb. The prevailing interpretation of my countenance amongst the contentious strand in the youth group was that I didn't smile enough; even worse, they claimed this meant I wasn't as accepting of them as I ought to have been. They were wrong. Nonetheless, I have always given them some slack, for they didn't have to be mind readers to be able to tell that I wasn't happy with how circumstances were developing, politically, in the church since I had arrived.

As the weeks and months passed, my uneasiness about everything at Grace Church multiplied. I didn't want the youth to have the inside scoop on the division within the leadership of the church, which was reaching the boiling point. From the way a few of the young people would stare at me, however, I wondered if they knew something I didn't. But there was an even more disturbing question: were they on to the fact that I was aware of what some of their parents were up to?

It was inevitable that these cascading difficulties overtaking the church would trickle into the entire youth ministry. It became my obsession to avoid any young person's awkward inquiries about the spiritual climate of the church—the gossip, the rumours, the lies. Consequently, I steered my priorities towards what mattered most: protecting my new marriage. We were already feeling insecure about our place at the church, and I was jealous to protect our alone time. Besides, Elaine was my world, and I feared that the quandary we found ourselves in would deteriorate further, permeating the sanctity of our home, which nearly happened.

Chapter 26

Affronts

After Pastor Williams left the church, I found the responsibility of balancing the youth ministry, with the associate pastor leftovers a bit thick to wade through. The young people at Grace Church were very demanding of my attention (as many teenagers are), and they were "reading" me at every turn. I've come to realize that that is ministry in a nutshell: people want your time as much as they want to see evidence that you care about them. If God's people perceive that a pastor is not demonstrative in that way, sooner or later the pastor will hear about it. Christians want to see their pastor's sermon tangibly applied in their own lives, and not just in terms of an application tucked onto the end of their script every week. At Grace, it wasn't that the youth weren't welcome at my home, not by any means; it's just that they were not welcome at *any hour* of their choosing, a practice they had been conditioned to taking advantage of with the previous youth pastor.

The nature of youth ministry calls for a certain type of flexibility that can ask a lot of its main leader. I may have sometimes given the young people at Grace the impression that I enjoyed time with my new wife so much that I had far less of it to spend with them, outside of regularly slated activities. I had the mindset that there should be nights when my door was closed, and that meant for the *whole* evening! It was trying for Elaine and me, being so new to the town, to feel like we were really a part of its people, who in general were lifers; they were born there, rarely left there, and were going to die there. Typically, small-town ministry has a flavour and scent all its own. There are political elements and social dynamics at work that make them very distinct from their big-city counterparts. As a result, I was learning at lightning speed just how much the approach I had taken with the youth group at First Community Church didn't jive with the batch from Grace Church.

The young people at Grace were far more restless, and often ambivalent towards buying into mission statements and group values. I was hired by Grace mostly on the laurels of First Community's recommendation, yet just after the halfway point of my one year at Grace Church, I was told by one of the elders that the search committee had pegged me wrong, and that youth ministry was not for me. All things considered, there was a group of teens a few hours away who would have debated otherwise. I could have taken this elder's opinion that I was categorically unsuitable for youth leadership as a blanket statement, something which wouldn't have been too difficult for me to do at that point. In any event, this leader's comment would actually prove to be quite prophetic.

I walked into a situation at Grace Church where I flat-out lacked the necessary resources in personnel and experience to face the troubles moving in and around me. To be fair, I was deprived of any governing hierarchy (the church was independently run and belonged to no denomination) whose presence might have been able to arbitrate through some of the conflicts in the church and bring some much-needed objectivity—not to mention sanity.

Before long, my initial excitement began to bottom out. Many of the key young people in the senior group withdrew, not only from the Bible studies but from the socials and events as well. The attendance at almost every youth gathering diminished week by week, almost inexplicably.

I was fed a steady diet of sketchy reasons as to why the young people were staying away. I was told that some of the teens had "other things to do," or "were at parties"; you name the event, there was an excuse for someone who wasn't there. I heard rumours that some of my youth functions were actually being sabotaged by informants. It became increasingly difficult to plan anything related to the senior youth ministry. One evening, I attempted to change things up by going a little off-script, putting aside the scheduled Bible study in favour of just hanging out. As my luck would have it, that had to be the same night one prickly parent showed up.

In front of the young people present, she proceeded to reprimand me for not doing my job. It just so happened to be the same night her teen finally came to the group, after a long absence, obviously expecting that a Bible study was going to take place. Absolutely nothing positive came from that unnecessary encounter.

Ron Mahler

I was shell-shocked from being taken down a few notches from a parent who thought I could use a good douse of humility. I got her drift that evening; in fact, really well! But I don't think humility was the intended effect of her tirade—it was *humiliation*. The only thing this parent's actions accomplished was to show the teens that it was okay to speak to the pastor with disrespect. The ordeal only further undermined my leadership. By that time, all I had left was a title, and certainly no respect or authority.

If I resembled a lame-duck leader before the incident, I was relegated to a cooked one after it. As expected, the elders were made aware of what had happened, and though they acknowledged that the parent's outburst was uncalled-for, they asked me to cut her some slack, considering the state of her family. This parent's frustration was judged to be mildly excusable. My feelings, and the embarrassment I suffered, didn't appear to matter as much. It left me with my pride more than a little sore. To my knowledge, no actions were taken to hold the parent accountable.

Rightly or wrongly, I chose to give this parent a wide berth as time wore on, instead of confronting her. I knew that she, as well as her spouse, was critical of me, just as she was of Pastor Williams. I didn't have the inner fortitude or heart's desire to have any of the elders (whom I didn't put much faith in) accompany me in visiting her. With my wounded pride, I resolved to do anything I could to save face.

I thought I could do that when I agreed to meet with another parent, who wanted to share his concerns about the youth ministry. Paranoid or not, I felt a little bit like I was going to be blindsided by a critique the size of a two-by-four. Man, was I right about that one! This parent was a person I had limited contact with, who was by no means ever visible at any youth event. He condescendingly opined that I should be wondering about the stability of my job. More than subtle was his jab that if I was unsuccessful in turning things around (as if it all depended on me), I would find myself swimming in the overcrowded pool of pastors looking for ministries.

I was disappointed in his brazen lack of discernment and tact. If I had given any indication of delinquency in my responsibilities or that I didn't give "two flying figs" about the youth, this parent's concerns might have been justified. If that were true of my ministry, I would have owned up to it and accounted for it. After I strummed up enough will to cordially thank the grumbling parent for coming in to see me, I was overcome by anger.

Enough

Divisions in families are as distressing as they are rife. Throughout the past fifteen years, I have encountered many. For instance, I once ministered to a single father who was always weary over how his children were going to be treated by their stepfather when they visited their mother. When the children returned to him, he would get suspicious of certain remarks they made; even certain looks were deemed to have been influenced by his ex-wife, her new husband, or the extended family. When a home is divided, the polarities can run so deep that a person may think they'll never get out from under it.

The same principle applies to the Church. After a while, pastoral couples who have had to endure divisive church environments can begin to irrationally dissect just about every minute detail of their day. It may seem quite natural for them (and I speak from experience) to assume that everyone is out to get them. They'll try to decipher any look for its hidden motive, and any comment for its intended meaning. Near the end of my time at Grace Church, I was wary of nearly everyone who frequented my office.

Everyone except one man, the father of one of the senior youth members. As I was accustomed to doing over the course of that turbulent year, I would sit at my desk and commiserate with him. I knew he could empathize with me. There we sat, with me bemoaning my lot, and him confessing to having been told he would not be the next senior pastor of Grace Church.

Ron Mahler

This man had a history of being a very politically savvy leader. Being a member of Grace Church, he was strikingly familiar with the personalities on the elders' board, just as he was with the combative parent who had not only plagued my existence but his as well, often trying to goad him into arguments. What made this man safe to share with was his obvious warmth towards me, not to mention that his children were some of my few outspoken fans. He also had a burden for the sin-afflicted state of Grace Church and the ability to gain the ear of even the most indifferent and reticent of members. He was the kind of individual that most people took notice of. Most of all, I was persuaded that if anyone had the tenacity to apply for the vacant senior pastoral position at Grace, it was him.

For his own family's sake, I was happy that he was ultimately an unsuccessful candidate. The powers that were probably wouldn't have been able to handle his pointed altruisms and firm principles. In hindsight, he was more valuable to the Lord for his role as resident mentor to any new incoming pastor than he would have been as pastor himself. He and his wife were part of a minority who staunchly supported my ministry and expressed equal disappointment for how my situation was being handled at the eldership level. It's no wonder the man wasn't considered for the vacant senior pastor's chair! He was not a guy to play the odds of popularity.

A poignant moment arose during our conversation. I took out my Bible and turned the pages to Paul's epistle to Titus, and read to him, *"Encourage the young men to be self-controlled. In everything set them an example by doing what is good. In your teaching show integrity, seriousness and soundness of speech that cannot be condemned, so that those who oppose you may be ashamed…"* (Titus 2:6–8)

When I finished reading the passage, I lifted my head and pleaded, as if to justify myself, "I have done this! I have obeyed what God called me to do here! So why has this happened?"

I thought I had made a solid case for my ministry at Grace. My point was that I had simply carried out what I had originally told the search committee I would do, and in a godly way. This veteran of church ministry calmly reminded me that things would not always be that easy in ministry, but that I could count on inheriting lives that were indifferent to how I ministered to them.

He was right. I have found that some people in the church will respond well to the touchy-feely type of pastor, while others tend to laud the merits of visionary leaders. Still others are disposed towards ministers who possess a solid preaching ability. Then there's the fact that youth seldom appreciate whether a leader is theologically sound, or educated, as long as they trust the leader to show a genuine interest in their lives, and to model Jesus.

As I pondered over my meeting with this friend and father of two, I prayerfully asked God to frisk me of all my tightly-held prejudiced views about my own leadership at Grace. The result was a loosening of insights and convictions that magnified the finer details of how I had shepherded the young people. Some of these insights left me feeling uncomfortable.

Could I have made more of an effort, to draw closer to the troublesome kids in the young people's group? I was willing to concede that maybe they were testing me, to see if I would still pursue them, despite their non-compliance to my leadership. Maybe they didn't need me to exhibit tough love as much as they needed me to love them in spite of their toughness? However, I felt I could balance my internal admissions of regret by reminding myself of all the times I had been stood-up after arranging to meet young people for coffee. Half the battle is making sure that we've done all we can do. People's lives, whether they are teenagers, adults, Christians, or non-Christians, are complicated; the ministry's task is to separate what is least important to overcome from what is most important, in fostering communication and trust.

As Christ-followers, we may not be able to be friends with everybody, but we can still make a difference in some of the lives we aim to touch for God. Ultimately, whether we are lay people or paid leaders, we are not always directly responsible for how people perceive and respond to our ministry. Perceptions can vary widely; someone may call orange what another perceives as gold, or call turquoise what could be perceived for ultramarine! Someone may gaze at an abstract painting and see a distorted resemblance of an old man, where another may spot a mule. Who is right, and who is not? Likewise, pastoral effectiveness is in the eye of the beholder. It's not always about whether we are right or wrong; it's people's perceptions of us that determine how they view us. We could offend a person and never really be aware of it.

Trials and criticisms are part of the "buyer beware" element of going into ministry. Opposition cannot and will not be avoided for very long, even in the best and healthiest of church contexts. It's the spiritual response these trials elicit in us that God is most concerned with. The growth we need to mature tends to sprout from the ground of our spiritual valleys—the disappointments, failures, and setbacks—rather than from the peaks of spiritual victory, where we feel so sky-high blessed that we can almost touch the floor of Heaven with our fingertips.

Ron Mahler

Just days prior to my resignation, I knew I had one more meeting to put together. There were questions about my leadership at Grace Church that I was not about to leave unanswered.

The elder I chose to meet with, whether he realized it or not, had the power either to encourage me to stay or to dissuade me from it. I trusted God would use him to confirm His will for me. If I didn't sense a hopeful olive branch on his part, I would resign that forthcoming weekend. We got together for coffee one night at a restaurant overlooking a large lake. A vast body of water was sprawled out before me through the window. The view paralleled the endless possibilities of my unpredictable future, both short- and long-term.

After we exchanged a few pleasantries, the elder made sure I heard what he wanted me to know.

"At least half the church has rejected you as a pastor here, Ron," he offered uninhibitedly as he sat sipping his java.

Where have I have heard this line before? I thought to myself.

"Are you serious?" I asked. "What have I done that's so wrong?"

He shrugged in response. "A lot has happened, Ron. People are people. That's ministry."

I was glad *he* had it all figured out. Suffice it to say that I heard nothing from him to give me the confidence to stay. The year ahead would be no better than the one that had just past. Whether I was gullible or not, my decision to leave the church was sealed. The only thing left to do was draft the obligatory resignation letter and to submit it to the elders' board. That experience, in itself, would be confirmation enough that I was doing the right thing.

Chapter 28

Heartaches

In life, there are moments when we wish that the people we've ministered to, in their greatest time of need, would recall our ministry when they are in the heat of conflict with us. I believe this is one of the hardest things for Christians to practice consistently. During my time at Grace Church, before all the disruptive trials, two of the elders had potentially life-altering crises strike their homes. On both occasions, and during the trials, I felt that I had faithfully ministered to these men and their families, even shedding tears for them in their presence, tears which I couldn't hold back.

None of these acts of kindness and sympathy appeared to count for much on the warm August morning in 1998 when I chose to submit my letter of resignation. It has been my experience that prior pastoral faithfulness doesn't always amount to much ministry credit. When fellowship in the church is broken, all that is left between Christians is animosity.

There's nothing quite as spiritually destructive as when the unity of God's people is shattered with such force that it splinters people's better judgement like shards of glass in one's hand. I hoped that the elders would show some benevolence towards me when I pulled the resignation letter out of my pocket, but instead they did the exact opposite. As I broke the news that I had reached the inevitable conclusion to leave Grace Church, nervous silence filled the room. On the letter of resignation, I left the date of my final day at the office blank, so the elders could suggest an appropriate last day for me. I still had some appointments and planning to finalize, not to mention that I desperately desired another paycheque before Elaine and I left the church.

As I proceeded to discuss a possible exit date, one of the elders (whom I had ministered to his time of trials) hastily blurted out, "You can make that yesterday's date!"

Talk about a hyper-accelerated push out the door! This elder's remark was not only spiteful, it hurt. It had been hard enough for me to sit through the meeting, knowing what I was going to reveal at the end of it. Couple that with the fact that I was performing two weddings that same weekend (my first two ever, at that), and one could understand why my nerves were a bit exposed.

Consequently, by the time the Saturday morning elder's meeting came around, I felt a bit wound-up. Here was my agenda for the weekend:

Saturday: Resign at elders' meeting (10:30 a.m.). Wedding #1 (1:30 p.m.).
Sunday: Last sermon (11:00 a.m.). Wedding #2 (2:00 p.m.).

Up until that point, I had never tangibly grasped how vital God's grace and mercy is for those who occupy the office of a pastor. That August weekend, I desperately needed to feel God's providential hand upon me. I shouldn't have been so amazed at just how strong God could make me when I felt I was at my weakest. Wasn't that what the apostle Paul boasted of? (see 2 Corinthians 12:10). If there has ever been a time in my ministry when God came through for me, it was during that ministry-heavy, spiritually burdensome weekend at Grace Church. Sometimes pastoral duties cannot be shelved in order to be dealt with another day, whether the one who ministers is hurting or not. People rely on pastors to be strong for them, even if that pastor feels worn down and unmotivated. It's one of the most challenging areas of church ministry—that is, how to be pastoral when you feel anything *but* pastoral. Thankfully, though, God is more gracious and merciful than any of us, even on our best day!

As the one elder's mean-spirited remark pertaining to my resignation date bit into me, my confidence in and respect for the leadership went out the office door, right then and there, and was never to be seen from again. I sat speechless and just took it. Only one other elder chastised the leader for his inappropriate words. The other elder (whom I had also ministered to his time of trials) sat with his head down, saying nothing. Only one elder, who was newly voted in, remained alone with me in the room after the meeting adjourned. At least he had a big enough heart to offer, "That must have been very hard for you today."

My Fanatical, Regrettable Tour of Ministry

Before Pastor Williams had left for another ministry, he'd slotted me in way ahead of time to preach a few Sunday sermons, and one of those mornings just so happened to be the day after my resignation. It would coincidentally end up being my last sermon, and last Sunday, at Grace Church.

It could have been an advantageous situation for me, to really let the leadership "have it" in front of the whole church. I could have spoken against their shaky and sometimes careless, handling of the problems at Grace, the welfare of my ability to minister included. I recall having to repeatedly deny those temptations, even up to the last minute before I took to the podium. It took everything in me not to sink my teeth into the fruit of verbal revenge! I had never seen the elders so nervous as they were that morning. They knew it was my last Sunday sermon, and that I could have selfishly made the *most* of it, if I had wanted to. One of the elders sat in the first few rows, looking tense and fidgety. His eyes pierced on me as if thinking, *I just dare you to say something*.

I'd had a conversation the night before with a fellow believer who I deeply respected and who has now gone to be with the Lord. He gently encouraged me to just "go out with a bang," not by shooting the leadership with criticism but by preaching my finest sermon. I was encouraged to let God's Word be the last thing they heard me say, not my own.

I took the advice to heart. With the service bursting with people I had not seen at the church for some time, I broke into my introduction with a determination to stay focussed on the topic at hand. When I wrapped up my conclusion, I knew in my heart and from the adoring look upon Elaine's face, that, indeed, the masses at Grace had just witnessed my finest message in the time I was there. I also delivered the message that I was not going to give the elders, or anyone else, any additional fodder to use against me.

The reason I gave when the time came for me to announce that Elaine and I were leaving Grace Church suddenly seemed to me to be as sad as it was succinct: I was leaving in order to explore other ministry opportunities. After a brief parting statement, I thanked everyone who had been praying for us, and trotted off the platform. I literally kept my chin up, and in gazing out at the congregation I saw people (more people than I would have thought) openly cry, sitting with a look of stunned displeasure on their faces. I immediately looked around the sanctuary in an attempt to spot even one elder to make eye contact with; I found none.

That day, I left a sanctuary that I knew I would never enter again and was promptly embraced not only by well-wishers and supporters, but by an embattled spirit within me. I knew the hardest challenge in my young ministry life still lay ahead: I had to choose whether I would let the sorry experience at Grace Church make me a *better* man, or a *bitter* one.

My resolve to be a better man was compounded when, just days before Elaine and I loaded up the truck to head back to Toronto, one of our beloved dogs was killed by a car just outside our driveway. There was very little *grace* at Grace Church, and now it seemed that the town itself was devoid of it. The pain of that incident was so blunt, and grossly jarring to our hearts, that we thought we might never get over it. It hardly seemed fair to have to hurt the way we did, in being so far from those whom we knew loved us. I couldn't press down on the gas pedal fast enough to leave town. Elaine and I, as a therapeutic measure, literally shook the dust of the town from our shoes. Even if someone who claimed to be prophetic had told me a year earlier that Elaine and I would go one-year-and-out at Grace Church, I would have thought they were totally delusional.

Absolutely bewildered and aghast at what had hit us at Grace Church, Elaine and I landed back in Toronto, where we were welcomed by friends and family like athletes who had won gold medals. We would stay there, as if in protective custody, for a period that would last almost two full years.

Chapter 29

Home Cooking

There's nothing quite like home. I had the privilege of going back to visit Cape Breton last year with Elaine and the kids. I was overcome by the feelings of nostalgia I got when I circled around the bend on the outskirts of the small town I'd walked as a boy. Though the place looked different, the reality was that I was home. It still felt comforting to explore and trace the paths I had taken some thirty-seven years earlier. The highlights of this nostalgic trip abounded as we made pit stops to visit the corner store, the local Catholic Church, and the farm where I had been brought home as a newborn baby. Soon it was time to visit with my cousins and extended family, which proved to be a real hoot when my children, Cassidy and Dakota, found other children to play with. It was a pleasure to go back home, to the place where it all began for me, and rediscover my roots.

That's how Elaine and I felt when we hit the turf of Toronto, which was our default home base. Whether it was for a lengthy stay or not, what mattered was that we were back home. Elaine's sisters took us into their townhouse until such time as we were able to get back on our feet, financially. We were incredibly broke, and worse, undeniably angry. If someone of influence at Grace Church hadn't suggested that they take up a "love offering" for us, we would have left there with nothing but wind in our pockets. On numerous nights, Elaine and I would lay in bed without much to say to each other. On many of those occasions, within the silence, we tossed around the same, unspoken prayer in our minds: "God, what are we going to do now?"

Ron Mahler

We were sapped spiritually, emotionally, and financially. Our situation was the perfect recipe for Elaine and me to put all our hearts' focus upon the One who could provide for those delicate areas of our lives. Both of us were hurting, afraid, and vulnerable; even more, we were wary of letting each other know that we felt that way. We may have had more questions than answers, more depression than peace, yet we took solace in that we felt more loved than we had for at least a year.

Elaine sought to find work right away, and landed a job as an administrative assistant in a doctor's office. As for me, I tailed behind for months, too wounded to even try to seek any kind of employment. I ended up spending too many long and unproductive days rehashing my misgivings of the past year, sifting through thoughts on how God would piece my life and future back together. I wondered whether any church would hire me again. My prevailing thought, swimming around in my fishbowl of a mind, was this: *Why would any church want me after I bombed so badly?* Though finding another ministry was what I thought I should have been doing, I began to seriously wonder if my one stab at pastoring was enough for me and if a "better" path of work was worth pursuing. I eventually caught on as an apprentice house-painter with a painting and decorating outfit. It was different work for me, but I was game for some radical changes.

When Elaine and I got back to Toronto, we were also deeply grieved to hear that two of our closest and dearest pastor friends were embroiled in their own ministerial waterloos. One of them was, unfortunately, Pastor Goodman from First Community Church. As I met with him, I was not sure whose heart was breaking more, mine or his. Goodman deflected attention from his own struggles long enough to let me vent about the difficulties Elaine and I were facing. Out of an underlying hope that I could somehow hold God responsible for what had happened to me at Grace Church, I asked Pastor Goodman whether it was possible that God could have "willed" me to be there only one year. Goodman crinkled his brow, grinned a bit, and gently rebutted, "The problem with that, Ron, is that it doesn't look good on the resume. God cares about your reputation." Pastor Goodman did raise the fact, however, that God was greater than my resume, and could still open any number of doors for me.

I had overlooked that fact while plying myself with a battery of negative thoughts. As my conversation with Pastor Goodman switched from my trials to his, I could read between the lines of his diplomacy. He was trying his hardest not to sound ungodly about some people in his own congregation who were giving him fits over some "changes" he had proposed. I learned that day that

My Fanatical, Regrettable Tour of Ministry

Pastor Goodman's long-running tenure at First Community was hanging on by the most tenuous of threads. For that, I was saddened. The church that had once given me such a terrific launch into the ministry had now deteriorated to the point where it eerily paralleled the sordid situation I had just come out of. As I sat across from Pastor Goodman that afternoon, one thing became obvious: the lines between counsellor and counselee were very blurred, indeed.

I realized that we both needed the unconditional support of one another, even though we both knew that the sobering realities of our individual situations were far from being squared away. Just as I had witnessed what happened to Pastor Williams at Grace Church, the fallout from Pastor Goodman's trials at First Community Church would inevitably result in him leaving for another church. Pastor Goodman was too good of a man to be out of ministry for too long. The same had been true of Pastor Williams.

As for myself, I would ride the bench of pastoral oblivion for longer than I would have liked. In retrospect, my wait for another full-time ministry was actually much shorter than what it felt like. Before I could reach that point, however, I needed my self-confidence to return. From time to time, God dusted me off and provided me avenues in which to remain active with my ministry gifts. Pastor Goodman wisely noted my need to get back on the bike, as it were, so my road to being active again in ministry appropriately began where it all started: at First Community Church.

Before I left the pastor's office that day, he offered me a preaching date at the church; I accepted, albeit with some hesitation. Pastor Goodman didn't owe me anything, and yet I walked away that day with everything I needed to begin my healing. Hurting pastors sometimes need to hang with other hurting pastors. They share a special affinity. Each one reminds the others that they are merely human, brothers in arms when it comes to their spiritual struggles in the ministry. The potential for explosive and mass-destructive power struggles are at the core of our churches. As I've come to understand, the issues surrounding our conflicts are rarely isolated anomalies; in fact, they're not even the real problem. The inherent pickle at the bedrock of many church disputes, rather, has more to do with *who* (or which camp) has control and who doesn't.

I personally know of no pastors, as innately flawed as we all are, who wish to thrive in their ministries by planning to routinely pick fights with their people. By the same token, I know of no church that gets ahead, or even remotely "wins," from shooing their shepherd out the door in an unwarranted fashion. Just as Pastor Williams didn't deserve the kind of treatment he received from some of his people, Pastor Goodman didn't, either. I would hope that now, years removed from the tensions, even some of their detractors could bring themselves to concur.

Unfortunately, upon my return to Toronto, I discovered that Pastor Goodman was not the only shepherd I knew who had fallen on hard times. Pastor Fellows (who was the one to counsel me long-distance to leave Grace Church, not to mention the one who officiated at Elaine's and my wedding) awaited me across town, for coffee.

As I drove to meet him, I wondered what I would find out when I got there. I felt that if I was to hear even one more bad church experience, maybe I should quit while I was ahead. The encounter should have been about my needing to be propped up and spiritually fortified; to an extent, it was. However, what I uncovered was yet another scenario where a pastor was putting on a brave, yet realistic face. I could hardly believe that two of the men who guided me out of Bible College were now reeling from their own storms in the ministry, when I had just come out of one of my own. There are all sorts of alarming statistics these days reflecting the number of pastors who are leaving the ministry. Some leave because of the unrealistic expectations that have been placed upon them; others leave out of frustration of their own unfulfilled expectations of the call.

For a brief span of time after hearing Pastor Fellows share his story, I entertained the occasional thought about discarding the "call" I had received, and exiting my life in ministry, a life which had barely gotten out of the starting blocks. Elaine and I felt it was best to attend Pastor Fellows' church for a time while we waited on God's leading. This allowed me access to meet periodically with the pastor while I picked his brain for wisdom. He put "bugs" in my ear, leading me to consider some options for ministering at the church until I knew what I was doing, as far as another church was concerned. Fellows observed that I was prone to sinking into multiple-day funks over my inability to shake my tattoo-like regrets over the events of Grace Church.

At one juncture, Pastor Fellows, who was floating on the waters of uncertainty himself, met with me, and told me flat-out that I needed to rise above my situation and be proactive in preparing for another ministry, even if the phones were not ringing. Fellows spotted some developing ministry traits in me that I didn't even know I had, as well as other pastoral strengths that I had long since put an A.P.B. out on. It was good to be home!

Chapter 30

Strengthened

It took weeks of counsel and prayer for me to scrape together enough nerve to send out a resume. As I saw it, I needed God's help to solve two problematic questions: what kind of church was I to apply to, and what position was best for me? Pastor Fellows was the first one to implant the possibility of seeking a ministry position that did *not* include youth ministry. Initially, I thought his advice meant that he thought I would be a repeat bust (I was assuming much those days, out of insecurity). The secret doubts I carried about my ability to lead youth ministry kept me from applying for many entry-level positions that I might have otherwise been able to get. Mainly, I needed an answer for the next search committee's questions about my quick exit from Grace Church.

The weight of this burden was so large and ominous that it seemed to hover over me every night. Far from counting sheep, or blessings, most nights I could only count the inquiries that would be made concerning my last ministry. I still remember the horrible day when I had to give an employment officer my reason for leaving Grace Church, so that I could receive unemployment benefits. Technically, I quit, a reality that could have made securing financial benefits more difficult (although one could have argued that I really didn't have much of a choice *but* to quit). The government official asked me to retell some of the more pertinent details surrounding the conflict. I explained how I felt that I'd been put in an untenable position, and that if I didn't leave it would not only have affected my health, but my marriage, too. That may have satisfied the government's inquiry, but my explanation reduced me to tears when I got back home.

That experience drove me deeper into depression. It seemed to shroud me with an endless cycle of hypothetical conversations, played over and over in my mind, where I would be forced to have similar interviews with another church. I was so torn up inside and disturbed in my spirit, because I couldn't shake the feeling that God had received a big, fat shiner that day at the unemployment office, and that it came courtesy of my failure. The feeling almost made me vomit. It was definitely one of the darkest hours in my life. My shame was raw and quantifiably real, for it made me recount all the ways in which God's witness was hurt. I knew, however, that I couldn't do anything about the past.

On more than one occasion, Pastor Fellows encouraged Elaine and me to just enjoy each other again. Laughter was sorely lacking in our life at the time. We had stopped having fun with God's people. For an entire year, we'd become so preoccupied with trying not to disappoint people that we forgot how to just be *one of them*. Consequently, Elaine and I resolved to do something that was somewhat frivolous by joining the choir at Pastor Fellows' church. It felt good to have some involvement again, where we could serve in church without having to worry who was pleased with us and who was not. (We were forgiven for any and all missed notes!) It was quite liberating for us to just be "us" again and not have to bear the expectations of being a pastoral couple. We also decided to piggyback choir practice nights with subsequent date nights, where we would make weekly visits to Taco Bell and stuff ourselves with burritos. It was the most fun we'd had in a while; we even joked at the indigestion we suffered those nights, as we tried to sleep.

We also enjoyed many nights frolicking with family and friends and would catch ourselves laughing with ease—even uncontrollably. The pain and memory of Grace Church began to dissipate, fading away like an island retreating into the distance as we rowed farther away from it. At the six-month mark in Toronto, even though I was still breaking down my hurts and appropriating them, the time seemed right to begin dreaming again, to pursue the promise and privilege of what it meant to serve God as a pastor. My heart was once again able to regain some of the hunger and awe I'd felt some six years earlier when I clearly sensed God's commission for me to enter into ministry for the first time. I was still undecided as to what exact role to aim for, so I applied to just about every feasible ministry position I could find, which included roles in senior ministry, associate's positions, and those with a youth focus as well.

My Fanatical, Regrettable Tour of Ministry

I tried to assure myself, in spite of my past misgivings and failures as an inexperienced young pastor, that God wouldn't overlook me forever. I recalled the biblical characters throughout history whom God had restored after they languished for a time in the pits of uncertainty and apparent defeat; Joseph, David, Samuel, and Elijah all came to mind. I longed for another church to validate my call to ministry, something which I was convinced could only be affirmed if I was given another crack at a full-time ministry position.

In those days, I lived close to the phone; every time it rang, it brought the hope that my time in limbo would soon end. A call *would* come in, and though the voice of the person calling was not the chairperson of a search committee, it was *the* voice God ordained to validate me as a servant of God, and as a pastor to His people.

Pastor Williams, who was now established in his new ministry, was on the other end of the line. We reminisced for a while about the past, but our conversation didn't stay parked there. Both of us were in better places in our lives. Pastor Williams shared about how blessed he felt to be where he was after the heartache of Grace Church.

Just as we were nearing the end of our discussion, he said, "Ron, has anyone ever told you that you didn't fail at Grace?"

I paused in a moment of contemplation before responding. "How did you know I needed to hear that?" I asked, with a voice that cracked with emotion.

Pastor Williams suggested that the best thing I could do was to continue my pastoral studies in seminary (which I had begun during my one year at Grace Church). He stressed that my being in school would be perceived positively when a potential church came looking my way.

Before hanging up the phone, Williams' last words lifted my spirit even more. "Ron, you have to trust God to lead you out of what He led you into. You have to trust Him."

From that day on, I trudged forward with a faith I had never tried on for size before. The ultimate demonstration of belief that God had called me to ministry was to press ahead with my studies and work towards completing my master's degree. Graciously, Elaine felt that whatever money we could scrounge together would be best applied against my tuition costs; this was confirmation that she, too, felt I wasn't finished in ministry.

The fact was that I had a lot of time on my hands, and a lot more to learn about pastoral ministry. I dug deep at seminary, and God blessed me by bringing into my life good, ministry-minded folks who plied me with knowledge, profitable insight, and sage advice, the substance of which I had never received before.

In early 1999, I experienced a ministry-altering moment while taking an advanced preaching course. Someone who aspires to preach well can't have enough tutelage on the subject! It was a night class during the winter semester; it was sometimes so cold, and I was so late coming home, that I disparaged of keeping on. I came close to dropping the course. I'm glad that I didn't. Not only was it beneficial in terms of its content and practicum, but I will be eternally grateful for the professor. If he reads this book, I hope he remembers it's him I'm talking about!

After a particular class, in which I preached a twenty-minute message, the professor walked alongside me on the way out of the room. In a matter of fact kind of way, I remember him turning to me and saying, "You have the potential to be a very good speaker. You have to work on some things, but you have something that can't be taught. You're the type of guy I could listen to every week."

The first thing that went through my mind was, *Does he really mean this, or does he say this to all his students to encourage them after they've been less than stellar?* I didn't think I had preached all that effectively in class that evening. I was tired, and I thought it showed in my sermonic mechanics, in the inflections of my voice and my body language. I might not have stunk out the joint, but it wasn't exactly my best, either.

However, the professor must have scouted out a gift, as a listener, that I couldn't see, as the deliverer. In all sincerity, I was completely blown away by my professor's affirmations, and I have never forgotten them; they have stayed with me, motivating me to be an effective communicator. On that January night of 1999, the professor's encouraging remarks also fed my growing sense that I was being built-up and prepared for a new area of ministry, one that would see my days as the "youth guy" become a thing of the past.

The Seeker Bug

ON THE CUSP OF THE NEW MILLENNIUM, ONE TERM DOMINATED THE THOUGHTS and conversations of a lot of people, especially doomsday theorists: "Y2K." It was known as the "millennium bug," or the Y2K problem, which pertained to how digital technology (computer data storage across the globe) would react to the changing of the calendar. Many computer codes represented the year as only a two-digit number, but the change in millennium would require a four-digit rollover. Depending on which expert one listened to, any and all sorts of global scenarios were forecasted. Way too many people (quasi-prophetic figures, overzealous clairvoyants, and even everyday Christians) were caught up in the apocalyptic implications. Many of them predicted the end of the world, and even the Second Coming of Christ.

Jesus didn't return when the year 2000 arrived with nary a glitch, which was, I must say, a totally anti-climactic way of putting to bed all the aforementioned hysteria. During that period, I was becoming more familiar with the "seeker sensitive" movement within the Church, another source of mass hysteria and speculation within the Body of Christ. Some genuine believers were convinced that the so-called seeker-oriented movement towards attracting unbelievers was apocalyptic in itself, in that it could spell the very end of Church as we know it!

One day, I picked up a copy of Rick Warren's *The Purpose-Driven Church,* and proceeded to devour it. Far from becoming a proselyte of any perceived movement, I've always preferred to read books (other than the Bible) to be informed, and not necessarily be conformed by them. However, keeping in mind Warren's Saddleback Valley Community Church, you can't, as the saying goes, argue with success (or, shall we say, with blessing).

The principles Warren lays out for spiritual and numerical church growth are proven, biblically-aligned, and spiritually effective. There is no doubt in my mind that God has been "in" the growth that Rick Warren and other visionary leaders like him have experienced in their much larger than average-sized churches. While Elaine and I waited for God to reveal His desired route for our next ministry, we busily attended seminars on building healthy churches and read books on the topic, seeking to comprehend why it is so important for more traditional churches to account for the unchurched people within their communities.

Then an opportunity arose for Elaine and me to join Pastor Fellows in establishing a newly-planted church. We were bursting with expeditious zeal to get back into a significant ministry partnership and saw this new initiative as a way for us to serve again in a high-reward, low-risk environment. The church plant provided us with a fresh forum in which to sharpen our ministry gifts and whet our appetite for frontline evangelism.

Elaine and I served in a variety of different areas within the new church, including stints on the worship team, performing Sunday morning service skits, and participating in an Alpha group. Our church's overarching biblical platform was simply to champion *commission* over *comfort*. In fact, anyone who called the church's office would hear the greeting, "You have reached *Such-and-Such* Church: A church for those who aren't into church!" I chuckled the very first time I listened to it (and every other time, for that matter), but loved the creative philosophy and transparency behind the message.

The leaders of the church were so amazingly and radically aligned with each other that every one of them seemed fraught with a lost-soul-sized burden to embody and fulfill the church's mission statement, carrying it into every ministry encounter God presented. In its early stages, the new church rode a wave of popularity and freshness. The excitement level reached a fevered-pitch in most services. People who had fallen away from the church, or who were wary of Christianity, were coming to know Jesus as the Lord and leader of their lives. Consequently, we all got to see how God was using a unique context and ministry philosophy to bring people into the Kingdom. "Remember," Pastor Fellows would regularly pontificate, "our ministry is beyond the church walls. It's out there, in the community, not in here." Fellows' exhortation was cutting-edge

My Fanatical, Regrettable Tour of Ministry

terminology for me. I had never heard the Great Commission communicated in that way.

Elaine and I were definitely on board with this new ministry philosophy, so much so that I resolved to pursue ministry in a seeker-oriented church, or one that was at least open to ministering that way. The seeker movement was like a bug that had gotten hold of me and infected my entire ministry outlook.

After being at the new church for about a year, and after nearly two years of prayerfully seeking God's will for the future, Elaine and I once again beat a ministry path to another church. It had been months since I'd made any inquiries about available pastoral positions. The reason was that we had become comfortably nestled in key serving roles at the new church. However, one fateful morning I fired off a resume to a mid- to small-sized church (I was told there were about eighty to ninety people), in a town about an hour and a half away. They were looking for a senior pastor.

It wasn't the first time I had applied for a senior pastoral position, yet I never failed to wonder if I was ready for such a jump. The resume was dropped in the mail just days before Elaine and I headed off on a much-needed vacation down south.

The church I applied to, Faith Church, had a fairly good history (from what I could gather). However, the church was, in fact, reeling from the simultaneous loss of both their senior, and youth pastors. The people at Faith Church, I was told, felt like they were in a position of rebounding and healing, and were looking for someone to help them grow, to serve and reach the community. In the words of a real estate agent I know, those were "buying words!" What pastor wouldn't be inclined to at least put some feelers out?

After being away from a paid ministry position for two years, there was no real hurry for me to make hasty decisions to return to one. Elaine and I were feeling good about ourselves spiritually and were getting by financially. It was the best scenario we could have bargained for, given how depleted we had been in those areas after Grace Church. Although we weren't making bags of money, by any means, we were rich in that life's demands no longer seemed to encroach upon us too greatly. We had moved out from Elaine's sister's home and had been living on our own for about a year. Our emotional frailties had been bound up, and were healing well. We were also doing a good job of leaving our past hurts and disappointments in their proper perspective—*in the past.* The number of house-painting contracts I'd received after branching out on my own were plentiful enough, and I was generally happy with how things had progressed work-wise.

Ron Mahler

Although we had been rocked by the roundhouse kicks of a ministry gone awry, we were not down for the count! Our individual self-esteems had returned to healthier levels, and more importantly, the knowledge of who we were in Christ once again took centre stage in our hearts and lives.

As much as the positives were piling up, however, I still could not deny the yearning within me to prove myself worthy of my call to ministry. Part of me continued to feel that I had let God down, and I was determined to not let such a thing happen again. I couldn't bridle my zeal to get back into a ministry role, no matter how hard I tried. Painting houses wasn't the hardest thing I could have done in life, and with my cliental increasing, it was difficult to fathom all the money I could have made if I stuck with it.

The strokes of my paint brush could cover a wall with a new colour, but they could never cover over what was so plainly written on the surface of my heart. Nothing could. I resolved that not only was I called to the ministry, but being in ministry was the only place where I could be at my best, as a human being, and be thoroughly happy. Two years after walking away from Grace Church, wounded and wondering whether we could ever do it again, Elaine and I settled into a peaceful place of wholeheartedly trusting in God's call for us to minister as a pastoral couple. The fact that I was even entertaining another ministry position was a good sign. It spelled the end of my spiritual exile, during which I had come close to burying myself in self-pity, thrusting me into the nether regions of indifference towards the church.

All I knew was that the resume I posted to Faith Church felt a bit like a peace offering to God, for His having stoked the fires of my hunger to be in ministry again. Peace offering or not, Faith Church received it with favour just the same, even though I'd gotten it in just under the imposed deadline. A well-established businessman in a high-ranking company once told me that there is oftentimes something peculiar to beware about the last-minute resume, which he claimed can turn out to be "the squeakiest wheel that lands the oil." Life, in general, can reflect that reality. You could have a room full of people lined up to audition for something, yet it's sometimes the one who makes the late entrance who causes heads to turn. Life is full of eleventh-hour revelations—some good, and others not so good. Then there are those revelations that are so hard to believe that they don't even seem real.

While I was sunbathing on the beaches of South Carolina, some two thousand kilometres away, Faith Church was busily vetting what few resumes they had received. It would come as an unbelievably pleasant surprise to me that my last-minute application to Faith Church ended up rising to the top of their wish list. Being overly eager to cut my teeth in another ministry, my priority was to get to another church as soon as I could.

Some churches that look for pastors accumulate resumes like they're air miles, whereas others are eager to jump on the first candidate who shows an interest; either way, the process of calling a pastor can be exhausting and agonizingly complicated. By the time I entered into a committed, courted process with Faith Church, I discovered that they were in no hurry to make any snap decisions over who they were going to hire. I was advised by a certain denominational representative very early on that if I, as a potential family man, wanted to be in a church by the time the new school year rolled around, I would have to engage in the candidating race by the early spring of that same year, if not even earlier.

It was good advice. I responded to the pastoral vacancy at Faith Church in the early part of 2000. Though we didn't have a family as yet, Elaine and I did have to be out of the house we were renting by that fall. Facing the prospect of having to move not only once, but possibly twice *if* a church came calling at a later time, Faith Church became an attractive option… and this, before I even stepped foot in the church.

CHAPTER 32
Tire Kicking

WHEN ELAINE AND I RETURNED TO TORONTO AFTER OUR VACATION, A PHONE message awaited me on our machine. It was an elder at Faith Church informing me that my resume was under review, and that it was a priority in their considerations. When I returned the call, our conversation concluded with the elder extending an invitation for me to preach at their church. After making some inquiries about the ministry, I proceeded to dissect the elder's opinion on where the church was currently at, both morale-wise and ministry-wise. I figured that I didn't have much to lose by accepting the invitation to preach.

After I hung up the phone, I had a feeling that perhaps Faith was the next ministry God had ordained for me to take on. My period of receiving "letters of regret" from churches who had declined my applications was coming to a close. My last-minute resume, coupled with how other leaders I trusted affirmed my spiritual growth through the trials I'd faced, acted as touch points and positive indicators that God's sovereign hand was about to move, guiding Elaine and I to Faith Church.

I arose early on the morning when I was to make the one-and-a-half-hour highway drive to preach at Faith Church. One of the first observations I made, as Elaine and I entered the church that morning, was how standoffish the people I first met were. They were cordial enough, but reserved; nice, yet seemingly a tad indifferent to our presence. There was an awkward moment when I kind of stood around, for what felt like an eternity, before the elder I'd spoken with on the phone, accompanied by another elder, came walking out of the upper sanctuary with hands extended.

"Ron and Elaine, it's good to see you! Welcome to Faith!" the elder I spoke with on the phone chimed.

That's more like it, I thought. The two middle-aged and conservatively-clad gentlemen were very warm in assuring that it was going to be a great day. I have always thought that the buildings we worship in say something about how we feel about the state of our ministries. Faith's facility was a lot like First Community's; it was very aged and cold-looking on the outside, and equally so on the inside.

The buildings we worship in should get some sort of makeover every now and again, to enhance their draw appeal. Perhaps the best and simplest question to ask would be, "If I was a visitor, would I be attracted to come *to* this place, and spend time *in* this place?" The majority of the worship music that Sunday, not too surprisingly, was sung from a hymnal; even their choruses were remarkably dated. I'd learned before my initial visit to Faith that the church contained the deep-rooted elements of being an "older" ministry, elements which were holdovers from their past. However, I hadn't a clue of just *how* old "older" was! If first impressions matter, then I had some prejudices impressed upon me at Faith. Fresh from my experience in a uniquely contemporary seeker-oriented setting, I imagined myself being an unchurched visitor in the pew that morning instead of a pastor. The internal thoughts I tossed around in my head about the complexion of the congregation and the whole vibe within the sanctuary, was telling: *If I was that unchurched visitor this morning, would I really return?*

There were some obvious red flags flapping as I sat through the service. In hindsight, I wish I would have taken more time to ultimately heed what those red flags meant. These early warning signs—that the ministry at Faith could be incompatible with my own, developing ministry values—should have slowed me down, and perhaps even halted me from moving ahead with the church. However, my overpowering desire to get back into ministry proved too brawny an obstacle. I couldn't put the brakes on the process. I was on the autoban, running through every precautionary red light imaginable. My mentality was, *Clear the track. Here comes the pastor who must get back in ministry.* Every church a pastor engages with, every church he or she could potentially accept a call to, has some subtle "bump on the road ahead" signs. Some of those signs aren't even very subtle. They just say "Stop!"

By the same token, some of the resumes that pastors send to search committees can just as easily announce warnings of potential bumps, and even stop a church from pursuing them as possible candidates. This is what bothered me about Faith's attraction to me. My scrawny pedigree in ministry was in plain sight for them to pick apart. Grace Church's phone number was on my resume for them to do their due diligence. They could readily research my very recent past. I explained to the leaders at Faith Church that my last ministry hadn't gone all that well, and yet they *still* gave me every indication that this wouldn't deter them from considering me.

Elaine's and my time at Faith that first morning went over well enough for them to invite me back to preach again. However, on the car ride home, you'd think that Elaine and I had just been to a heartbreaking funeral. In all honesty, though the people at Faith Church were extremely sincere, we felt let down.

Elaine was particularly unsure about what she had just sat through, and wondered if Faith Church was the right place for us to go. She was justified in feeling that way. We were still steadily (and happily) serving as laypeople in the refreshing new church plant we were part of. The anonymity of just being faces in the crowd was precisely what we needed. Our participation on the church plant's start-up team wasn't merely an opportunity for me to keep using my spiritual gifts; it rendered me a warm body to a potential search committee, enabling me to hit the ground running when another ministry position presented itself. Elaine and I were spiritually reinvigorated, and had gained back a lot of the energy and zeal that had been mercilessly siphoned out of us by the unfortunate events at Grace Church.

As we arrived back home from Faith Church and parked in the driveway, the ensuing silence brought with it a glum reality: we had no problem believing in our doubts. Maybe God wasn't calling us to go there. The ministry appeared to be too old, too tired, and too much work for us to try turning it around. We estimated that the lion's share of work—coming up with ideas, spearheading them, and seeing them through—would most likely fall on us. In the long run, we would be right.

As a young pastor who had not even completed seminary, I was still trying to evaluate my strengths and main areas of giftedness. A big part of that was deciphering how God had wired me as a leader. Nothing about the ministry at Faith Church seemed to be even remotely magnetic, or hold a lot of enticement for us. The fact that I had been asked if I wanted to come back to preach at Faith, immediately after the service that first day, put me on the spot a bit.

It felt just as awkward as the question an excited elder posed to me a short time later: "So! What do you think of the church, Ron?"

I walked around under a cloud of confusion and unsettledness within my spirit for a couple of weeks. The excitement level that consumed me before my initial preaching appointment fell flat. However, I kept a flicker of hope alive within me that Faith Church would work out, even though the last thing I wanted to do was waste any more of the church's time or money. Even as I prayed about the ministry opportunity, I feared that if it wasn't God's will for Elaine and I to go further with Faith, that would usher in a longer waiting period for me, a possibility I would have not only despaired of, but resented, too.

One thing became abundantly clear as we got closer to my second preaching date at Faith Church. Whether or not Elaine and I eventually landed at the church, our first encounter didn't exactly leave us projecting ourselves as a ministry couple there. Despite that hesitation, I couldn't corral myself from going further, even though we both had more than a few reservations.

A friend in the ministry once noted that sometimes God's will is "nothing more than the mirror of our common sense." Over the years, I've come to accept that assumption as being true oftentimes. When it came to the issue of whether or not I should have been moving forward as a pastoral candidate at Faith Church, I was in need of a little common sense!

What kept me interested with Faith Church had less to do with its ministry, than it did with the absence of any other ministry option. Aside from that, the house we were renting was being taken over by its owners, which left us facing the prospect of having to look for other accommodations. A move to another ministry, even if it was to Faith Church, presented a viable and timely way out. It would also provide a good financial solution to our situation—a steady, guaranteed salary! As pragmatic as that plan sounded, even today, it might have been more beneficial for Elaine and me to have moved on to another "tire" to kick.

Candidating...Again!

By the time of my first preaching invitation at Faith Church, I had already sent out numerous resumes to various churches around Ontario. In doing so, I applied only to those regions and areas where I wanted to live. I also made a pact with myself that I wouldn't go to a church that I didn't sense an irresistible pull towards, just for the sake of being *in* a ministry. Well, you know what they say about the best laid plans… The fact of the matter was that the longer I remained without a full-time ministry position, the more attractive *any* ministry began to look to me—even Faith Church. It was as if I awoke one morning feeling so desperate that I made up my mind to lower my standards.

In the realm of politics, people sometimes vote a particular candidate into office not as an actual endorsement of that person or their policies, but rather as a statement against the opponents that person is running against. The opposition I was facing at the time, as a ministry-obsessed neophyte, was God's waiting room, and I was growing all the more desirous to elect any church (even Faith Church) as my way out. I had grown weary of counting the holes in the room's ceiling tiles, as it were. I saw my circumstances reflected in how Abraham failed to heed God's promise of providing him with an offspring (Isaac), by complying with his impulsive wife's suggested detour, to secure the promised child not by steadfastly waiting upon God for it, but by hitting the hay with her maidservant, Hagar (see Genesis 16). There was a twenty-five year gap of time between God's

My Fanatical, Regrettable Tour of Ministry

promise to Abraham and its eventual fulfillment. In comparison, I only had to endure a two-year wait between ministries, but I, too, resorted to scouting out a few shortcuts to get back into ministry.

Though I couldn't claim with integrity that God was, indeed, leading me in the direction of Faith Church, there was something about feeling wanted again that I believed could be interpreted as God's blessing. I figured that with Faith keeping their door open for me, even with the level of hesitancy we had about the ministry, it was worth my while to take another shot at going there to preach. I aimed at getting an ear-to-the-ground synopsis of their past, as a ministry, by asking some pointed questions over lunch with some of the more prominent couples of the church. During the course of the conversation, in which Elaine and I sat with eight other people from Faith, I was adamantly told by one leader that there were no power-broker people at the church. The crazy thing was that I actually believed him. In perfect hindsight, however, such a comment should have caused me to ask if there were any sinners at Faith, even if such a response would have made me sound somewhat cynical.

The topic of politics arose as I opened up a tad about some of my trying experiences at Grace Church; I figured they needed to know, upfront, where I was coming from in terms of not wanting to feel so vulnerable again as a leader in ministry. On a positive note, every church member that afternoon was complimentary, if not gushing, over Elaine and me, and their desire to have us come there. After finishing lunch, we parted ways and walked back to our car. Elaine and I were that much more convinced that we might have been selling the ministry at Faith a bit short. Perhaps we were underestimating God's ability to change our hearts. God is certainly not limited or subject to the odds of any situation; He is able to change the hardest of hearts. Still, trying to be in tune with what the Spirit of God is saying to us in any given circumstance can sound more like a drone of a thousand voices than the still, small voice it ought to.

Thankfully, the Bible guarantees us that God will not keep our lives out of proper order, for He is *"not a God of disorder"* (1 Corinthians 14:33). I may have interpreted the lack of an overall response to my resume as a need to not let the opportunity that Faith Church presented get away. In reality, however, God may have been nudging me to escape the advances of Faith Church while the window of my doubts were open wide enough. Nothing leads a Christian down compromising paths in life like a lack of trust and faith in God, who is more than capable of providing the ideal path. If we choose to suppress the voice of God, take matters into our own hands, and try to control a situation that wearies us, we are at the mercy of our own fears and finite wisdom. This can be true of the churches and ministries that pastors agree to take on.

Sometimes we miss out on sale prices because we were willing to buy a certain item while we knew it was available. In the same way, sometimes we, as pastors, settle for ministries when perhaps God would have been fine with our passing on them. It's not that some churches are less worthy than other churches of being taken on, it's just that the existing structures within some churches are so dysfunctional that they set up the prospective pastor for a no-win situation, and possibly even a painful ministry. I have learned that one the hard way! If I had grasped that ministry dynamic more keenly ten years ago, I probably would have walked away from Faith Church the very first day I preached there. However, the lessons we learn in the overall arena of life are ultimately those which God allows and accounts for in His sovereign purpose to mature us as His people.

If the sovereignty of God is depended upon to guide both search committees *and* pastors in the process of issuing ministry invitations, perhaps it is reasonable for both parties to correctly hear God the majority of the time. At other times, it is plausible for one party to hear Him more clearly than the other (when either the pastor or church says no). God did not lead me, with hands tied behind my back, to accept the invitation of Faith Church. Whether or not God's guidance was clear to me at the time, the loudest voice, the one that seemed to win over my will, was that of my impatience. As a result, the process I was in with Faith Church went forward. I would preach there a third time before finally engaging in more serious discussions about the position. While sitting before a roomful of people from the church (a good portion of whom I had not yet seen), I was given an opportunity to break the ice with those who had not had much exposure to me.

These curious people, who had stood passively on the sidelines during my previous visits to Faith, were interested in stepping into the church's search process at full throttle. They proceeded for forty-five minutes, taking their best shots at their would-be pastor, firing question after question with the flare of a media scrum. For a church that had initially come across as reserved and shy, even disinterested in my candidacy, they became decidedly vocal. Their questions were as odd and unfair as they were interesting and revelatory.

"How long are you going to be here, if you become our pastor?" one lady asked.

My mouth helplessly dropped open at that comment. Silently, I'm sure I was thinking, *What a dumb question!* I replied, with a bit of a chortle, "I wish I could tell you, but I would hope I'll be around for a good while."

My Fanatical, Regrettable Tour of Ministry

Other questions stood out to me—some of them for their subliminal undertones. "What do you think of the purpose-driven movement?" asked a young person. "How do you plan to serve outside of your regular pastoral duties?" wondered the wife of a prominent leader. Then there was the predictable inquiry, intended for my wife: "What area of ministry, Elaine, do you plan to serve in?"

Though many of the inquiries were good, and necessary, I was more interested in hearing what they thought about the drastic drop in their church's attendance over the years. However, the answers that came back fell short of the real reasons I thought were responsible for their thinning numbers. Their answer—"People just don't want to go to church today"—though that may sometimes be the case, cannot be true of *all* people all of the time.

A wise person once said that in order to arrive at the right answers in life, one must first ask the right questions. I thought that this attitude applied to Faith Church's decline. They needed to ask hard questions about their ministry, such as, "Are we too beautiful here, for the down and out? How are we showing this community that we care for them? How many people in the church forge intentional relationships with the spiritually lost? Are people walking into a time warp when they come into our church? Do we speak in a heavenly language too lofty for their earthly ears to relate to?" And perhaps the biggest question of all: "Is evangelism a priority in our budget expenses?" There's always a reason for a church's lack of growth, and though it may be indicative of the times and culture we live in, sometimes the reason lies in the times and culture of the church.

The trajectory of growth (or lack of it) at Faith Church had taken a gradual but unabated and disconcerting nosedive. Thirty years previous, the same church boasted a swollen Sunday morning attendance and an active and respected presence within the blue collar community it was a cornerstone of. By the time I got there, Faith had become an enormous reclamation project. The people associated with the ministry had disappeared faster than snow in an oven! Not all of them flew the coop, however; a good number of them had "flown north"! The previous pastor had done a record number of funerals, yet I would have broken that record—had I stuck around longer than I did. The unfortunate reality was that those numbers were not being replaced. The glory of the good ol' days had long passed them by.

Sadly, Faith's ministry was not unique in that way. They were in the good company of many once-flourishing, God-glorifying ministries that end up possessing the echo of emptiness, which comes from having more pew space than bodies to fill them.

Ron Mahler

As the meeting neared its end, I was asked to share where I thought Faith Church was at. Questions of that nature can become a booby trap for any unsuspecting ministerial candidate. They can close in on them, seemingly providing no easy way out. A pastor's response to such inquiries can be deemed the deciding comment, the one that either sways or dissuades a church member's final vote.

Like any other area in life, honesty is always the best policy in the interviewing process, even if a little bluntness is in order. The cold, hard truth of the ministry situation at Faith Church was that things didn't look too encouraging. After observing the dynamics of the church's leadership, and hearing the hearts of many of its people, it was obvious to me that a large gap existed between where they were and where they wanted to be. Given the church's rapidly declining attendance, a lack of core, ministry-minded young people, and their longing to reach young families in the neighbourhood, my charge to them was quite serious and pointed. "You need to get young, fast," I advised. My diagnostic response seemed to be well-received, despite the fact that the room was predominantly filled with people of an advanced age. Though my "two cents" was far from profound, it was plainly obvious and duly accurate. If nothing else, the senior crowd was still smiling at me after I told them that I thought the age of the average church member had to *lower*.

Elaine and I left that meeting for yet another long, contemplative drive home. We mutually decided that though there was a huge challenge ahead, the people gave every impression that they were up for it. However, though we felt needed, we were not quite ready to pull up our stakes and pitch our tent there.

CHAPTER 34
Saddled Up

I HAVE NEVER BEEN A FAN OF CANDIDACY MEETINGS WITH SEARCH COMMITTEES. Something about them just feels so pretentious, where both pastor and church can feel a bit wary of letting their guards down. They want to be themselves, but they're not quite sure the other will really like that "self." When I was before the elders of Faith Church, I wrestled with the temptation to be someone I wasn't. This was due to my own insecurities, my feeling that I was getting in over my head. The alternative was to come across as decisive and unflappable. A few weeks after I preached at Faith for the third time, and after two substantial meetings with the people, another meeting took place between Elaine and me and the elders.

We were moving ever closer to a possible vote on my candidacy, and the leadership of the church thought it best for us to meet one last time. At the advice of a trusted friend in the ministry, Elaine planned to ask the elders how they would handle conflict that was directed at the pastor, as well as how they would protect me. This was a personal issue for Elaine, as the debacle at Grace Church was still a recent and at times sensitive memory. Incredibly, that question would eventually be used against her, when our relationship with the leaders of the church became strained. I could discern from the elders' scrambling to decisively answer the question that it had taken them by surprise. Then one of them spoke up and promised what sounded like a sincere assurance: "We stand by our pastors one hundred percent."

Ron Mahler

All things being equal, Elaine and I wouldn't forget that response. We would later hold the leadership of the church accountable. By no means was that elder's answer an iron hand in a velvet glove, as the saying goes. None of us in the room that day could have possibly foreseen the unfortunate events that would come to mark our ministry at Faith Church. Before the meeting concluded, one of the elders (who along with his wife happened to be close friends with a couple from Grace Church) confessed that he had done some checking up on me. The elder was informed by the couple at Grace that Elaine and I had left an "indelible impression" on them.

It may have been a satisfactory endorsement for the main leadership, but it was up to the people of Faith Church to make it a marriage between us and them. I was told that a vote would take place the following Sunday. Surprisingly, I didn't find myself hanging off every ring of the phone that Sunday afternoon.

The call inevitably came in, from the chairman of the elders' board. "Ron, we'd like to invite you and Elaine to come to Faith," he said. "You've received a one hundred percent vote!"

Despite being thankful for the outcome, I remained somewhat conflicted about the church itself, and felt marginally uneasy. However, in the hours that followed, and into the next morning, whatever misgivings I was toting around faded into the background of what suddenly felt like promising days ahead. The reality that *I* was the pastor of my own church was growing on me!

One of the factors that played a substantial role in our decision to take on the ministry at Faith was the advice we got from other pastors and leaders within our sphere of influence. "It might be a good place to get your feet wet," said one person. "Just go and preach your head off, and see what happens."

Just prior to moving into the smallish townhouse we purchased in our new, adopted ministry turf, some friends of ours got together to give us a bit of a send-off. The evening turned out to be more joyous than I had anticipated. When we'd returned from Grace Church, Elaine and I had sworn that it would take a lot for us to ever again leave the kind of family and close friends that we were accustomed to having around us.

And yet, once again, there they were, unselfishly cheering us on and seeing us off in grand style. The event included food, laughs, and even some unforgettable moments. Among them, a friend read Jesus' words to Peter, in how Satan desired to sift him as wheat. He punctuated the next part of the passage in which Peter, after overcoming a time of sinister testing that could have left him spiritually laid waste, strengthened the other followers by his own obedience to the Lord

My Fanatical, Regrettable Tour of Ministry

(see Luke 22:31–32). Our friend then turned to Elaine and me and applied the passage to our experience at Grace Church. With the wisdom we gleaned from that ordeal under our ministry belt, we could go to Faith and build up the believers, growing the church. The mini-sermon was appropriately affirming. While it moistened my eyes, it produced in me a sense of unworthy honour.

The reality of spiritual warfare in the church was one that I hadn't come into much contact with before. Ironically, even though our friend's words spoke of the past tense, of the struggles we'd faced at Grace Church, their words would come to apply, as if prophetically, to our time at Faith Church as well.

The early days at the church were predictably warm and giddy, with the "honeymoon" stage in full flight. Both sides got what they were hoping for. Faith Church got their man, and I got to sit in the pastor's chair once again, enjoying my new role as a re-established servant in the ministry.

One day, not long after I started at the church, one of the elders poked his head in my office and said that he wanted to get out some glue for my chair. I got his drift; it wasn't that the chair needed repair, but that the elder didn't want me going anywhere anytime soon. Like all of us, he was enjoying the love-in and feel-good atmosphere that encamps the services and meetings of newly-called pastors.

One of my first orders of business when I took on the position at Faith Church was to make contact with the homes and families in the surrounding neighbourhood. I wanted them to know *who* I was, and that I was going to make it my business to get to know *them*. To accomplish that, I fashioned a letter, with its top line reading (in a bold, block font): "I DON'T WANT YOUR MONEY!" It was important for me to let the community know that there was a new minister at Faith Church, and that it was equally important to me that I hear their thoughts about the ministry. It was a priority for me to get out of the starting blocks on good, community-friendly footing. That was as big an imperative as getting off on a positive note with the church itself. How you start in ministry is just as vital, for impact value, as how you finish.

My trek around the neighbourhood was met with some polite indifference, as well as with some scepticism. Some even exhibited a mild curiosity towards the church. Although I can't say for certain if any of the people I spoke with gave me the time of day, I hoped they wouldn't soon forget the gesture.

These new beginning seasons in pastoral ministry are amongst the most desirable and enjoyable. Like brand new shirts, new pastors have a distinct, unblemished freshness about them. New ministries possess novelty and promise during the honeymoon period. Those whom the new pastor on the block gets to know during that time, both in the church and in the neighbourhood, usually make them feel accepted and needed; dare I say, they even give the pastor the impression that they could be their B.F.F.!

The new pastor is equally eager to gain the respect and confidence of those whom God has placed in their pen, as sheep they need to shepherd. One of the best ways a pastor can do that is by putting down a good foundation for their ministry in terms of solid, biblical teaching and preaching. Though it may not be as important for some believers at the end of a pastor's tenure, an effective teaching ministry from the start will get people's attention and attune them to the spiritual depth of their leader.

Having left my previous ministry on such a sour note, it was vitally important for me to get off on a good start at Faith Church. Fortunately, I did. The couple of years I spent away from full-time, vocational ministry afforded me the freedom to be able to preach in various churches and ministry settings. It wasn't until a few years after that I came to appreciate just how spiritually profitable that particular time period was.

During those two years, I honed my pulpit skills as obsessively as possible. I studied various preachers, sermon structures, and even dabbled in different delivery modes and styles. There were occasions when I bombed in my experimentations, while there were other days when I was able to pull it off. I was like a sponge soaking in as much as I could about the discipline of homiletics, while making great strides in the preaching craft. My progress in those areas matched my ever-growing passion to impart God's Word. One of my seminary instructors told me that I could tell if I had been bitten by the preaching bug. "It doesn't hurt *when* it bites you," he said. "It only hurts when you're *not* preaching." Some of those who had heard me preach could tell that the preaching bug had chomped down on me pretty good.

One Sunday morning, at a church where I was asked to fill the pulpit, someone remarked to me that they thought I came alive when the time came for me to preach. It was the first time anyone ever complimented me like that. Not knowing how to take it, I blushed, responding, "At least I wasn't comatose, eh?"

Preaching was also the one facet of my ministry that was the first to be noticed, and applauded, at Faith Church. All the hard work I'd put into becoming a more effective communicator was paying off, and better still, I had gotten off to the good start I was looking for. Whether it really had anything to do with my preaching or not, for the first few months at Faith our service attendance increased. It felt good to be using my gifts of teaching and preaching every week. People were appreciative of Elaine and me, and I could have bet all the money I had (which wasn't much), that we would be at Faith Church not only for a good time, but a long time.

CHAPTER 35
Test Drive

THERE'S A SAYING IN LIFE TO REMIND US THAT WE CAN'T ALWAYS ACCEPT THINGS AT face value: sometimes things just aren't what they appear to be. When I bought my first new car about twenty years ago, the advertisement listed the small sedan at $9,999, which was a highly affordable price for a single guy with a fair-paying full-time job. What made the price even more buyer-friendly was the fact that I had saved a good chunk of money for the down-payment. As it worked out, what I thought was a sizeable down-payment turned out to be a mole-hill compared to the mounting price of the vehicle after the taxes and some "extras" were factored in. Indeed, though the initial price sounded good, I drove out of the dealer's parking lot not *feeling* too good! I was lighter in the pocketbook, and for my consumer efforts I would get a monthly reminder of just how much *things aren't always what they appear to be.*

How many times in life have we been standing at the bottom of promising rainbows, only to uncover a pot of something other than gold? For a while, I thought I had it made at Faith Church. On my first year anniversary at the church, I took some solace in that my tenure there (though still a short one) was arguably a great milestone compared to where I had been at the same time in my ministry at Grace Church (out of a job). I was Mr. Popular, and the church was enjoying a good bounce as a result of having had a full-time pastor for a year. There was a general feeling that the ministry was going somewhere.

Cue the saying at the beginning of this chapter: "Sometimes things just aren't what they appear to be." Though all may have been quiet on the Faith Church front (there were no upsets, no flare-ups), that didn't necessarily mean things were really "going somewhere," either.

The trend of optimism within the church, and the ethereal atmosphere of the services, couldn't—and wouldn't—last. My *modus operandi* was to be cautious, even to a fault, in how much new stuff I introduced, whether it had to do with music, drama, video, or different Bible versions being read. Most of the people at Faith Church had become all too comfortable with the same old, same old, and after the shine of having a new face upfront began to wear-off the attendance fluctuated, and eventually decreased. People from the community who had come to check things out came once and a while, but then left again. After my first year mark at Faith, I found that just being an appreciated preacher was no longer a satisfying perk for me. There was more to me, and much more that needed to be addressed at the church, that beckoned my inner, budding leader.

It's one thing to sit in a newly purchased car in the parking lot at the dealership, knowing it is ours to go places with; it's another thing entirely to press the gas pedal, get it in gear, and drive onto the road. As a leader, it's one thing to test-drive a ministry during the candidate process; it's another thing to get it to perform well, to get it to move in the right direction! Churches can be like snails, in that they hide inside a protective covering. They're in no particular hurry to get anywhere; at least, that's how I came to view the overall mindset at Faith Church. When I began to drop a few subtle hints to the elders' board that I was praying about certain initiatives that might mobilize the ministry a bit more, the leaders' hackles went up. It was then that the *real* Faith Church began to stand up and be counted.

Some pastors bulldoze into their ministries by introducing too much scary change too early, and at too rapid a pace, for older, more established churches to digest and accept. However, even if I made that mistake at Faith Church, I know of churches that are completely closed to change, regardless of its pace. Although that didn't appear to be true of Faith Church from the outset, it turned out to be the case in the end. A respected friend in the ministry once counselled me that, in his opinion, even if big-name pastors occupied the pulpits of many churches today, their people would still buck at the notion of straying from the more traditional forms of church ministry.

Sure, no church wants their pastor to commandeer the ideas they have for the ministry in a manner that oppresses the Body of Christ, yet neither does any pastor want to be relegated to the status of some clerical automaton who just follows orders and does as he's told. There has to be a balance in terms of allowing a leader to lead, and giving God's people the inspiration, not to mention the time, they need to follow their leader. As the saying goes, "If no one is following a leader, that leader is not really leading." However, just as it is possible for even well-intentioned pastors to overrule their people, it is possible for churches to selfishly snuff-out any spark of vision or initiative within their pastor that doesn't dance to the beat of their own will for the church. How many times have pastors heard from an obstinate board member, "That's the way things have always been done here, and that's the way they'll remain, even after you're gone."

One doesn't have to be a big-name pastor, of course, to come across those kinds of shutdown statements; many no-name pastors hear their fair share of them. Regrettably, on more than a few occasions, so have I. The first church where I experienced this was at Faith Church, at the hands of a senior leader. When the divisive dust of mismanaged change settles in the church, the fallout is often tragic. The Body of Christ can easily be ripped up, causing God's witness to grievously suffer. The pastor is often forced to sift through the post-mortem of ministry guilt resulting from their good intentions either being misinterpreted or incorrectly perceived as power-driven. Casting an enduring vision to fulfill the Great Commission takes impeccable timing in the lifecycle of a church, not to mention enough people who have bought into the vision to see it through.

However, one cannot underestimate the foundation of Solomon-like wisdom, Nehemiah-like prayer, and Paul-like discernment that is required from a church's leaders. I also believe it takes some pastoral fortitude to lead a church in vision-casting, especially if the pastor senses there is enough of a vocal minority *opposed* to it to cause ripple effects. I came upon a rather humorous bumper sticker one time that read, "If you want to be wise when you're old, you first have to be young and stupid." On the surface, the saying does seem to reflect a profound truth about life; it even applies to one's leadership abilities. Young, inexperienced leaders in the church are going to make mistakes; if nothing else, they'll make those mistakes out of an overzealous desire to make a difference for the Kingdom of God. The *severity* of those mistakes will not only dictate their consequences, but also how wise they may become as a result.

I've had a lot of time to deconstruct the anatomies of my mistakes at Faith, and I'm willing to concede that I may have been a bit too *young* in my ministry life to paddle my way through the topsy-turvy tides of church politics, and too *stupid* perhaps to quit trying so hard! It was always my heart's intention to make a godly and positive impact at Faith Church. Sadly, though, I was either unable

My Fanatical, Regrettable Tour of Ministry

to clearly communicate that ideal to the people, or it was lost in the persistent whirlwind of conflict that came to characterize my turbulent second, *and last,* year there.

No church I have ever been associated with, whether as the leading pastor or not, did *not* want to grow numerically. In my experience, it is *how* the growth comes, and at what *cost,* that either sways a church to embrace it or reject it. The acceptance of change in any given church involves a few factors. How much is the Body of Christ asked to flex? Who represents that new growth? Will the church still be recognizable to the long-standing faithful during and after the process of change?

Perhaps I was near-sighted in my leadership by thinking the main need at Faith Church was a quick turnaround in their fortunes, attendance wise. For certain, the changes I was hoping to see were not merely for the sake of change or appearances. I wasn't solely concerned about how things looked to the casual visitor; I was burdened about the results of the changes in the church's ministry. As the preeminent leader, I felt responsible to grow the church by being an agent of change. I resolved that a growing church would speak volumes of my leadership and presence in the pulpit, a perspective that was not nearly as ego-driven as it was pride-driven. What I overlooked was that I had inherited a group of God's people who were insecure and in much more need of being accepted than being issued spiritual pep talks. When I went to Faith Church, a desire to be stretched wasn't even on their radar. I thought they were looking for something to get them excited about church life again, and for an injection of something to jumpstart their lacklustre ministry.

A pastor's leadership and the mission of his or her church are inseparably intertwined; for what use is there in having a leader if that leader fails to lead God's people by the very biblical priorities that have rendered them a people of God to begin with? What resulted was an all-out campaign on my part to see to it that Faith not only had better services and programs to offer its community, but a newly-drafted philosophy to match it.

By the latter half of my first year, I had already begun the charge towards revamping the church's tired, stuck-in-a-rut layout of ministry. I implemented (with moderate enthusiasm amongst the people) various forms of creative evangelism. Even more daring was my intent to introduce contemporary, upbeat worship music in the services, an initiative that yielded only marginal acceptance and maximum headaches! An insightful pastor I often had coffee with in those days shrewdly noted, "Ron, we have as many bosses in the church as we have people!" The longer I ministered at Faith, the more spot-on that pastor's comments seemed to be, for there were as many priorities and opinions concerning my responsibilities as the pastor as there were people in the church.

In order for a ministry to be substantial and viable, not to mention for it to hold any promise for potential growth, it cannot be a one-person show. If a church is to be truly united in a common, corporate vision, it needs what I call *buyers* and *sellers* (those who come to believe in the direction a church is taking, and those who are willing to encourage others in it). Getting to that point is a huge spiritual workout. When everyone has their own idea of what the church should be, chaos ensues. A pastor's spiritual gifts and missional heart can only take the Body of Christ so far; the people have to want to take it the rest of the way. I wasn't confident this would happen at Faith Church. I had spent the better part of my first year trying to accomplish all the right things: I had preached hard, prayed for direction, and tried to get to know the people.

I was convinced that some wholesale changes were in drastic order, and that I was just the man to do the changing! Three hundred and sixty-five days of letting Faith run itself were enough for me. Day number three hundred and sixty-six would have been too painful! At the very least, I felt I had to test the resolve and sincerity of the church's leadership, in order to know where I stood with them. Would they back up their words that they wanted to move forward and reach the community? Would they shrink back from that line in order to dig their heels in, proving it was nothing more than a platitude? Would the leadership hunker down in the abyss of the status quo?

Most importantly, I was looking for them to surprise me by rallying the troops at Faith Church in choosing commission over comforts. One thing was for sure: I was looking for a quick fix, not a marathon of maybes or uncertainty. I had to know if the people were truly with me before I could take the ministry ahead.

CHAPTER 36

Inventory

AT THE ONSET OF MY SECOND YEAR AT FAITH, I NEEDED TO CHECK A BOX ON MY to-do list. I had to elevate the value and visibility of the few young people the church had left. I often wondered why they still hung around Faith Church when there was so little there for them. Whatever their reasons for sticking around, I was thankful that they did. I saw them as the future of the church, a future that had finally arrived when I took the job. There were two couples and just a handful of other college-and-career-aged kids. Not only did they need to be heard, they needed more involvement in the ministry. I wasn't content with the young adults just being seen at the services, and neither were they. Little did I realize just how ready and willing they were to become a greater presence in the church's ministry, if only they could be encouraged to.

After listening to them pour out their hearts about the ministry at length, I immediately knew we needed to use them, or the church was quite literally going to *lose* them. And use them, I did! From reading scripture to doing drama, to getting involved in bringing the church bulletin up into the twenty-first century, I utilized them. I managed to talk the elders into turning what always felt like an obligatory (and poorly attended, I should add) Sunday evening service into something different. Then I was able to convince a couple of very shy and inward twenty-somethings to join me on the platform in a choreographed dance to the Gaither Vocal Band's "Satisfied." Leading up to the night, we practiced our moves and lip-synching the words of the song. Though our rehearsals felt silly, as did the whole idea of what we were preparing to do, it did manage to build a bond between Elaine and me and the young adults.

On the Sunday evening we performed the act, it was a hit! In fact, some of the elderly busted a gut so badly that I thought I might be responsible for putting them in the hospital—or worse, in the grave! Even the elders couldn't maintain their composure, casting aside their usual rigor-mortis-like exteriors. They soared in approval, becoming giddy men. I'm sure the main leaders couldn't believe what they were seeing as some of the young people who were usually hidden away in the back pews came out of their veritable cocoons to take centre stage. I went home that evening feeling justified in that I had broken some ground by giving the church a taste of what cultural relevance was like. As the weeks went by, almost every other service contained some new element of surprise. I rationalized that if God is a God of creativity, a God who puts a new song in our mouths, and a God who calls us to observe Him doing something new in our midst, then we at Faith Church needed to be open to anything new He wanted to do in the Sunday services. After all, the services belonged to Him, and were for Him.

We are the ones who limit His movement and Spirit, by the fortress-like traditions we erect to keep us feeling safe in our Sunday pews. The God I know and worship will not, and cannot, be restricted to any liturgy; if we try to harness God, we miss out on all that He has in store for us. In essence, what makes a church old is not the age of its people as much as it is the extent to which we discard the new things that God may be doing.

That was my mindset at Faith Church. Regardless of whether or not the people were prepared for some new things, I was more than prepared to bring them out. Consequently, out came the mimed and dramatic skits. Out came the guest singers, as well as the actors and the video clips. In fact, out went snippets of the old in the services (fewer responsive readings, fewer announcements, less formality), and in flew the new and improved.

We painted the foyer and upper interior of the church, and even refinished an antiquated banner that had greeted the people who entered the front doors for years. These changes reflected the new order of the day. Besides having some appropriate scripture put on the banner, with calligraphy, we painted the expression: "Loving God, Loving People."

That wasn't the extent of the changes. Even the hymnal, which had become a bastion of the church's traditional worship experience, was relegated to "now and again" status, in favour of flashes of "praise" music. On top of this, the worship team was fortified with additional people to accommodate the fuller sound I was after. Anyone and everyone who could sing in tune or play a few chords could join in and take ownership.

That said, it was never my intention to outlaw the singing of hymns! Rather, my intention was to have the elders of the church realize that there were three different functions throughout the week (one being the Sunday morning preservice) at which the elderly could enjoy the exclusive singing of hymns. But the time had come to break that pattern in the weekly worship service. My argument was that not everyone found older hymns to be a meaningful worship experience. I assumed that the elders and I concurred that if we were to get younger at a quicker rate, we needed to showcase a new and intentional philosophy in our services, one that embraced generational and cultural divides and sensitivities.

For me, rightly or wrongly, it was more about reaching our target audience (young families in the community) than about pleasing the people who were already in the church and knew Jesus. In other words, if the demographic from which we desired to grow were young families, and if those families who had visited the church were deciding not to come back (partially due to the music), that was enough reason to address the type of music we played on Sunday mornings. If the worship service is a vehicle God can use to draw people to His Son, I don't think it would be heretical to say, "Whatever it takes, within biblical boundaries, so be it!" Sure, I could have been like some people at Faith Church who had chosen to pay no mind to those "one and out" attendees who came to the service only to leave and never come back. I could have shrugged my shoulders in self-righteous indifference and resolved that if someone didn't like the church, tough noogies for them. We cannot know with absolute certainty why every person fails to return to our church after having visited just once. However, churches sometimes need to be more concerned about why they can't retain certain age groups.

If I accomplished anything of substantial value at Faith, I would like to think that it was how I disturbed the complacency of the people enough to get them to view their church more objectively. I shared with them how people they came into contact with every day, as a part of an impersonal world, were seeking authentic community. I taught that the church had to stepup and *be* that community. I shared with them that people (Christians or otherwise) who visit are asking, "Do I belong here?" and "Do people here care about me?" I wanted the people at Faith Church to see that some of their traditions could no longer pass the test of the changing times. To be blunt, they weren't working to draw the lost, and drawing the lost was not only Jesus' business, but the church's business. Even if we as believers are supposed to be out of sync with the times spiritually, we have to keep in sync culturally in order to remain relevant to the world. I was willing to go to the wall with any leader on that issue.

This came with a heavy price.

In the late summer of 2001, just over a year into my ministry at Faith, Elaine gave birth to our first child, Cassidy. It seemed like the best of times in our lives. The thrill of becoming parents was untempered by trouble brewing in the church. The early days of Cassidy's arrival— and all this entailed, including late-night feedings and the diaper changes—distracted me from the burdens of ministry that were popping up at Faith. I didn't find myself worrying as much about the subtle opposition I was experiencing over the direction of the ministry. I thought being a new parent might actually help my cause at the church, if they saw me as a harmless family man with a baby carriage. It didn't. My time of parental reprieve soon came to a crashing halt, and gave way to the worst times in our lives.

Around that point, after some prayer and hearing the leaders share, I discussed with the elders how I felt we needed to form some kind of vision for the next few years. I explained that it would mean having to meet periodically to revisit, assess, and possibly dismantle any of the church's ministries which were no longer serving a productive purpose but which required much time and manpower. These initiatives only served to clog up other opportunities for ministry and outreach. It was my opinion (and not necessarily that of a lot of others) that at least two ministries needed to be put out to pasture; clearly, they were not yielding any fruit. In the book *Seven Practices of Effective Ministry*, the authors touch on this exact subject: "When individuals tie their identity to a program they've created, they lose the objectivity that is necessary to evaluate its effectiveness…Failing to eliminate programs that need to be purged can stunt a church's growth and tie up important resources."[6] The powers that be seemed too sentimental about some of their long-standing ministries to be able to judge their spiritual usefulness and vitality.

After the elders and myself spent some time dissecting the various elements of Faith's ministry, the fact surfaced that we were heavy on "Bible" and heavy on "fellowship"… but there was precious little else to support a well-rounded and balanced ministry. That was when I pulled out a piece of paper and marked out what are generally perceived to be the five main components of a New Testament church. In large letters, I wrote down the words: *outreach, spiritual formation, community, worship* and *leadership*, with lines separating each word. After giving a brief definition of each, all the leaders agreed that the church was lacking in a few of these categories. It was never my intention as the pastor, nor was it the will of the other leaders, to do an out-and-out restart of the ministry or take away those programs or functions that were meaningful to the older crowd.

At one board meeting, I could hardly suppress my excitement about the initiative we were taking to explore how we could become a healthier church. The others around the table, to a lesser intensity, just seemed willing; one elder, who was conspicuously quiet during the discussion, said nothing. I was hesitant to pick his brain, for fear of what he might have been hiding. Judging by his countenance, I thought he would be the quintessential fly in the ointment, a leader who seemed to enjoy holding his political cards close to his chest. Unfortunately, in time, I would be proven right about my hunch. This particular leader often held to a more conservative slant on all things spiritual. As he kept his head down, I kept from pressing him any further. I assumed that with the endorsement of the two other elders, I had the necessary confidence and blessing to keep moving ahead with the reconstruction of the ministry.

If there is a leadership lesson to be had in this, it's that one should never interpret silence as a "yes," under any circumstance. There is no substitute for hearing the verbal affirmative from a fellow leader. Pastors must press their fellow leaders for comments and not let any leader get away with ambivalence on such an important issue as a church's vision. A verbal "no" from a fellow leader, even if it is not the desired response, is always better than a disguised rejection. After all, it's the quiet ones you've got to watch out for!

CHAPTER 37
Bull's-eye

I ABSOLUTELY ABHOR PLAYING DARTS. PERHAPS I FIRST DISCOVERED THIS AFTER receiving a dart game one Christmas when I was thirteen. I placed it on the closet door in my bedroom and, standing four feet away, flung the darts as close as I could get them to the bull's-eye. I was such a poor aim that I ended up freckling the closet doors with holes which far outnumbered the holes I made in the dart board itself. Although my game has not improved much since, I've yet to hit anyone standing close to a dart board; however, if I were them, I wouldn't press my luck. Give me a dart, and I'm bound to stab something I shouldn't. As God's people, we are not beneath acting like reckless missiles flying at their intended targets in the form of our discontentment.

Have you ever noticed how we're always complaining about something, or someone, in the church? It's far too easy to do, and too prevalent a reality today. We can get upset over the child who made too much noise in the service, the person who looked at us the wrong way, or the worship leader who repeated a verse one too many times. We can feel put out over the weak after-service coffee or by the sermon (even if it was good) that was way too long. We get a bee in our bonnet, so we take out our dart of discontentment and let it rip. It's too easy sometimes for us to hit-and-run with our complaints and criticisms, stabbing people for the sole reason that we *can*. Oftentimes, those easy targets are our leaders. Pastors and leaders of any organization are going to have complaints come against them. Justified or not, every leader has a target invisibly endowed on their back. The reality is that some of the people we lead will be tempted to take aim and fire at our turned backs.

By the midway point through my second year at Faith Church, I'd become more acclimated to that kind of leadership heat. Even though I was used to periodic criticism and complaints, it stung all the same whenever a new one landed on me. A good amount of the criticism that reaches a pastor's ear is unfair and totally unfounded. However, sharp complaints not only prick the hearts of pastors, but their spouses as well. Elaine, and other ministerial spouses like her, could tell you firsthand just how real the pain of ministry criticism can be.

Elders, deacons, and pastors need to be able to decipher and separate what constitutes a real concern from what doesn't. Some concerns within the Body of Christ which have the potential to blow up can be diffused on the spot, if they are dealt with graciously and succinctly, before they have the opportunity to spread and latch onto other people who may then take offense. Complaints and criticisms from God's people are sometimes byproducts of their sinful nature.

Much discernment is required of a leader when they are asked by a church member to be the messenger of their discontentedness. During an elders' meeting at Faith, a complaint was raised by none other than the silent elder. Apparently, this leader could no longer remain silent.

"People are saying that you preach too long, and that there are not enough hymns anymore," he said.

In response, I readily conceded that those who brought the complaint about the length of my sermons were probably right—most of time.

I assured the elders that the length of my sermons was symptomatic of my overall zeal for preaching, and that I didn't mean to purposely drag out my messages or take advantage of the people's time. I also mentioned that I was still learning how to "K.I.S.S." (Keep It Simple, Stupid), in terms of my sermon content. Saying more by saying less is a challenge for most people—not only preachers!

As far as the other complaint was concerned, I acknowledged that it must have been difficult for some of the older people to get accustomed to newer choruses and praise tunes. I tried to take the complaint in stride, assuring the elders that I would discuss the issue with the worship team, if they felt it was in the church's best interest. The worship ministry of a church is such a personally formative aspect of one's spiritual experience. Consequently, when someone feels they are not able to engage that way, or kept from being edified in their expression of worship, musically, it can trigger the most ungodly of actions and attitudes.

Ron Mahler

My fear was that the worship music complaint would only serve to weaken the worship team's resolve to keep pressing for flexibility amongst the members of the church. One of the elders on the worship team didn't sense an extreme urgency to discuss the issue with the worship team, so he and I agreed to hold back for a bit, a move that would later on prove to be a mistake. The issue was never addressed with the worship team, formally, largely due to the fact that I misinterpreted the absence of any further known comments from the silent elder. I thought the case was closed. I couldn't have misread the situation any worse. The unrest over the music didn't boil over into a greater problem right away, even though the evolution of the worship style may have been tolerated for too long already.

In attempting to deal with the complexities surrounding the style and generational preferences of worship music, it's not good enough to just say, "God doesn't care what we sing, or how we sing it, because it's not about us." Though that may be a theologically sound argument, it's also a convenient sidestep often used to escape having to sort through the contentious issue of worship music. A blanket statement such as, "God doesn't care what we sing…"—though it is biblically accurate—falls short of solving the true issue with worship. Even if God doesn't care what we sing *in principle*, we inevitably need to see what that looks like *in practice*. When it comes to who is doing the singing, to a degree it unfortunately becomes about us. Though the church needs to be sensitive to those people who have more traditional leanings in worship (hymns), it must still be responsive to the present time, and to our culture's ever-increasing value for different genres of music and the arts, so that we may be able to utilize God-honouring, contemporary worship music to make relevant connections with people.

Blended worship services, in my opinion, don't always guarantee musical equality in the eyes of the congregation. Giving everyone what they want is not always the panacea for "worship wars." For instance, if four choruses take precedence over two hymns, the hymn-favoured crowd might rightfully feel a prejudice against them. However, that argument can cut both ways. If the number of hymns or older choruses in a service were to outweigh those of a more contemporary style, those who prefer the newer, upbeat praise songs will feel restless. This is the potential outcome we face when we try to blend music out of a fear of offending different sides. Even equally dividing the number of contemporary and traditional songs in a blended service isn't a sure-fire formula for satisfying everyone's worship needs.

What's the solution, then? Do we separate God's people by age-appropriate brackets so that they can worship before the same throne at different times? Will we do that in Heaven? The Book of Revelation doesn't appear to suggest so. Then again, our perfect eyes will be focussed entirely on Jesus, and not on ourselves, as they currently are. In the church today, we seldom realize that we worship God imperfectly in all aspects. This is certainly observable by all the selfishness contained in our preferences over music. It has been my view that a church should choose a course and complexion for their worship services, and stick to that template. If you need two services in order to accomplish worship unity, do it! If a church can succeed in having two, separate worship services—one being solely traditional, the other contemporary—and have the people resources to see it through, go for it!

However, in small church settings, as was the case with Faith Church, it's hardly practical to have two separate worship services. Whatever model a church utilizes for music ministry, the leadership should be given the task of preventing any hijacking of it, especially if it has proven to be a spiritually effective and relationally cohesive strategy. I've noticed in some of my own travels how a church's worship music has gone from being a thematic primer for the content of the sermon to being a showcase of its target audience, mission statement, and core values. It may not be a recipe to make everyone happy (which isn't possible anyway), but at least you know that those who come to your church, and who stick with you, are there because they identify with your vision. However, it's key that the leadership be unified in how they want the Sunday morning worship service to reflect the vision of their church.

At Faith, hymns hadn't been stricken from some sort of "eligible songs" list for Sunday morning worship. There was no outlawing of hymns whatsoever; it was just that the hymnal was no longer the focal point of Sunday morning worship. This position had been agreed upon by the existing worship team after my arrival, which admittedly I had a hand in influencing. It was also a position that one of the more progressive elders gave his assent to, as a member of the worship team himself.

When I joined the worship team at Faith Church, there were at least two to three hymns tucked into every service. I wasn't the sole person who picked the music every week, as I shared that task with two other people, both of whom were much older than I was and whose musical choices reflected that age gap. In the first few months of being on the team, it felt a bit like I was forcing my will upon them, and that maybe I should have sat back and became one of the pew-worshippers.

Ron Mahler

The fact was, Elaine and I were invited to join Faith's worship team the moment we got there. Not doing so, I figured, could have made us seem like we were holding back our gifts and talents. In hindsight, however, it probably would have been politically prudent for us to have waited for a period of time before hopping up on the platform. Indeed, the worship team appeared more than happy to give Elaine and me the reins. The last thing we wanted was to be perceived as being in takeover mode, yet we had a lot of time and energy on our hands in our pre-children days, not to mention our desire to make an early contribution. To my recollection, there were no ruffled nests in the transition of the music ministry's leadership. Our aim was to compliment what the existing team was already doing, and not to get in the way, bind their hands, or retire their favourite songs.

Unfortunately, the latter was what we would come to be accused of doing, despite the fact that when complaints began to arise over music preferences, Elaine and I believed the worship team was of one mind—that a new, more contemporary approach was needed. Though many of the old standards from hymnody were retained, a few of the worship team members were enthusiastic to learn new music. If I was reading them right, they were discouraged at seeing the trickle of young people and families at worship services. Like me, they attributed some of that to the style of music being sung. At the outset of the new millennium, the Christian worship music scene was changing. It was bursting with new and different artists and forms of worship music that were suddenly deemed to be congregationally friendly. They were making their way from the airwaves of Christian radio stations into the playlists of worship bands.

All the changes I had envisioned resonated with the comments I was hearing from some of the younger church members. Though my part in blazing a new path for the music ministry no doubt put a bull's-eye on my back, I gladly accepted my role (in spite of the complaints that came along with it) as the kind of leader who led by keeping the church's mission foremost in mind. Numerous churches I knew of at that time were experiencing gross divisions over the issue of music—more to the point, over the perilous tightrope of change management. Faith Church wasn't immune to that reality, and was in fact about to be numbered among them.

Devil's Manifesto

While Elaine and I were away for a week's holiday, the worship team held a meeting during which it was felt that all the members of the team (eight people in total) should be able to pick music. It wasn't the first time a group of people at Faith had met to discuss things involving me without my having any knowledge of it, and it certainly wouldn't be the last. On another occasion, someone leaked the news to me that a meeting had been conducted between the elders and some people in the church who were "unhappy" with me. When I confronted one of the elders about it, he informed me that there wasn't anything clandestine behind the furtive meeting; however, he didn't seem to appreciate my displeasure at how suspicious the meeting appeared to me.

I felt warranted in not catering to the agenda I perceived coming from the elders, who clearly didn't feel the need to consult with me, so I didn't answer the questions for me they'd cooked up in their secret meeting. To some degree, it was similar to the move I had witnessed with the elders at Grace Church, who also had kept their pastor in the dark. I didn't do myself any favours on the board level by my decision to clam up. The elders were visibly heated, annoyed that I wouldn't respond to their efforts to give ear to complaints about me.

Two particular members of the worship team requested to have every member (some of which were very young and inconsistent in attendance) have a turn at picking music. It seemed to me this would lead to having "too many cooks in the kitchen." Was having four people involved in picking the songs for Sunday worship not enough? Reading between the lines, however, I discerned that this request was really just a front for their underlying motive to cater to the older, more traditional crowd.

Suddenly, I found myself in a place I never thought I would end up in, with a full-blown controversy over the worship music. The fact that we, as God's children, can fight against one another over the way we sing to Him makes no sense. More often than not, in such situations, the Devil wants in. When the people of God give Satan leverage from which he can propel his motives and intentions into our squabbles, he can divide us using the very music and lyrics we use to praise his archenemy (God). Sadly, when that happens, the Devil wins a moral victory, even as God is worshipped. Satan doesn't care about who might be right or who might be wrong; all he cares about is that God's people fight over their rights.

If Satan can disrupt unity in the church by convincing Christians that their worship needs are more important than those of other Christians, he'll try to work that angle. This is what makes change in older, established churches so very difficult to execute. The Devil is good at brainwashing people into thinking that fooling around with worship music is akin to giving the gates of hell a foothold in their church; therefore, it should be resisted at every turn.

It's ironic that this is, indeed, one way that the enemy *can* get into the church and wreak havoc. It was important to me for the elders, and the church as a whole, to see that a transition from an older, antiquated way of doing ministry at Faith was crucial and could be exciting for the people. However, as the saying goes, it's not always about the law; sometimes it's about politics. Sometimes it's not about embracing the Great Commission, at all costs, that really counts; it's about the comfort of the great *omission*.

Sadly, reaching the lost for Christ can mean very little to some believers if they aren't happy with how their church is going. There's nothing like the landmine that awaits us when a pastor steps on the preferences of how some people want to worship God in song. There's nothing like a congregational brouhaha over worship music.

At yet another elders meeting, one of the leaders straightened up in his chair and, looking at me, communicated that some people wanted things to go back to the way they had been before I arrived. I thought to myself, *Where have I heard that line before? Wasn't it when the Israelites wanted to ditch Moses and go back to Egypt?* Yeah, that would have been a good move on their part! Perhaps the onset of some unsettling changes at Faith, and the prospects of further

My Fanatical, Regrettable Tour of Ministry

amendments to the ministry, had some people thinking that I was leading them to wander in a wilderness of their own.

I was surprised by the elders' revelation that some people in the church not only wanted to digress from further changes but wanted to repeal the changes already in place, especially in the areas of the Sunday morning worship service, and in the employment of two small groups that had replaced my presence at the poorly-attended Sunday evening worship service. To this day, I regret not pressing all the leaders, right then and there, into telling me what *they* wanted.

During this same meeting, the "silent" elder (who wasn't as silent anymore) got into it again, stating that I should make a practice of reading my scripture before I preached and not start into my introduction before doing so. "The people want to know what part of the Bible you're talking about," the same elder continued to chirp. As mild complaints go, I found *that* one to be a bit strange, since every sermon title and accompanying passage was listed in the Sunday morning bulletin for all to see.

Before I had an opportunity to address the comment, oddly enough, another elder came to my rescue. "Well, at some point he does go into the scripture," he said, before concluding, "Besides, the passage is up on the screen." I thought the leader responded adequately, and I essentially reiterated his sentiments. In any case, I took the complaint for what it was, an opinion of one person's preference. Nothing more. That said, the touchy elder's comment was a sign of things to come. What was so disconcerting to me, as time wore on, was how arbitrary and petty some of the concerns and complaints became. They seemed to invade the board meetings with such volume that they sucked the joy out of what I really wanted to discuss: how to progress in finalizing a vision for the church.

I didn't have my head in the sand. I fully understood that forward progress in a church could not come about in the best possible way unless interpersonal relationships, and the root issues related to them, were worked at. Unfortunately, instead of actually solving problems in the church, merely managing them can sometimes be seen as success. The regurgitating of concerns and complaints during the elders meetings were beginning to sound more like children's excuses as to why they couldn't go to school. Whether it was something about a service, about a comment I made, or something that someone said to an elder, it got to the bleak point where the constant badgering more closely resembled a scrum of reporters than a board of elders. If you've ever watched members of the media ask an athlete questions unrelated to their game in order to pick away at some controversial issue in their personal lives, you'll know that the player, after humouring the provocations for a time, usually snaps, cutting them off with such comebacks as, "Who here wants to talk about hockey?" That became my adopted pushback. I would say, "Who wants to talk about evangelism?"

At one point, at my request, a representative came to Faith Church from a Christian organization that specializes in mobilizing churches towards healthy reproduction of leaders and spiritual growth. The seminar was open for all the leaders in the church. It was interesting to see their reactions to some of the statements that the representative made, which more or less affirmed the direction I was encouraging them to take.

I thought that hearing from a passionate expert on the topic—and not just from their own droning pastor—would cause the leaders to see the importance of shaping a vision for the church, for properly structuring its ministry in order for them to advance in its mission. The person leading the seminar was preaching to a choir of one (me). A good number of the other leaders had some difficulty getting in tune.

Before we recessed, I felt compelled to get up and tell the leaders present that I wasn't afraid to lead, but that I needed willing followers. Let's just say that my best rah-rah speech ultimately failed to light an inferno under them. Some of God's people at the church were knee-deep in the revolt while others didn't know what to think. Some of the more immature and emotionally-driven leaders played the power card, or the ridiculous sympathy card, by resigning their ministry positions. Others either stopped tithing or stopped coming to church altogether.

Even now, years later, it's difficult for me to fully accept that the sheep at Faith Church were solely responsible for taking down the vision I was attempting to implement, one headache at a time. There was also an unseen, underestimated party who sought to kick the legs out from under my ministry initiatives: Satan himself. I am thoroughly convinced that my unrelenting zeal to turn the church around afforded Satan the opportunity to not only play on the fears and anger of some of its people, but on my own pride and feelings. My inexperience in managing change in an established church didn't help the overall situation, either. The church had dug its heels in, and I lacked the tangible support I needed, as well as an objective mediator.

It's not that I didn't consult God in prayer or in reading the Word, or that I didn't seek or take the advice of those who had been in similar situations in the past. It wasn't like I neglected to take into consideration comments made by my co-leaders, who had dropped more than a few hints that they were conflicted in

My Fanatical, Regrettable Tour of Ministry

their ability to make objective decisions. It's not like there weren't any indicators showing that the changes weren't yielding fruit and spiritual gain.

In all sincerity, I was sold on the fact that I was persevering well, in terms of my ministry philosophy and leadership style, as well as in my ability to articulate to other leaders the church's ministry priorities and initiatives. I had explained early on, as far back as the interview process, that I intended to assess the ministry strengths and challenge areas of Faith's ministry, to help map out a strategy that would hopefully move them closer to their desired future. It was also my feeling that the changes I had prayed for and hoped would take place at Faith were in the best interests of the community we were trying to reach. They also represented God's best for them, as a church. However, in my excitement (and maybe my ignorance), I wasn't seeing the look on most of the faces in the church, the faces of people who didn't really want to change. I couldn't help but feel that my overzealous wings were being pinned when I really wanted to fly.

What Elaine and I had to endure for the last six months of our time at Faith Church pushed the limits of our understanding about the realities of spiritual warfare. For more than a hundred and eighty days, we would experience a kind of dark ugliness that would rival, if not top, what had already happened to us at Grace Church.

Stringent Opposition

Though my time at Faith Church has come and gone, the further I move away from that experience, the more I find I am willing to own up to the fact that I made some tactical mistakes there. Sometimes we only figure out what works best after we've gone ahead and done the opposite. Although some of the comments I made to the leaders at Faith Church were conveniently misconstrued, I can readily admit that there were times when I came across as being less than diplomatic. For starters, my expectations of the leaders were vaulted too high to be met by them.

The best example of this is the way in which I expressed at a mixed deacons and elders meeting how disappointed I was in some of them for their lack of attendance at our Friday morning prayer meetings. Though I couldn't see it at the time, my sentiments embarrassed some of them, causing that moment to burn within their hearts for months afterward. I lost those guys that day, and in all probability also the ones who I'd calculated were "with me." My rationale behind the piercing comments was born out of sheer frustration, if not spiritual dog-tiredness. Not only did it seem like I was carrying the bulk of the burden for church growth, but I had to pull teeth over getting key leaders to pray about it with me. Along with a few other guys, I had sacrificed, on a weekly basis, some very early, cold morning hours getting into my car and driving to church to intercede for the ministry of Faith and for each other. It was supposed to be a time of bonding and building camaraderie as men of God. There were at least three leaders who I thought could have made it to these meetings, but who never seemed interested in even trying to.

If I could have done it over, I would have taken the time to do the personal, pastoral groundwork of meeting with these men individually, to get to know them better. In that way, I would have had a better shot at earning their trust, and hopefully their respect, *before* I went about instructing them as I did. All that my board room comments bought me that day were steely-eyed glares. In addition to that pastoral flub was the content of some of my sermons, which may have reflected a subtle rebuke of those who opposed my campaign to revamp the church's ministry. I was rather effective at proving my theological and spiritual position, yet it was unnecessary for me to use the pulpit as a forum to score points. Some of my choice sermon content, I knew, was bound to hit hard those who openly defied my leadership efforts. The end result was that they were intermittently taken to task.

Despite all this, at no time did I ever intentionally call out anyone in the church or refer to specific church struggles from the platform—something I ended up doing at my next ministry. I never did anything or said anything that would have led to me being disciplined. Certainly nothing I did warranted the kind of treatment I received from some of the believers at the church.

"I just wanted to grow the church," I later told a counsellor after leaving Faith. "You'd think I killed someone."

"But you did, Ron," the counsellor responded.

I was told that most likely there were people at Faith cheering me on, but that there were also those in the church who perceived me as someone who threatened to kill and bury any semblance of the ministry they had once known and been comfortable with. Talk about wounds from a friend being trustworthy (see Proverbs 27:6)!

It was an accurate assessment on the counsellor's part, for it made perfect sense of how the church had overreacted towards me. As a friend would tell me later, "Even lightning rods need lightning to make sparks fly." The people at Faith Church who opposed me didn't *have* to react the way they did.

I did my best to bring about positive change, because the infrastructure of the ministry didn't allow for the probability of much sustainable growth, in terms of equipping the saints for ministry, having the appropriate building blocks to do evangelism, or maturing new converts. I had spotted these sorts of problems going in. Faith Church was so focussed on their Monday night kids program (run by almost every member of the church) that there was little to no energy or interest in pursuing other programs to reach adults. I once came close to being stoned by the leaders of the kid's ministry when I said, "We don't have a lot of money as a church, and kids don't tithe!" I dug myself a deeper hole by adding, "Adults need to be saved, you know!"

In my opinion, it was obvious that God was blessing some of the initiatives that had been put into place. Unfortunately, even though some of God's people can see the spiritual value of growing pains, others either can't or won't; all they can see is what they had to give up on account of it. Sometimes they even become militant.

When I agreed to pastor Faith Church, it had looked like a rite of ministry passage, not the trapdoor it turned out to be. I couldn't have known what I was getting myself into, and I surely didn't know how to work my way out once I was in it. However, as someone wise once said, "If you're going through a rough period in life—*keep going.*"

What happened at Faith that was so bad for its ministry? For one thing, the church's membership increased. In my two years there, a number of people who had previously rebuffed the leaders' attempts to get them into membership finally decided to become members of Faith Church. Fresh interest appeared to be generated in the community (even if it was marginal), as pockets of new faces began to attend services. Elaine, as well as a few other women from the church, started up an outreach ministry specifically geared for women, which drew a good response from some of the parents of the children in the kids program.

Over and above that, we made a decision to advertise more and increase our visibility and presence in the community. A revised church bulletin was constructed, exhibiting a new logo which reflected the new direction the ministry was taking. We also instituted an elders-in-training program for men with potential leadership ability. We even managed to hire a part-time youth worker to fill the needs of some of the older teens. Besides a newly developed college and career ministry, the beginnings of small group ministry were introduced, which I hoped would eventually replace the dwindling and painfully-drawn out evening service. Aside from all the aforementioned additions and changes to Faith's ministry, the true gauge of how God was at work in the lives of people in the church, despite the upheaval, was that a few new Christians showed evidence of measurable growth and were willing to be baptized.

You may be thinking, *All that came about in two years?* Yes! As a result, the church entered a season of perceptible spiritual and numerical growth, which generated modest excitement that hadn't been there for a long time. My goal was to have the church redirect its energy from getting bogged-down in maintaining Faith's ministry to becoming more fluid in its operation, to becoming outwardly-focussed instead of inwardly-focussed.

However, the problem wasn't the growth that the church was experiencing; it was the speed and all-consuming nature of that growth. I was perceived to be ignoring and discarding the needs of the older crowd, which got the ire of some of the more obstinate and vocal pillars of the church. To this day, I'm not sure if a lot of the older people actually felt that way, or if a token few of the disgruntled crowd told them that they *should* feel that way!

Nonetheless, I had to take the charge seriously, for it was never my intent to segregate anyone. However, I resolved to come to my own defence by reminding the older crowd that I had spent a good portion of my first year at Faith conversing and ministering to their age group. I realized that the changes were not going to come about easily, nor were they going to be accepted with arms wide open. I likened what was happening at Faith to the slogan for Buckley's cough syrup: "It tastes awful. And it works!" For some of the malcontents at Faith Church, it didn't seem to matter that the changes seemed to be working. The plain fact was that it wasn't leaving a good taste in their mouths. Some of their ministry roles were no longer the main focal points of the ministry; everyone was asked to join in now, to share in the church's ownership and the overall identity of the church.

As time went on, a growing camp slowly but visibly pulled their support of my leadership. I had noticed that these people were the same ones who seemed to value the way things at the church used to be. Consequently, anything that smacked of change, even if it was biblical and God-glorifying, appeared to be unwanted—and they let me know about it in very creative ways.

One Sunday morning, I was awakened to how silly things had become in the church. When I walked into the church that day, I could tell by the sudden silence coming from a holy huddle that its participants were hiding knives behind their polite, Academy award-winning smiles and greetings. It felt a bit like I had become the Julius Caesar of Faith Church, and there I was, standing in front of a bunch of Brutuses and the rest of the Roman Senate.

It got worse. People who I suspected were unhappy with me made little attempt to hide it. Insensitive slights and slicing verbal barbs were not spared on me, or even on Elaine. They came from both the young *and* the old. What disheartened me even further was that, after all I and the elders had been through in trying to remain unified, the gossip was so concentrated in the church that it ended up dividing the elders from myself.

Ron Mahler

Coming on the heels of my leadership trials at Grace Church, I couldn't believe it was happening again. One Sunday morning, I could keenly see that I was nearing the finish line at Faith Church. I received a call from an elder who was away with another elder at a retreat. In a tone that was totally out of character for this person, he proceeded to ream me out. He pretty much demanded that I not go through with inducting a certain couple into membership during the service that morning, because two of the three elders weren't there. I wasn't going to take his command lying down.

"Am I not counted as a teaching elder, at least?" I shot back. "Did these candidates for membership not agree with the church's doctrine and values? Have they not been supporters of Faith's ministry for many years?" Go figure! No one became new members that day. I thought it best, in the interests of making peace, to make a concession by refraining from inducting any new members that Sunday morning. I hadn't just fallen off the watermelon cart, so I discerned that it probably wasn't about which elders were or weren't there that morning; rather, it was about *who* was coming into the membership. They were vocal supporters of me, a fact that made me, and a few others, suspicious.

There were a few raised eyebrows over the elder's call that Sunday morning, especially on the faces of the husband and wife who were slated to become members. They never did, nor did they stick around Faith Church a whole lot longer.

CHAPTER 40

War Rooms

By the time the two-year mark of my tenure at Faith rolled around, it seemed as if I were still in the "first period" at the church. However, the already visible cracks in the ministry began to stress even more. Everything was imploding around me. At least one month before I eventually left the church, I was desperately seeking a reason as to why I should remain at a church whose powerbrokers acted like they wouldn't miss me if I left! A meeting was held between me and the pastoral ministry superintendent from the church's denomination. This person was very familiar with the complexities of Faith's ministry, as well as with some of the difficulties that the church was facing as it struggled to remain a viable ministry in its community. The superintendent was also well-schooled in the history of the church, and with its tendency in times past to buck change.

There had long been talk at the denominational level of possibly merging the resources of three separate but small ministries in the same area as Faith Church to form one more substantial ministry (Faith being one of the three). I shared with the superintendent (a former pastor himself) that Faith had a congregational meeting planned in one week. After filling him in on some of the pertinent struggles going on at the church, and divulging some of my own misgivings, he advised that in his own experience a situation like the one I found myself in rarely ended well. He told me that it wouldn't look good on me if the only reason I stayed at Faith was to roll up my sleeves.

Ron Mahler

He also encouraged me to avoid the temptation of kicking the windows in, if and when I chose to leave. I could feel the flow of his wisdom permeate the island of confusion I was marooned on. That's when I had a moment of clarity, a moment which dispelled the blurry haze of wondering when I would know for sure that I needed to leave. The superintendent told me that pastors such as myself who were embroiled in deep conflict tended to have such watershed events. I took his guidance and experience to heart. I wasn't up for fighting any longer. By that late hour, I was looking for a way to exit the church without any further, unnecessary conflicts.

A week later, the day of the congregational meeting dawned. Waiting for it felt like the calm before the storm of having to go before a jury of my peers. The results of the after-service meeting would, indeed, seal my decision. I was called by the elders to address some concerns and finally defend the changes that had become a part of Faith Church's new ministry fabric. It had sounded like a great idea when it was proposed; in practice, however, the meeting fell far short of accomplishing its desired purpose: to hopefully unite the church. In hindsight, I would have had at least one of the elders lead the presentation that day. If talk of change had come from another person's mouth than just mine, news of the ministry's direction would have been perceived by the church as being spearheaded by the *leaders,* collectively, and not by a certain *leader.* At the very least, I wouldn't have been the sole object of some people's anger.

An ominous sign before the meeting was the sudden appearance of one woman, who had stopped attending the church because of her dislike for some of my and the elders' ministry decisions. Her husband was a compromised man, which rendered his judgment of her behaviour biased at best. He was in a difficult position, and I felt for him. It was out of design, I'm sure, that he was not at the congregational meeting that day. After some weeks of giving this woman a wide berth, I was accused by the rest of the board of ignoring her and not running after the one sheep who had strayed from the others. Granted, it had been a few weeks since I had seen her, but I felt the board's sentiments were more a display of melodramatics than real concern. All of us at the boardroom table knew what we were dealing with: a disgruntled person, a woman who was choosing to handle her discontentedness by making a statement that would put immense pressure on me. She wasn't the only woman in the church who had broadcasted her displeasure with me.

On a few unfortunate occasions, two other women made their points known to me by taking not so subtle jabs. The last time I had attempted to meet with one of them, to sort out some issues (even in the presence of her husband), she treated me to an hour's lecture so sharply condescending in its delivery that her criticisms scraped my heart, hurting me quite badly.

In particular, I was wary of any conversation with the woman who had chosen to stay away from Faith Church. Even though I knew such conversations could easily go off the rails, I agreed to call her. I didn't trust many people at that point, and she would have been almost the least trustworthy person of all. Our conversation was more civil than I expected, yet what struck me was her insistence that she had nothing against me. Her only admission was that she was upset that the church just didn't feel like "her church" anymore. She was absolutely right on that point, for the church was *never* really hers in the first place! We ended our brief talk, agreeing to pray for one another in the hopes that any disagreements could be laid to rest.

In the end, nothing was resolved between us. As the members of the church began to trickle into the sanctuary, my eyes spotted the contentious wife that I had spoken with on the phone only days earlier. I didn't like the look of her—arms crossed, stone-faced, and looking so perturbed that you just knew a tantrum might break out. Just a few weeks before, I had done a funeral for a family outside the church, which she had attended. When I worked my way over to civilly greet her, it took everything she had to acknowledge me.

Halfway through the congregational meeting, the inevitable moment arose. She stood up and gave me more than a piece of her mind; she gave me both lobes! Sure enough, she had vats of ammo and had no problem pulling the trigger on her weapon-like anger. Whether she realized it or not, she rallied the emotional heartstrings of all those at Faith who had been attending the church for longer than I was *alive.*

Everything from her words to her body language and gestures worked together, to incite the people. With staccato force, she alluded to the past, conveying that for years Faith Church had functioned very well, but that I was changing all that. Then she looked right at me, and with the use of three fingers rhymed off, "All the people want is a hymn, a prayer, and a message." To me, that was exactly the problem at the church. For far too long, Faith had stuck to the predictable, concrete template of just giving people a hymn, a prayer, and a message. Perhaps it had never occurred to them that such a service structure left certain people (predominantly those of a younger generation) wanting more than just rigid, hard-and-fast religiosity. I cannot fully recollect my response to her that day, but I can recall the response of every single leader present: *silence.*

Ron Mahler

While I came away from the meeting feeling whipped and scolded, Elaine was ready to sell the house and get out of Dodge.

If I had left the church that day, I would have avoided a very painful moment that would have spared us further heartache. A few months before the congregational meeting, I had been approached by a couple in the church who were two of what had become very few of my remaining supporters. The husband made a habit of praying with me on a weekly basis. The couple often offered timely and calming words of encouragement, and even supplied me with my favourite coffee, as well as books to read. I loved that couple to pieces; without them, my more difficult moments at the church would have been harder to take. Roughly six years ago, the husband passed away and I shared my feelings about him at his funeral. It was only then that I found out just the kind of friend who had invested in me while I was at Faith Church. He was a prayer warrior if there ever was one, and a man with unbelievable spiritual discernment.

One morning while entering the church building on his way to prayer, he shared that he'd begun to have trouble breathing, to the point where he was even gasping for air. Even though he was elderly, he assured me that he had never experienced anything like that before. He also informed me that after he regained his breath, he demanded out loud, "Who is this?" An audible answer, from a spiritual nether region, responded to his inquiry: "I'm the closer." For a stretch of time, even before I came on the scene, Satan had been acutely active in Faith's ministry, in ways that even the godliest and well-intentioned Christians there may have been unaware of. This faithful couple suggested that a group of prayer intercessors from another ministry come into the church to combat the satanic oppression that had overtaken it. Initially, I was hesitant, sceptical at the prospects for success.

After doing some checking up on the ministry of these intercessors, I gladly agreed to have them come. I didn't need much arm-twisting on the matter, for I had already experienced the spiritual heebie-jeebies while I was in the church building alone. Case and point: while I was in my office one day, I felt an uncomfortable presence come upon me. The presence left the impression in my mind that my preaching ministry at the church would be constricted as long as I remained there. It was undeniably a satanic attack upon me, after which I felt so fearful that I almost ran out of the church. I never shared that with the leaders, for fear that they would think I was off my rocker. However, I know what I felt, and I know that it happened. A close friend of mine suggested that there were obviously some serious strongholds in the church, and that I needed to go throughout the building and have people pray aloud, anointing different areas with oil.

My Fanatical, Regrettable Tour of Ministry

When I eventually explained this incident to the intercessors, they were only too willing to go with me through the building, praying and anointing the church. It was the first time I had heard of a Jezebel spirit being present in the church to intimidate godly leaders. They also informed me of how I could break the power of destructive words that were being levelled at me.

To this day, I struggle to get a full, theological handle on such a teaching, yet it made perfect sense at the time. Besides, I was revved up to break a few things at Faith! The intercessors told me, as we met in my outer office, that two people who had just walked through the church's front doors (absolutely out of their view) were confirmed detractors, and that they would be leaving the church. They were partly right, for the same couple would return to the church once I was gone. I couldn't believe how the intercessors could have known who walked in, and whether they were supporters of mine or not.

The intercessors proceeded to pray over me, read scriptures aloud, and to prophesy directly to me while proclaiming the powerful call of God upon my life. It was quite an eye-opening experience, if not a spiritually exhausting one. I still hope some of what they said comes to fruition! It was too much for me to take in all at once, though the day left me feeling like I had done all I could to take the fight to Satan, in the event that his counterfeit workings at Faith Church were as real as they appeared to be.

However, just as Elaine and I were not allowed to leave Grace Church without experiencing grief upon grief, we would not be afforded that luxury at Faith Church, either.

The Violence of the Lambs

MINISTRY IS POCKMARKED WITH SO MANY DISAPPOINTMENTS AND UNPREDICTABLE detours that it can be truly tough to even see a couple of weeks down the road. One thing I never saw coming at Faith Church was how profoundly disturbing, spiritually, the actions of some of God's people could be.

I shared in an earlier chapter how Christians can be used by the Devil, on any given day of their life, to tear down fellow believers. The inconvenient truth is that if we lend our ears to too much gossip, tittle-tattling, and speculation in the church (and in life generally), we may soon find our minds being invaded by the bidding of Hell itself. My last days at Faith Church were so heart-wrenching that I debated whether I could include much of it in this book. A very nice person, whom I had close contact with at Faith Church and whom I had ministered to, made a terrible error in judgement. This person was so taken by the case some of my critics had built up against me that they took up their offenses and actually put words to a tape recorder. The taped words seemed to be designed to sully my character and punish me.

Had the derisive tape been manufactured by any one of my known detractors, it still would have shocked me, though it might have been a tad easier to stomach. However, it came from someone whom I had never thought would ever stoop to such malevolence. About a week or two before I resigned, an elder phoned me and asked me to come to a meeting. I was informed that it was over a personal matter. It was yet another meeting that I simply did not want to attend.

My Fanatical, Regrettable Tour of Ministry

Even as I spoke to the elder on the phone, I could feel my heart beat up and into my throat. At that juncture, I'd had about enough of the elders' rhetoric, and of the fact that they had become faithful mouthpieces for certain people in the church who couldn't have cared any less about me. The only reason I agreed to go to the latest meeting was that I felt I needed to have one more shot at trying to work things out, at least as far as they *could* be worked out.

By the end of my term at Faith Church, church attendance was dropping every week; even more crushing is the fact that the Spirit of God was being terribly grieved in the process. Those who did show up on a Sunday morning must have wondered if *God* was going to. Going into the meeting, I would have just been thrilled for a week off—without pay even!

As I entered the room with a heightened sense of suspense, one of the elders quietly and grimly revealed, "We want you to listen to something on a tape." They warned me that what the person had to say was vile, and that it was about me. "We all thought you should know about it," the elder explained further.

Another elder, who was holding the tape recorder in his hand, pressed down on the play button. I won't go into a lot of what I can remember was said. Suffice it to say that the words shed serious doubt on my call to the ministry and my credibility as a leader in the church.

Does this sound remotely familiar? They were in the same league as the kinds of postulations that were made about my character and ministry while I was at Grace Church. As I sat listening to the unbelievable words on the tape, I didn't know what tore into me more—the comments that were made about me or the mouth that was delivering the venomous words. All I will reveal about the unfortunate recording was that I was accused of being a dictator who longed to have "a puppet ruler" to work with, and that I wasn't a real shepherd but a hired hand. To be called such things by your own people once in a pastor's lifetime is disturbing enough, but to be told it twice in the span of two and a half years is, well…you think of a word. After listening to the tape for longer than I should have, I motioned to the elder with the recorder, signalling him to stop it.

Though the tape—bereft of any grace, tact, *or* truth—may not have gotten me fired, it did burn within me enough to cause some major self-doubt. For days after, I pondered whether I was the kind of man I was being accused of. I asked the Lord why these sorts of malice-laced criticisms seemed to follow me around in ministry. Elaine threatened me not to entertain, even for one moment, that I was the kind of man some misguided and deceived people claimed I was.

Ron Mahler

Incredibly, I was able to get together with the person who made the infamous tape a short time after. The elders and I agreed that the two of us should get together alone, but in a neutral, public setting so that we could both be tempered in our dialogue. I thought it might be an uncomfortable meeting, filled with the temptation to reach over to this person and plunk them on the nose—in the name of everything that was right! Thankfully, I was able to let go of some anger by simply resolving to leave Faith Church for good.

Before I could even say a word to this person, he wasted no time in beginning to weep and asking me for forgiveness. As a pastor, I have prayed with troubled Christians and counselled emotionally sensitive people, but never have I witnessed the kind of repentance that this person displayed before me. I asked him why he had done it, and if in any way they had been coaxed into it.

"No," he confessed. "I acted alone."

He also fessed up to being deceived into listening to too many beefs that some people had about me. Elaborating a bit more, he explained that he had simply chosen to believe what those who were in opposition to me were propagating. It was important for me to hear that this person didn't *actually* believe what he had said. However, he did confirm what I had sensed all along, when he told me that there was a push to get rid of me, and that the people behind it wouldn't stop until I was gone. I told him that I had gotten the hint. Pastors can usually tell the difference between the times when their people are merely unhappy with them, and when they are overtly trying to jettison them from the pastor's office.

Although he tried valiantly to compliment me and encourage me not to let those who were stepping up against me get their way, my mind was made up. It was time to bid Faith Church, *"Hasta la vista!"* It had been good knowing most of them, but it was even better leaving them. In the final analysis, I felt sorrier for this person than anything else. That said, it took a long time to shake off his chosen words, and the spiritual tone of them (as if the evil one was speaking himself). I can still hear them if I try to remember hard enough.

Sometimes, the words people say about us in foolish haste can be quite persuasive, even if the things they have said are the furthest things from the truth. The tape was a byproduct of what was in the hearts of some of the believers at Faith Church.

It was necessary for the elders at Faith to hear from a concerned pastor's wife. Soon after, Elaine met with the elders to call them on the carpet for failing to live up to their previous assurances that they would protect me. That particular

My Fanatical, Regrettable Tour of Ministry

meeting went nowhere. The elders felt that Elaine was the one who had come across in the beginning as "chippy" and "threatening." I was never able to accept their perspective on that, for I thought that Elaine had been remarkably diplomatic in communicating her reservations about my role, due to my prior hurtful experiences. Oddly enough, the elders also implicated our pastor friend, the one we had chosen to be the speaker at my induction service, citing that he had baited the church by telling them to treat us well and not to hurt us.

I wondered to myself how the leaders in the room could have been so dense as to not appreciate where our pastor-friend was coming from. He had simply called for Faith Church, in their dealings with us, to take into consideration all the difficulties we'd been through at our previous ministry. There was nothing even remotely inappropriate about the comments he made; unless, of course, his comments ended up coming back to sting the elders with conviction. Elaine and I sat, bristled; we were dumbfounded by how these men seemed to be able to turn everything back on us. There was hardly any willingness on their part to take responsibility for the things we perceived they had done wrong. Roughly a week or so after tape-gate, I gathered the elders in my office and gave it to them straight, that I had preached my last sermon at Faith Church.

When I think back on that memorable moment, I wonder if my decision was determined more in haste—perhaps even disillusionment—than affirmed in prayer; after all, my abrupt departure from the church, once again, put Elaine and me in a financial bind. Putting aside my need for a paycheque, I knew that my working relationship with the elders at Faith was severely handicapped. It was all over for me long before it was *literally* over. I was depleted of any will to carry on, in a position. I had nothing left to give. Gone, almost overnight, was my zeal to make a difference at the church. My working relationship with some of the church's leaders took a huge hit as well.

What I know, for certain, is that I disappointed a number of the people at Faith. At the same time, however, a number of them flat-out let me down. A rather small, but amazingly combative group also hit me when I was down. Pastors may reach a point where they feel like they cannot go on, yet it can sometimes be more a case that they *shouldn't* go on. If pastors and other leaders get concussed by too many conflicts in the church, the long-standing effects may leave them overly defensive in their role. The vertigo-like effect of paranoia can subtly kick in over the slightest of criticisms that are directed at a leader, leaving them dizzy. Pastors need to know when enough is enough, and when carrying on in a specific ministry can only serve as a detriment to their marriage, and a threat

Ron Mahler

to their spiritual well-being. Even a boxer who has been battered and bloodied has to choose whether or not they will answer the bell for another round. Most of them want to live to see another payday in the ring.

As I left Faith, I wondered whether I would live to see another ministry come my way. I only realized after I'd left the church that my exodus probably should have come sooner than it actually did.

Chapter 42

Exiting

Months would pass before I could sleep through the night without waking up at some point, angry. It would take a much longer time before I could forgive myself for being a two-time failure as a pastor. While there were spurts when I thought I might have left Faith too soon, it was probably more a lack of a paycheque talking. Not only was I disappointed with so many of God's people at Faith Church, people who had unnecessarily ganged up on Elaine and me, not only had my relationship with the elders become estranged and weakened by distrust, but all the efforts I'd made to introduce change seemed for naught. I had to face the fact that a lot of the reforms and fledgling ministry initiatives I had instigated would fall apart without my steering presence to look after them.

Discord will always exist amongst Christians. We are so sin-soaked that even the best of relationships between Christians has the potential to be affected by selfishness. When fellowship is broken in the church, it's like we as believers won't allow ourselves to see that we are fracturing the hand or foot of Christ. It's hard to fathom how individual believers can get to the point where they no longer want to have communication with each other, let alone encounter one another. In many respects, church infighting has become the way the world perceives Christians. The casual unbeliever may think, *If they can't get along, why do I need to join them?* Unfortunately, those outside of the faith often come to know God's people by their factions rather than by their love.

Ron Mahler

In the wake of all the spiritual carnage at Faith Church, the minister who married Elaine and me, Pastor Fellows, made a gallant effort to console us. He reminded us that even Jesus was misunderstood, passed off, and then even crucified (at least *that* didn't happen to me). He assured us that we, by virtue of our trials at Faith, could take heart in knowing that we were sharing in the sufferings of Christ. I know there's only one Man (Jesus Christ) who was worthy of the holes He bore in His wrists. If He couldn't turn some people around, after all He did for them (and without sin), how could I, as one who had no holes in his wrists or feet, have ever imagined that I could turn them all around?

The night I said my goodbyes to the elders, I was filled with a surprising mix of emotions. Collectively worn out from months of meetings and heated arguments that had affected our hearts and homes, we shook hands and strummed up enough godliness to part on amicable terms.

After the meeting, I left the church for the last time, wishing I had never been on the same leadership with these good, decent men, for outside of the boardroom I am sure I would have gotten along famously with them. They were the type of guys who would have given you the shirt off their back. They had been faithful to keep the ministry at Faith Church going long before I set foot there. While the doors at Faith Church had revolved with servants and pastors coming and going, these elders had remained, even if the church's evangelistic lustre faded and its ability to attract people declined. I liked those guys, but I just couldn't take any more of the toxicity that had come to choke our working relationship. This saddened me greatly.

If forgiveness and forgetfulness were all it took to repair my relationship with those men, we could have carried on together, yet I didn't have enough will left in my tank to allow for the amount of time that would be needed to glue back together the broken trust. The danger of experiencing unabated conflict, whether we are pastors or not, can produce sinking amounts of mistrust in us, so much so that we inevitably need to step away from the clash and place our hurts at the foot of Jesus' cross, so that we can fully pardon people and learn to trust again.

Being human, and hopefully sensitive to God's Spirit, I am given over to momentary lapses of thoughts and feelings of regret that things did not work out better for us at Faith Church. Sometimes I think we were *that* close to turning the corner. When I first grasped that the elders were showing signs of resistance to some of my ideas, I had consulted Pastor Williams, from my days at Grace Church. I had shared with him that I was hitting a wall with my leaders, trying to get them to see things my way. My main concern was how to influence them to follow along with me, in a unified oneness of purpose.

"Think of them like a string," Williams had suggested. "A string will move and follow you if you gently drag it along. It won't if you try to force it forward."

After it was all said and done, I still believed that I had made some humble and prayerful attempts to gently pull the elders in a healthy direction, but there were times when I probably forced them forward a bit too much. What was obvious to me was how lacking a number of the leaders had been in their leadership gifting. This can be true of pastors as well. Though sometimes we need to work with the willing, regardless of their strengths, abilities, or giftedness, not every person in the board room is cut out for the leadership role. Honestly, however, the pastor is the person in the church who most often feels that way. God's shepherds feel the blunt trauma of their failures more intensely than the satisfaction of basking in the glow of their successes. I failed in various areas of my ministry while pastoring at Faith Church, though I would like to hang on to the belief that I brought about some good as well.

Most importantly, I left with the church predominantly intact. Though a marginal group of people left over my departure, the pillars of the church who had pulled political stunts and who made statements by boycotting the services, eventually returned. Despite how my legacy there might be remembered, I take a grain of satisfaction in that I helped the church accomplish some kingdom mandates for the Lord. I challenged them to think outside the proverbial church box, and dared them to dream that the glory days of times past didn't have to be tucked away in the history books. A new day of rebirth could be realized with God's blessing.

One evening after Elaine and I had been away from Faith for a few weeks, a thought occurred to me as I was reading through the Books of the Prophets. The chaos was calming down in our lives, and we were better able, from a distance, to sift through and process all the what-if's from our time at Faith Church. I raised my sudden thought to Elaine, who was sitting on a couch next to me.

"God only sent so many prophets to warn His people before the end would come and His judgement fall," I told her.

How profound! she must have initially thought.

I was referring to how the ministry at Faith had become a morgue for many well-meaning, change-seeking pastors like myself. In saying this, I am not in any way inferring that I am, or was, another prophet-type sent to Faith as a voice calling out to them in their desert of stagnancy. However, it was still possible, in my mind, that God had been trying to get the attention of the leadership there to listen to a voice for change before it was too late for them. How many more pastors would God send to a church like Faith, which now had the dubious reputation as being known as a "jump-off" church for pastors?

I don't know if I was off in my estimation of things, but today Faith Church no longer exists as an independently, functioning ministry. The name of the church has been changed and the purpose of the ministry has been taken over and restarted by its denomination. In the end, God would have His way with Faith, and He would give them a bold new course to chart. As it would turn out, the very changes I tried to implement were eventually forced on them by their denomination—a great irony.

In a twist of circumstances, I would yet again come face to face with some of the individuals I was in conflict with at Faith Church. An elderly woman who was a longtime member of the church later passed away, and her daughter requested that I officiate the funeral. I deeply cared for the deceased, and had visited her on many occasions. This would make seeing some of the people at Faith again even more emotionally challenging.

CHAPTER 43

Aftermath

IT WAS THE FIRST TIME I SAW MOST OF THE PEOPLE FROM FAITH SINCE THE LAST Sunday I preached there, a year or so earlier. Talk about nerve racking! With my legs feeling weak and shaking beneath me, and my stomach queasy, I stepped behind the podium. Holding it tight, I looked up to face a crowd of people with whom I had never resolved my past issues. It wasn't an appropriate occasion, of course, for me to make any references to that.

The awkward reality of the moment added to the elephant-in-the-room feeling that permeated the whole service. It felt more like a blast from the past, like I was preaching a sermon at Faith Church, than like I was ministering to a family in mourning. However, God used the moment as a witness to my pastoral care for the deceased person. It was my hope that with some time behind us, those I had battled at Faith would be able to see a different side of me. I wanted them to see that I was quite comfortable with demonstrating compassion, and that I could even cry real tears, if it got to the point.

By this time, Elaine had given birth to our second child—a son, Dakota. Our family was growing, but our bank accounts weren't. Like with all couples whose breadwinner spouse loses their job, we struggled to pay the mortgage. There were moments during my period of unemployment, which lasted close to a year, when Elaine and I fretted over whether we could keep our financial heads above water. While she continued to work in offices, I made so-so money from taking on house-painting jobs; in the long run, it wasn't nearly enough. At the insistence of the denomination associated with Faith, I had been given a generous severance upon my departure. It was my hope and prayer that I would find some other work before our financial parachute gave out.

I managed to send off a few resumes to churches. I didn't see my decision to apply for positions at other churches after leaving Faith Church as an act of casting my bread upon the waters. Sending out resumes felt more like dropping a morsel of bread into a puddle; I never really thought I would get so much as a church's nibble, let alone a full bite-down. In fact, for a time, I couldn't have cared less if I ever heard from another church ever again.

When we had left Grace Church, we were in a rental situation and could leave on just a few months' notice; there were also no children to account for. However, when we left Faith Church, we were parents and had the blessing of a family. Naturally, that meant added financial challenges this time around. One thing was for certain, though, ministry or no ministry: I couldn't be out of full-time work for very long.

My employment insurance benefits had their end point, and Elaine and I barely made enough to cover our bills.

One November morning about four months after making the break from Faith Church, I recall looking out the back window of our townhouse and feeling depressed, like I was an utter failure. I had probably hit as close to rock-bottom, mentally and emotionally, as I had ever been. While friends of mine were being ordained, inducted into new ministries, or in the process of getting churches, there I was, once again relegated to a watch-and-wait desert. I fell into the misery of a spiritual slump for weeks.

In fact, for the better part of the year following my departure from Faith Church, I would dip in and out of discouragement so intensely that I even contemplated making a sharp turn in career paths. If all I had wanted was to make a contribution to the Kingdom of God, why did I have to end up out of ministry, not to mention out of money? This was just one of a torrent of rants that poured out of my heart against God in those fragile months. It meant precious little to me that Elaine and I could take consolation in the fact that we had been dealt very difficult ministry cards. Neither did it rate all that high on the comfort meter that we couldn't have known what we were walking into by agreeing to minister at these dysfunctional churches. The cold, hard fact remained that, even though I'd had three ministry jobs, I had virtually no quality references from the last two with which to seek another ministry.

My Fanatical, Regrettable Tour of Ministry

All things considered, I prematurely convinced myself that I had earned a bad reputation, which would surely mark the death of my call to the pastorate. By no means was I totally writing off a return to ministry, yet I didn't possess the confidence or will to pursue my calling, not right away. I wasn't even sure whether I had what it took to be a leader in a church, let alone venture down that road again.

I dumped all my frustrations one day on the desk of a valued mentor. I can still hear his comical tidbit of advice: "Just go into a forest somewhere and scream!" It sounded great, actually, and I probably did it a couple of times.

I knew such a therapeutic suggestion wouldn't get me another job, but it might make me feel better. My mentor also gave me a bit of a more practical suggestion, though, which was that I should consider pursuing "a good associate's role," so that I could learn from another leader for a while. That idea sounded good, too, but I could recall another denominational figure giving me opposing advice: "Really good associate roles are like hen's teeth; they're rare."

It was hard for me to imagine changing gears that way. Though I knew, undeniably, that I needed to keep evolving in my leadership abilities and broadening my avenues of mentorship, I still felt I could do the job of a senior pastor, if given the right situation. Besides, many associate roles I had pursued in the past had resembled errand-boy mop-up jobs more than specialized, gift-specific ministry opportunities.

However, being away from a full-time ministry role for a prolonged period, did have its benefits. My ability to focus on other things, apart from getting back into ministry, was the key to my sanity. At various stages of life, things of lesser desire are more important than things of greater desire, even if those great longings are good and valuable in themselves. It's great to be involved in vocational ministry, even with all the unpredictable hazards that come along with the role.

The pastorate, as rewarding as it can be, is not *everything* in life. I've been able to see that more clearly in the times when I've been away from the ministry. One advantage to spending a lot of time at home was that I could share some quality time with our daughter, Cassidy, who was in her toddler stage. She was old enough to stay in her stroller while I walked her almost daily to a nearby park. We frequented the same route so often that Cassidy came to memorize the specific turns I made around the streets. She even predictably stuck her little finger out as if to say, "I know the park is this way, Daddy!"

Those were memorable times, even though they were bittersweet. As much as I thought it was great for me to be able to be around my children a lot in their early years, it would have been greater to be in a position of gainful employment, even if it wasn't in a church. I'm a typical human being; I've never been good at waiting on the promises of God to be fulfilled. I searched the scriptures quite often in those days, looking for God to give me a word to confirm that He still purposed to use me in pastoral ministry. I was in a hurry for an answer; He wasn't. I received plentiful counsel on the matter, but it was confusing at first, for as many who told me to get out of pastoral ministry, or go into missions, there were just as many who exhorted me to hang in, that God must have something really special for me to have allowed me to go through such a trial again.

That, in essence, was the crux of my struggle. I spent months trying to iron out these mental wrinkles. I wondered how much of everything that had happened at Faith Church I should have owned. Was I the author of my own heartache? Had God hardened hearts at Faith Church to show His recalcitrant children something of great spiritual gain? How much of the mess in the church had I been the cause of? Even more bothersome a question was why God had permitted me to be so injured by another ministry, especially when it had taken so long to get my confidence back after my first pastoral beatdown.

I could have thought up questions all day, but it wouldn't have changed the fact that I had no recourse. What happened at Faith Church had happened; I couldn't change it, and neither could they. Dwelling on my regrets, blaming myself, and staying fixed on what I *could have* done differently wouldn't put food on my table. It was time to move forward and take with me only that which was profitable in terms of lessons learned; the rest (accusations, unresolved conflicts) had to be left behind.

Some of my favourite scriptures from that period of my life were Paul's liberating words to the church in Philippi: *"But one thing I do: Forgetting what is behind and straining toward what is ahead, I press on toward the goal to win the prize for which God has called me heavenward in Christ Jesus"* (Philippians 3:13–14). However, the fact that I had gotten a healthy grip on the past didn't automatically translate into me gaining a clearer picture of my future.

It's easy when we feel like we're drifting on a raft of uncertainty, with no solid dock in clear view, for the periscope of our pain to show us nothing but the possibility that God may have abandoned us. Even though some of these conclusions we come to are totally unbiblical, they don't seem any less real to us, especially when we're being stretched beyond our comfort zones. I needed a spiritual transfusion of grace. Not only did I need to be easy on myself, but I needed to cling to Jesus' invitation in Matthew 11:29–30: *"Take my yoke upon you and learn from me, for I am gentle and humble in heart, and you will find rest for your souls. For my yoke is easy and my burden is light."*

In fact, God's grace would come to me from areas I never could have predicted.

Chapter 44

Grace

The Greek word for "gift" in the New Testament is *CHARIS*. What I really like about this word is not how it sounds but what it means. The word *charis* means "grace." The apostle Paul referred to this word a few times in his letters to the early churches. To the Corinthian church, Paul wrote that the manifestation of the Holy Spirit's gift to believers was an act of God's *grace* (1 Corinthians 12:7).

Supernatural abilities are, of course, not the only gifts God bestows on us to live the spiritual life. Spiritual durability comes from when the onslaught of trials meets up with the graciousness of God, to help us through. If we can expect anything from a gracious God, it is grace! I needed to get into a better frame of mind, mentally and emotionally, and achieve some spiritual momentum if I was to ever contemplate ambling out into the ministry once more, a prospect that would have been unimaginable to me in the months following my exit from Faith Church. Divine grace was just what the Great Physician ordered!

I was abreast of my need to continue working through some of the things that had gone down at Faith Church, letting go of a lot of things from that experience. I had gone through the same process in the wake of leaving Grace Church. In life, we have to be cautious not to carry any unnecessary baggage from old breakups into new relationships. The same is true of ministry. Anything we take with us from our prior ministries (hang-ups, bad habits, hurts), things that weigh heavily on us, needs to be unpacked rather than taken with us still kept under wraps. A new ministry, in many respects, is a clean slate. Therefore, it is both unfair to the congregation we are inheriting, as well as unproductive for us as leaders, to project anything of the residue from our past (including pastoral disappointments) onto a new church.

It took a while for Elaine and me to settle on a church to attend as we waited for our next move, whatever that would be, and to see if God willed for us to be in another full-time ministry situation. I still thought it was a long shot. We didn't have many close relationships in the town we had been living in for over two years (the same town where Faith Church existed). Moreover, we weren't inclined to share very much about our lives. We feared personal embarrassment, even rejection, as a result of the events at Faith, and despaired of shedding negative light on our witness as Christians.

As we toted our past hurts with us, we found that there were a limited number of people who could adequately relate to what we had gone through. There was an even smaller contingent of people (outside of professionals) who we felt we could be ourselves with, who we could trust to bear our dirty laundry.

Thankfully, God brought such people into our lives, including a couple of local pastors. Elaine struggled at first to find women she could have a rapport with to freely share her pain. However, after about a year, we began to feel stronger again. The church we attended played a significant role in our progress. The floodgates of pent-up wounds broke wide open. Although we sought to be appropriate in the disclosure of our personal struggles, it was very liberating to be able to share our hurts without fear of being judged. We would spend hours bemoaning our lot in ministry, rehashing our stories to listening and caring ears. Elaine and I were conscious, however, of not wearing out people's compassion; consequently, we made a point of not dumping on people for too long. The last thing we wanted was to be seen as "needy."

That said, it was a great feeling, personally, to be a counselee (and not the counsellor), to have my choice of pastors to "talk shop" with, if I so desired. As I spent time with a few weathered warriors of the ministry, they reminded me not to make myself out to be some kind of pastoral criminal who should be confined from being allowed to see the light of day in church ever again. Though my situation was unique, there was wisdom in balancing my experiences with those of many good men and women who had been through similar struggles—even the very men who I was looking at across the table! The more Elaine and I remained realistic about our pain and the disillusionments we'd encountered, and the more we kept our eyes and minds on God's goodness, and not on His people's shortcomings, the more we found our hearts filled with encouragement for the future.

With our hopes stirring again, we believed that we might be able to dare dreaming about ministering in another church. Like a mother who forgets the physical pain and exertion involved in giving birth after she has held her newborn child, the sensitive nerve-endings surrounding my memories of conflicts and ministerial abandonment began to dissipate as I grew in my understanding of the perils inherent with leadership, becoming more familiar with the ministry principles I needed to incorporate if there was a "next time."

Elaine and I came to the point where we settled on serving in one of two churches which we were hopping back and forth between. Unclear as to what the Lord's plan was for us in the future, we determined to keep moving ahead. We mutually decided that we had spent enough downtime just showing up for Sunday services, absorbing sermons and licking our wounds. We longed to get back to serving as a lay-couple in church, wherever and whenever we could.

I felt it was imperative for me to be discharged from the sick-pastor ward and once again get into the operating room of the church. It was a newly-planted church just down the road from our house. Do you see the pattern here? It had been our involvement with Pastor Fellows' church plant three summers earlier that had whetted our appetite to see God work in new and fresh ways. Now, this new chance to serve in a church plant seemed too tantalizing an opportunity to squander. Whether it was for a few months or for a longer duration, we felt we should throw ourselves into this new ministry without reservation. From that point on, we enjoyed months of much-needed and consistent fellowship.

I formed a close bond with the founding pastor of the church plant, who was at least twenty years older than I was. Our friendship gave me a venue in which we could bounce our individual thoughts and passions about ministry off each other. His stories were very enriching and quite a bit more amusing than my own. However, what I appreciated the most was his genuine concern for Elaine and me and our young family. He had a mild-mannered exterior, but by no means was he a pushover. He had been around the block more than a few times to be able to see how churches can be caches for the worst kinds of spiritual issues. This man had seen firsthand the sorts of disguises that churches and their leaders put up to gloss over the potentially serious issues that incoming pastors have to deal with.

One day, as I met with him over coffee, I discussed my rising hopes of getting back into the ministry. He semi-jokingly offered me a position at the church—

when they had enough funds to pay me! He made me promise him, however, that I wouldn't play the blame game if another church was to contact me. The only way I could disqualify myself from a future ministry, he remarked, was if I nursed grudges and harboured bitterness.

"No church," he warned me, "would call that kind of guy." Over time, through our association with the church plant, which blessed us with new friendships, compassion and the exhortations of God's people, the sharpness of our angst from church ministries gone sour dulled greatly.

Though I was asked to preach a couple of times at the new, infant-like church we were attending, I found it surprising by how okay I was with remaining a background figure. Being immersed in the church-plant ministry felt like a can't-lose situation to us as we prayerfully entertained the odd calls from different churches, inquiring about my availability. I tried hard to postpone stepping up my search to find another ministry, but Elaine and I could sense that, as much as our time at the new church was a welcome refuge, it was probably not a long-term stay; it was only a warm-up. There wasn't any skywriting from Heaven being sprayed over our house, revealing the coveted will of God for our future. There wasn't a banner announcing the terms of where or when the next ministry would take place. We just had a feeling that my days of wearing the pastor's badge hadn't yet reached their conclusion. Suffice it to say that we simultaneously sensed by the Holy Spirit's prodding that God's plan was just around the corner.

I highly doubt if I have ever prayed as consistently and intensely as I did during those fourteen months between the time I left Faith Church and when I eventually heard God's call to pastor again at another church. The dilation of my heart towards accepting whatever it was that God had for me was greater than ever.

There are thorny points in our lives when we have to take Him at His good Word, and trust Him. As Elaine and I sought to rest in God's never-failing promises, we felt His strong arms cradle and carry us through that lean season when money was fashionably scarce and prospects for even nominal employment scarcer.

Though we were once again regaining our spiritual footing, balancing previous setbacks with present reprisals, the reality was that we were nearing a crisis. Elaine and I were in real danger financially; we were in the express lane, headed towards the possibility of losing our home if something didn't come our way pronto. During the stressful time of having to endure another bout of unemployment and wade through the stresses that came from Elaine having given birth to our second child, our bank balance reminded us that we couldn't realistically live on love alone. It was God's providence, however, that a spattering of people who had subsequently departed from Faith Church felt compelled to graciously contribute to our needs from time to time. Even some of God's people in the church plant we were at insisted on providing for our most pressing needs.

During one desperate phase, we flat-out ran out of food for the first time in our six years of marriage, which prompted me to call a fairly large church in the area where we lived, whose pastor I knew, to request for some assistance in groceries. We didn't want to burden the church we were attending, to sap any more of their resources and goodwill. That was a tough day for me, personally, as a man. Admittedly, my pride was bruised, and I knew it was a call that I didn't want to make ever again. Unfortunately, the bleak period caused Elaine and I to relive all the agony of what happened at Faith Church, after a period of our seemingly having put it to rest. Our depleted cupboards, and wallets, had us wishing we had never gone to Faith in the first place. It was one of those regrets that was dying a slow death!

We were tired of our circumstances dictating our decisions, in taking on churches that perhaps we would have been better off passing up had we not been so desperate for full-time ministry work. Something is wrong when bill payments or ominous bank statements play major roles as to whether pastoral couples take or leave a particular church. Pastoral ministry isn't like the average job where one can start and then leave just like that, without incurring huge costs; rather, such jobs require couples to sell and buy homes, to move, and to uproot children from school, not to mention all the social elements involved in changing location.

Just as Elaine and I edged closer to financial ruin, out of the blue we got a call from a precious couple we had known for years. They told us that God had put it on their hearts to sacrifice a certain amount of money per month. They wanted to send that money to us, in order to keep us afloat until we could sustain ourselves again.

It was an extremely difficult exercise in humility for us to accept their incredibly mind-blowing offer. We thought the amount to be too much, but they wouldn't have anything of it, choosing to smooth over our objections by responding, "It's only money." That, from a couple that wasn't exactly floating in it at the time, either. Amazingly, the six cheques they predated and sent us would last just long enough for us to meet our last mortgage payment—*before* the eventual sale of our home. God orders and arranges the affairs of our lives perfectly.

The selling of our home coincided with the opening of another ministry door for us. Almost a year and a half after Elaine and I said our goodbyes to a pair of successive painful ministry experiences that left us questioning my suitability and personal adequacy for the pastoral role, God confirmed my simmering suspicion that He willed to use me in yet another church ministry.

Transition Redux

IN ALL THE DOWNTURNS AND DARK TIMES I'VE EXPERIENCED IN MINISTRY, I've come to appreciate more and more that shepherding Jesus' church is a privilege as much as it is a spiritual gift to be used to serve God. Even though I have strived through the years to take myself less seriously—after all, the Kingdom of God will not fall if I fail—I do take the accountability of the pastoral role *very* seriously. As it turned out, God wasn't nearly finished with me in the pastorate, despite what I had thought. Though it took months upon months of wishing, wondering, and worshipping my way through the ebbs and flows of uncertainty, I would again reach the point of interviewing for another pastoral position.

I spent a great deal of time researching ways in which I could put a positive spin on a resume that looked like bombs had gone off on it. My relatively short portfolio in pastoral ministry was long on mistakes and longer still on question marks. A church wouldn't have to do much scouring before raising more than a few eyebrows at the short amounts of time I had spent at my previous churches.

Our resumes speak for us before we get the chance, and if they are the swan that attracts employers to beautiful possibilities, then mine was the ugliest duckling of them all. My credentials were just plain homely, and no amount of facelifts could cure it. When I got to the point of intentionally applying to churches again, I did my level best to refurbish my weak resume.

For my efforts, I received two main prospects to consider. The first was The Believers' Church, seven hours north of where we were living before we sold our home and moved. The second, Northern Bible Church, was only three and a half hours away. Elaine and I would eventually settle on Northern Bible, whose ministry opening was listed as an interim role. However, before Elaine and I would get to that church, the other ministry (The Believers' Church), which was a *full-time* position, informed me that my name had come to the top of the pile. This revelation absolutely stunned me, for it seemed more like a cruel dream than the result of a search committee's prayerful consideration.

The Believers' Church was a larger ministry situated in a scenic, good-sized town with lots of potential for growth. The only knock Elaine and I had against it was its considerable distance from our closest family. However, what I found so interesting was the rapport I seemed to be naturally developing with every passing phone conversation I had with one of the elders there, who also happened to be the chairman of their pastoral search committee. This individual and I would end up forming a close friendship. The church was willing to have our family stay in the town for a few days while I preached, met with the leaders, and became more familiar with the ministry. While the beginnings of that process were going on, Northern Bible Church was also in warm pursuit of me. They had me come to preach at their church as well. Indeed, the candidating process with Northern Bible, largely due to the position being an interim one, went fairly quickly.

Our matchmaking would scratch the backs of each other's need. My eventual decision to go to Northern Bible would provide a pastoral presence for them, since they were currently without a pastor heading into the fall months. Their hiring of me would provide Elaine and me with a badly-needed injection of finances after having moved back to Toronto for a short period while we waited for God's clear direction.

With the reality that I was burning the candle at both ends, being pulled in two separate ministry directions, the day came for me to preach at Northern Bible for the first time. I was deemed a guest speaker who was also being considered a potential pastoral candidate for their ministry opening. As it would happen, that particular day left Elaine and me near exhausted, and more than a little freaked out.

It started out as a very warm and sunny August day; it would end with a darkened sky giving way to a violent rainstorm. With two kids in tow, we made the three-hour journey to Northern Bible Church. We had to use my mother's tiny old sedan, as a result of our car being in the shop. During the ride, our son Dakota suddenly took a colic-induced crying fit of such proportions that it left both Elaine and me totally annoyed. Our nerves were shot from listening to a steady bellow of blood-curdling cries for nearly an hour.

Not only did we misjudge the travel time, but Dakota's crying caused us to stop a few times. Another hurdle for me that day was a physical one, in that I was suffering from a rather terrible cold. I was so sick that my plugged sinuses affected my ability to breathe normally. I had decided against cancelling my preaching date with Northern Bible, however, for fear of setting a bad precedent with the church. As a result, my sniffing and coughing caused my sermon delivery to be less than stellar. The people were quite understanding of my health situation, though, and my performance in the pulpit that day (which was not up to par, by my standards) didn't stop them from having me come back for an interview.

It was then that I made the search committee aware that there was another church (The Believers' Church) interested in me, and I in them. The leaders at Northern Bible assured me that this would not be a problem and referred back to the fact that their commitment to me was only for an interim period, which might only last for six months anyway. The understanding allowed me to feel like I wasn't being unfaithful to them by keeping the other church, another four hours away, on the backburner.

After our initial exposure to Northern Bible Church, Elaine and I were glad that we would only be there for a short time. At first glance, the ministry had "Faith Church" written all over it; change a few things here and there, and it could have been first cousins—maybe even fraternal twins—with Faith. In other ways, however, the two ministries differed quite a bit, especially in terms of the facility. It was a newly-built but small, country-looking church set atop a hill, overlooking a picturesque lake. Inwardly, however, the ministry at Northern Bible wasn't in any way a reflection of its breathtaking surroundings. It was an older and predominantly conservative congregation that seemed to be content to exist just the way it always had. The previous pastor had enjoyed a good, lengthy tenure but had moved on under what I perceived to be mysterious circumstances. It didn't help my inquiring mind, nor treat my slight reservations, that no one on the deacons' board or search committee was quite able to give me a satisfactory answer as to why he and his wife had suddenly left them.

The pittance of an explanation I received was nowhere near adequate. I was informed that their previous pastor's departure had come as a surprise to them. In thinking back, the lack of a quality explanation was telling. This mystery would be filled in some more as time wore on. Isn't it funny how we readily stop our vehicles at red lights, but as pastors we sometimes just keep on going straight

My Fanatical, Regrettable Tour of Ministry

ahead even when the red glare of alarms light and the warning sirens sound? Perhaps it's because we want to believe that the last guy *was* the problem and not the inherent culture of the church. Though any pastoral candidate will freely acknowledge that no church is perfect, some really believe that they will fare much better than the last pastor did.

In my last few days at Grace Church, I had a brief opportunity to meet and speak with the incoming pastor who was to replace Pastor Williams. Given the irksome affairs at the church, I specifically encouraged this leader to contact his predecessor in order to hear the other side of the story and gain a clearer picture of the situation he was inheriting. The pastor, though appreciative of my concern, didn't see the need to do this. "In my opinion," he reasoned, "I don't think that is ever a productive thing to do." Of course, due to the extenuating circumstances at Grace Church, I had to disagree with him on that one. Considering everything that's involved in making a move to a new town, a pastor owes it to himself to at least put in a call to his predecessor, especially if the previous pastor left under duress.

If it's fair game for search committees to do as much homework on prospective pastors as possible, why shouldn't those prospective pastors do just as much homework on the churches they are to represent? Despite the warning signs, I resolved that I probably wouldn't be at Northern Bible Church long enough to uncover anything of their past. This was a huge miscalculation on my part. As far as I was concerned, being in an interim role meant that I was made of Teflon; nothing was going to *stick* to me! Besides, I was a smarter and more cunning leader now. If Northern Bible was a short stop on my way to the other, more promising full-time ministry, I could live with some temporary dysfunction. It was just refreshing to have options for a change, to not be so dependent on one church for employment.

If I had only known that our drive home after preaching that first time at Northern Bible would be symbolic of things to come, I would have stood the church up quicker than a bad blind date! The drive home resembled something out of an Alfred Hitchcock movie. First of all, I ran over a partridge on a two-lane highway; it would have been better off in its pear tree, but there it was, mangled and convulsing in my rear-view mirror, its feathers flying everywhere. The thud it made under our car, alone, was enough to give you chills. Normally, it doesn't bother me to gaze upon road kill on roads and highways, but it was me who had slayed this bird, and it bothered me perhaps more than I thought it would.

After that, Elaine and I began to experience car trouble; we stalled whenever we had to slow down to a stop. That was just the beginning of our bizarre drive home. We had to make a stop in the parking lot of a restaurant to fix some things in the back seat that were bothering the kids. As we were making the adjustments, we were overcome by flies that attacked us and infested our car. If that wasn't enough, the skies grew dark and it began to pour down rain and hail, causing the kids to be quite upset.

As I gingerly drove through the buckets of water being dumped on my windshield, our car stalled once again at a stop sign—just as we noticed that we were nearing the point of needing gas. We headed towards the nearest fill-up station. Once there, we discovered as we parked at the pumps that I couldn't locate my black leather wallet, which had camouflaged itself pretty well down between the two front seats! To make matters worse, Elaine couldn't spot any change or credit cards in her purse. She then realized that she had changed purses that morning and that all her cards had accidently been left on the counter at home. By that time, Elaine and I were madder than wet hens. I already felt under the weather to begin with, and it didn't get any better as the hours passed. The last thing I felt like was playing nice. Thankfully, after locating my hidden wallet, I paid for some gas so that we could make it home.

On arrival at our place, we parked, sighed, and found the whole ordeal more than a tad strange. We wondered for days afterward if anything of a spiritual nature had been working against us on our trip to Northern Bible Church. The day seemed so long that, by its end, my morning sermon seemed an eternity ago. I have never been one to be overly preoccupied with omens, but the events of that day taken together were as bad an omen as I could imagine. The ghastly ride home was, indeed, a portent, for it was a sign of the challenges and trials yet to come our way. God may not have been done with me in pastoral ministry, but I thought for sure that I was finished with all the headaches and heartaches.

I was wrong.

Inquisition

I DEVELOPED A FRIENDSHIP IN THOSE DAYS WITH A MINISTRY VETERAN WHO WAS in an interim pastoral role with a mid-sized church. To him, such a limited role was a plus, in that it was like having the best of both worlds; he felt that he had nothing much to risk by coming in and picking up after the last leader. He confessed that the ministry he had taken on was hardly a pick-up-the-pieces kind of job, though it did possess its skeletons. However, he shared how meaningful his role was, in that he was able to preach, counsel, marry, and bury without having a vested stake in relationships, existing politics, or leadership dynamics. My chat with him heightened my interest in going forward with Northern Bible Church. It seemed to be a freeing proposition. I calculated that such an interim role was like being a middleman; the church's history and future were more God's problem to deal with than mine.

I knew that doing church in a rural setting, regardless of the duration, would present a real test for my faith. I was convinced that my sole sore point would come from having to tolerate the insipient insects that came with the glory of living in a bountiful country setting. By this time in my life, while in my late-thirties, although I had bounced around geographically, I absolutely considered myself a city slicker in every sense of the term. I preferred malls to barns, and the bright lights and buzz of a bustling city to the droning of mosquitoes and lonely country roads. And yet God's call to us, if we are really open to Him, is unmindful of our wants. There are times when God's will for us comes laden with His divine sense of humour. However, it *always* comes our way, with the promise of His presence. There really is no place where we go for God, that His boundless grace won't go with us.

In any event, faced with the prospects of doing rural ministry, I was just thrilled to have two potential ministry irons in the fire, with possibly one big decision to make. Either way, I was once again in the desirable position I had aimed for: to be wanted by a church who believed in me, and who trusted in me enough to let me lead them.

The afternoon finally arrived for my one and only interview with the search committee of Northern Bible. As I sat in a cool, sterile-looking room in the basement of the church, surrounded by eight committee members, for some odd reason I felt less confident than I'd imagined I would. During the interview, it was my take on the situation that I was effectively fielding most of the inquiries batted my way. I even touted the fact that I was in the process of teaching myself New Testament Greek. Though I thought that news sounded impressive, it only managed to induce a few nods of acknowledgement amongst those in the room. *This is a tough crowd,* I thought to myself.

Before too long, I ran into the inevitable question pertaining to my ministry at Faith Church: "Tell us about your last ministry. You were there for two years. How did things go there?"

I really wanted to respond to those questions by saying, "I intended to soar with eagles at Faith, but I had to settle on running with the turkeys!" However, such a response, even if it would have been a humorous lead-in to a glum conversation, probably would have been interpreted as being disrespectful. I had anticipated this type of question and had rehearsed my answer for it ad nauseum. Prior to any potential interview, I envisioned myself sitting in front of a church leadership, talking my way through, and then out of, what had gone on at Faith Church—and at Grace Church, for that matter.

I had practiced my response like an actor goes about committing their lines to memory. Whether it was in the shower, while I was walking, or while I was driving, I massaged the answers I knew I might have to give one day. I did it until I'd honed it into an airtight, crack-proof response. With a good measure of bulked-up, healthy self-confidence, I resolved to stick to the story I had decided to offer as an opinion of what had transpired there. Carefully and calmly, I recounted the pertinent details that led to the eventual disintegration of my ministry there.

A pastor I knew who had been through a few tough interviews with parole-board-like search committees had coached me not to understate the consequences that my previous ministry misadventures had produced, both in me and the church I had left. He also advised me not to play the victim card, even though I may have felt like one. My overarching task was therefore to communicate the disappointments of my past ministries in light of the wisdom I had gleaned from them. It would have been all too easy for me to bash the leadership of Faith Church, and just as easily the leaders at Grace Church, yet that kind of act rarely, if ever, garners much respect or sympathy in the eyes of another church's search committee.

My game plan had to be to focus on what God had *taught* me from my austere ministry experiences, and how Northern Bible Church could benefit from that by hiring me. I proceeded to explain what I believed were my areas of giftedness, how the leadership and myself at Faith Church had been in the process of developing a five-year vision before opposition eventually led many, including the elders (who I was never sure were all for it), to pull from under my feet the rug of their support.

I mentioned nothing of the personal attacks on Elaine and me, or the waves of demonic activity that had engulfed the church. I felt that my appraisal of the goings-on at Faith Church, from my perspective, was the truth as far as I could decipher it, albeit *my side* of it. I concluded by reiterating that in all of the frustrations and unfortunate tussles over changes in the church, I had never lost my good intentions. I also emphasized the actual headway we had made in making the ministry the best it could be, as God's expression of His Body, in the town in which it existed.

My overriding objective throughout the interview was for the search committee to view me as remorseful about my past mistakes, and yet see me as unhindered, fully capable of initiating and dreaming in the future. I desired for them to see me as being realistic about the challenges in ministry, but still hopeful of being successful in whatever capacity I ministered in. It was a tricky balancing act, but I felt I pulled it off. I may not have said enough to get me hired, but I was positive of the fact that I had said nothing to harm my chances, either.

I wrapped up my debriefing of the time I spent at Faith Church by intimating that I had failed to see how far out in front of them I had gotten. In the fog of conflict, I explained, the church mistook me for the enemy. If there was one lasting imprint I aimed to leave on the search committee, it was for them to see that though I was willing to take tangible blame for what had transpired at Faith, I was not willing to bear the brunt of it.

Whether I came across as humble or not, I'll never know, yet I found that day a new resolve to stop feeling sorry for my past, to stop feeling so judgemental towards myself. As the afternoon interview came to a close, as if to pronounce a final verdict on my candidacy, one committee member, prematurely affirmed, "That's good enough for me!" I was relieved by that comment, even delighted; however, I found my eyes wanting to rove around the table, to study the other facial expressions. I wasn't sure that everyone at the table was as cool with some of my responses as that person was. Some of the best poker faces I have ever seen have come from members of search committees! Northern Bible's was no different; they weren't giving me enough to make an accurate read.

I once heard someone remark, "There's no easy way to ice a burnt cake… sooner or later, someone will take a bite and know what's been covered up!" If all I had to do was explain away the ugly realities of my time at Faith Church, it would have been a piece of cake. Not many pastors who have been around the block a few times can boast of accident-free records. Most search committees will excuse a sordid ministry story coming from a pastoral candidate; perhaps they even expect to hear at least one. One trying ministry experience can be one too many, but having to account for *two* consecutive ones—in the span of three and a half years—was like a ball-and-chain at every subsequent interview after Faith.

I knew there was a very real chance that Northern Bible might do their own exploratory check-up on my time at Faith Church. I was truly at the mercy of a convincing, sovereign God to go ahead of me and open new ministry doors. If I was to be hired by any church, let alone Northern Bible, I knew it had to be God's doing, not as a result of any masterful spindoctoring on my part. Although I believed in principle that God's willing hand had reached into the decisions of search committees in the past, as I awaited Northern Bible's decision about my candidacy, I knew without a doubt that this time I was living it.

As the interview broke up and everyone prepared to vacate the room, one of the members stood up and halted everyone in their tracks. "Do we even need to wait on this? Can't we vote right now?" he prematurely pleaded.

The other members of the search committee, however, were not as keen on inducing such a decision, and promptly shot down the idea. I didn't know how to take his comment, either. However, I was banking on it being a good indication that my days of rehearsing answers to defend my less than exemplary track record were behind me—even if it was just for an interim position.

CHAPTER 47

In the Moment

I realize it isn't the case for more people than we might expect, but my favourite time of the year is the Christmas season. There's something about the anticipation leading up to the day—the sounds, the smells, and the sights—that has always provided an escape for me. No matter what might be going on in my life, there's always the Christmas season to hide myself in. Call it a stab at trying to make time stand still, but I call the weeks leading up to Christmas a gift *before* the gifts! All I have to do is put on a CD of holiday music, watch a classic Christmas movie, smell some of Elaine's sugar cookies (which should be boxed and sold), or stroll through a nicely decorated mall carrying my favourite blend of coffee and I am in my happy place. Maybe you can relate, in that you could just curl up and hibernate during the Christmas season, like a bear with no cares. That's me. The season that has a reason has always made the pressing distractions and disappointments of my life seem stripped of their dead weight.

A lot of the things that grab our attention, including our imagination, are sensory. The day before my first hour on the job at Northern Bible Church, our family moved what we needed of our belongings into the garage of a bed-and-breakfast owned by some people who frequented the church. It was their way of putting our family up for a few weeks until we could find other, more long-term accommodations. The place was nothing short of fabulous. It was spacious and featured plenty of room for our young children to roam around.

Ron Mahler

The night we moved in, the appetising smell of hot chilli filled the upstairs. Also on the menu: apple crisp. My favourite! I liked the arrangements of our new digs immediately. The place was warm and every room was filled with the smell of a wood stove burning. The inviting, rustic interior resembled something of the best decorating shows I have ever seen. Outside, we could enjoy the sights and activities of the small town, which sat perched on the shores of a mirror-like lake, reflecting a palate of autumn colours.

Even my office in the church was like a hideaway: a place where I could open my books, make calls, plan, and comfortably glide back into the pastoral role at an easy pace. Compared to how my last church had me free-falling out of a ministry role, the immediate peace and satisfaction I felt at Northern Bible, where the expectations upon me were minimal, provided the ultimate soft landing. As I walked to my car one day during the first week after leaving the church building, gentle snow began to fall and litter the ground, a sight so postcard-like that I despaired of not having a camera on me. The next day, while in my office, I turned around at my desk to face the window, where Rudolph and Bambi got up close and personal with me on the other side of the glass. I could see the texture and detail of their skin; they were that close.

Those early days at Northern Bible were like a sanctuary. I believed I was truly being blessed once again by a God whom I resolved owed me nothing. If I had done anything right at Faith Church to deserve any earthly reward, I was convinced that our time in this beautiful new town, even if it was for a brief term, was exactly that.

I wish my time at Northern Bible Church had ended on the same lighthearted note on which it started. I wasn't in my new interim role for too long before I began to grow a bit restless. I didn't know how long I would be at the church.

This much we can know with crystal clarity: no church that a pastor inherits will be fully ideal. Some ministries embody congenital dysfunctions. For sure, all ministries come with "best before" dates, cycles of vitality, limited-time warranties, and absolutely *no* guarantees for the pastors who take them on. It would be wonderful if pastors and their families could go somewhere where they could minister forever, but we'll leave that much-sought after congregation, for Heaven! As much as there are no idyllic pastoral assignments out there, there are many whose pastors would, if they could, return to God and get their money back.

Suffice it to say, Northern Bible Church, like my previous two ministries, was yet another such place. Far from remaining the great pastoral ministry option that

Elaine and I had come to see it as, the church began to evolve into a whirligig of trials and traumas over the year that I would last there.

I sometimes hear church leaders say that they've "seen it all" in ministry. That's something I believed of my own career and calling after bowing out of Faith Church. More than a handful of people concurred that in light of what Elaine and I had gone through in each of our ministries so far, how much worse could any church be after that? Across the board, we were all wrong on that one. Northern Bible Church was *supposed* to be a nice respite for me as a tried, tested, but slightly tender leader, a place where I could get my leadership legs again without having to be too concerned about the church's ministry in the future. It was *supposed* to be a stepping stone where I could get revved up in my zeal again. It should have acted as a confidence-boosting vault horse, holding promise for better things ahead.

I made my peace with the fact that if my time at the church was relatively uneventful, even dull, that would be okay with me. If the people at Northern Bible appreciated my preaching and pastoral care, that would be enough kudos to keep me going. Conversely, if the people didn't like my personality, it wouldn't matter much to me. In any event, my predetermined escape plan was to take on The Believers' Church, located a few hours north of where I was at the time, which continued to reach out to me as their prime pastoral candidate. However, life in ministry is like life in general: it affords us no crystal ball to peer into to see what possible detours, disappointments, or devastations may lay ahead of us.

The Bible prescribes us to live by faith and be spiritually near-sighted enough to live, as Jesus said, by not worrying about tomorrow (see Matthew 6:24). We should sojourn in this world by daily staying in close consultation with God. Israel's prophets spoke of things in the future, things which they often didn't understand. Why then do we think we could do any better with our own futures? If I would have had the privilege of seeing a few months down the road when I dove into my ministry at Northern Bible, I would not be where I am in life and ministry today.

As a finite people of faith, God's wisdom is for us to live by concentrating on one day at a time, by not burdening ourselves with the tomorrows and next-years of our lives. All we can fathom is one day at a time. That's all we can handle.

As it would turn out, one year at Northern Bible was most likely all that any pastor could have endured if they had walked in my shoes. I left after one year, but that wasn't on account of my "interim" label expiring, nor was it a result of my accepting another pastoral position. That was how it was *supposed* to work out, but God doesn't operate by what is *supposed* to be, but rather according to what He *purposes* for us. God's ultimate spiritual outcome of our earthly problems is to use them to mature us, as His people, to ready us for when our faith shall be "sight," when we one day see our Saviour face to face. For that spiritually nutritious reason, we are allowed to experience pain.

If our hearts remain mouldable and receptive to being broken by God, He will use our trials as if they are clay to shape us into richly ornamented and useful vessels that resemble the beauty of His Son. When we're glued to a trial, it's sometimes hard to accept that anything good can come of it. However, there is no trial which God cannot redeem and glorify Himself through. The eternal hands that made the universe out of nothing also extend deep into the dark voids of our lives, making something out of our hopelessness. We need pain in our lives, and though we tend to shrink back from any onset of it, God wills to bring about refined servants from the kilns of suffering He allows us to be in (see 1 Peter 1:7). After all, if Jesus was made perfect through obedience that required suffering, why should we expect any different as His sin-prone people? (see Hebrews 5:8)

Never in my wildest dreams could I have scripted that any good would come from what would eventually go down at Northern Bible Church. What transpired in the course of the lone year I was there knocked me down with such brute force that it nearly put me out for the count as a pastor.

It was an experience from which I almost didn't get up off the mat. Northern Bible Church would prove to be my greatest heartache yet—a prospect that was altogether inconceivable to Elaine and me before we jumped on board.

Sparring Partners

Northern Bible Church was situated about twenty kilometers from the nearest town, which in itself boasted a population of only five thousand people. Being a ministry that was somewhat out of the way was a problem in terms of visibility for the church. It was also the reason why my city-boy views of ministry sounded a tad like an alien language to some ears at the church. A few of its leaders, from their own admissions, were wary and suspicious of those who came from the city, with "their way of doing things." Such comments seemed inconsequential to me, especially as someone who had no thoughts of ever being their permanent pastor. I was determined to see myself as someone who was just passing through. Admittedly, during the interviewing process at Northern Bible, I was always a step ahead mentally, distracted by the other church (The Believers' Church) I had applied to, which held more of my interest. Though it was hard not to look over the shoulder of Northern Bible, it was harder still to wait for the day when I could know for sure where Elaine and I would eventually end up.

Within my first few months at Northern Bible, though some well-meaning congregants held their own agendas, it was the consensus of the church's leadership (at their denomination's urging) not to entertain any ideas of asking me to consider the permanent position. "A church should never hire the interim pastor," one of their denominational executives insisted. It was thought to be unfair to the pastor, especially if the one they were following was around the church for longer than ten years. Indeed, my job at Northern was to put some time between their last pastor and the full-time one who would come after me.

However, that philosophy didn't keep some people in the church from dropping a few subtle hints wishing otherwise. After one Sunday service, a fellow I was in conversation with turned and inquired of a deacon within earshot, "Why are we looking at anyone else?" At other times, a few older ladies would use a handshake as an opportunity to pull me close and whisper, "I hope we keep you." Certain people's support and adoration of me was even voiced in board meetings.

Having a popular interim pastor on their hands posed a dilemma for the search committee, as well as for the deacons' board. Though my knowledge of how favourable I had become in the eyes and hearts of many fed my self-esteem, I kept looking ahead, hoping for the other church to open for me. There were moments when Elaine and I had lengthy Sunday afternoon discussions where we arrived at the mutual observation that Northern couldn't be our church, even if most of the people desired that we stay. Elaine and I had spent too long a period of time harbouring regrets over not heeding the check in our spirits we had felt with respect to our decision to go to Faith Church.

Three months into our ministry at Northern Bible Church, I was invited to preach at The Believers' Church. It was the ministry where I ultimately aimed to go. Things seemed to be lining up for Elaine and me just the way we had thought they would.

My candidacy at The Believers' Church was an experience in itself. This church had a bloated search committee of sixteen individuals, and they were the first test in finding out if it was, indeed, God's will for us to go there. Miraculously, perhaps, all the members were unified in going forward with me, after interviewing me twice.

Being unanimously accepted by a search committee wasn't a new deal for us, of course; what was new was the fact that sixteen people were able to get on the same page. The church had a core of over one hundred and twenty people, which lent to us feeling a trifle intimidated. Because of its size, we thought about all the different personalities and possible power dynamics that would be involved.

Then there was the matter of one venerable, influential elder who pulled his support of my candidacy just prior to the congregational vote. This came about as a result of an all too familiar conflict that arose over a question I issued the elder's team in a private interview with them. The unanticipated tempest that disrupted my near "in the bag" status spawned from something as silly as it was sad.

My Fanatical, Regrettable Tour of Ministry

As I sat with the elders a few days prior to the vote, I thought it prudent to gauge the openness of the six men to allow multimedia presentations to be played in their services, as a cultural vehicle from which to bridge spiritual truth to the perceived spiritual needs of non-believers. I was told that from time to time they would have non-Christians sit in their services, some of whom were married to believing spouses in the church. There I was, consciously going down the seeker path once again, only this time I was determined to rock the boat before I dared boarding it, to see if such a proposition (showing video in the church) was a dealmaker or a dealbreaker. I may as well have insulted the man's character! The aforementioned dissenting elder was so offended by my inquiry that he couldn't keep himself from releasing a diatribe of sentiments over my proposal to bring "secular" movies into God's "sanctuary."

"Why would we do that?" the stirred-up elder interrupted. "You are bringing the realm of the world into the church by doing that!" I knew right then and there that my inquiry had touched a real bugaboo in this person's life. It was obvious by this elder's quick, sharp response that the topic was a sore spot, and an area of contention for him. I respected that, on the spot, but it didn't stop him from carrying on with his thoughts. Not only did the elder tell me what he *really* felt, but the colour of his face turned a few shades redder with every passing theological point as to why the realm of Satan could not be allowed to compromise the church. By that point, I didn't know whether I felt more sorry for raising the subject or if I was just plain embarrassed. However, I couldn't help but feel that this man wanted me to put on my theological boxing gloves and fight him, right then and there.

I took the bait. Perhaps unwisely, I gave him what he wanted. I poked at this gentleman a bit more, tried to dialogue in such a way that forced him to hear me out on the issue. I mentioned how I had once played a segment of the Mel Gibson film *The Patriot* in a church service, in order to show what courage looked like in a tangible, visible way. It was part of a message I'd taught on God's charge to Joshua to be strong and courageous as he led the Israelites over into the promised Land of Canaan after the death of Moses. My argument, however, only served to upset this elder even more. As some of the other elders jokingly ribbed him for his revelation, that he and his wife didn't even go to watch movies in theatres, he became volcanic in his anger. He was royally ticked. The feeling in the room grew more discomforting by the second. By the end of the meeting, I didn't think he liked me very much, and I was convinced that any form of media (be it video, interpretive dance, or drama) were off the table.

Ron Mahler

I can remember feeling a simultaneous mixture of disappointment and relief over the fact that the blow-up had taken place before I took the job. The chairman of the search committee and head of the elders' board took me aside after the meeting and frantically asked me if not being able to bring creative media into the service was a deciding factor for me. I didn't hide the fact that what had just occurred in the room was a troublesome sign. The other elders encouraged me that the lone elder's outburst was isolated, that they didn't believe that he was representative of the leadership's greater views on the subject. They told me, in addition, that they didn't have any problem with me introducing video footage into their services, so long as I used the appropriate discretion in my choices. We agreed that should I be voted in as their pastor, we would try to revisit the idea at a later time, when the people had had a chance to get use to me.

By the way in which the chairman spoke, it seemed as though he felt my being voted in was a foregone conclusion. He also communicated that his support of me, as well as that of the rest of the search committee, would probably remain intact. This was the person I mentioned earlier, the one with whom I eventually formed a close friendship. He was a deeply spiritual man who was burdened not only for his own spiritual growth, but for that of his own older children.

Unfortunately, one hairy experience seemed to lead to another in the days leading up to the decisive congregational vote. There are some setups that a pastor just can't see coming, when they accept invitations to people's homes during their candidacy. This happened to me the day after my foiled meeting with the elders.

Due to my interim status at Northern Bible Church, I had been allotted enough time by them to visit with the other church before I preached for a call there. In total, our family spent five days at The Believers' Church.

While our children were being watched by a babysitter, Elaine and I accepted an invite to have lunch with a couple from the church who could have tried a bit harder to disguise their obvious purpose in having us come to their home for a visit. The husband happened to be the brother of a rather high-profile member of the church. The invitation to lunch, however, was a bit of a front for a private interview which this husband desired to hold with me. His brother had a reputation for being a bit headstrong in his ultra-conservative ministry views, but it was his brother and his wife who would be his mouthpiece on this day.

A few questions were lobbed at me as we began to eat. We weren't too far into the first course when the husband inquired, "So, Ron, what are your thoughts about where Jesus stands with other religions?"

I could tell this man found it difficult to grapple with the possibility that God might work in other faith backgrounds, through Christ, to bring people to Him. I was quizzed with such questions as "Are Muslims going to Heaven?" and "Does God hear the prayers of people who aren't Christians?"

My default answer, as is the case with many Christians, was to leave that decision to the ultimate sovereignty of God. "Only God knows for absolute sure where each person is with Jesus," I replied. "Including a Muslim." That said, I reminded him of what Christ said: *"I am the way and the truth and the life"* (John 14:6), and, *"Whoever believes in the Son has eternal life, but whoever rejects the Son will not see life, for God's wrath remains on him"* (John 3:36). More often than not, such a response dismantles the kind of theological snap-trap I was about to step into.

Silly me, I couldn't let the situation go by without at least issuing some form of challenge to this man. Perhaps it was my tussle with the irate elder the day before that had me feeling a little worked up. As a result, I was in the mood for some theological sparring over this guy's borderline self-righteous bigotry. In response to his question, I took a deep breath and blurted out that if Jesus were around today, on earth, He might even go to a mosque with His Muslim friend.

Elaine swivelled sideways in her chair and looked at me. Out of her peripheral vision she seemed to say, *Be careful, Ron.*

"Oh, really?" the husband came back with, surprised. "What makes you think that?"

I could tell the guy didn't think a whole lot of the hypothesis. "Jesus was seeker-oriented," I went on. "The Lord might have figured that His Muslim friend, though very religious, needed to hear what prayer sounded like, as petitioned to a personal God. But Jesus might have said something to the effect of, 'While you pray, I will pray to my Father, and to the One whom I know hears prayer.'" The point I was making was that prayer crosses over religious boundaries, if one prays to God the Father, in Jesus' name.

By that time in our discussion, the hole I'd dug for myself was so deep that the guy tried to bury me in it. "I don't agree at all with you," he said with a hint of arrogance. Addressing his wife, as she removed dishes from the table, he said, "I can't believe a Christian pastor could have such a view! Jesus never entered pagan temples to pray. How could you say such a thing?"

"How can we know with certainty where Jesus chose to pray and where He did not?" I shot back with the fervour of someone who enjoyed playing the

Ron Mahler

Devil's advocate. "Don't you think it's possible that He took fieldtrips with His disciples to observe how the pagans worshipped, and used those teaching moments to draw spiritual applications?"

I was trying to show this individual the possible lengths to which Jesus might have gone to reveal people's need for the love and mercy of God, which was available to them in the Kingdom He was bringing, qualities which He embodied as the Saviour. For a second, I thought this man would brand me a heretic and accuse me of blasphemy. He shifted in his chair and shook his head, as if he was ready to ask me to leave. I concluded my heated debate with this man by confessing that the thoughts I had just shared with Him were not my own. I revealed that they were simply a point of view, one which I felt had merit, and that if he had any further disputes about them, he could take them up with a well-established and respected faculty member of one of Canada's most prominent conservative seminaries, where the thoughts originated. I left the lunch feeling a little bit like I'd gone the distance with this man, who would vehemently oppose anyone's theological suppositions as long as they didn't match his own.

Don't misunderstand what I'm saying. We need to be scripturally sound and not waver on theological non-negotiables, but this guy had such an air of religious dogmatism and smugness that I felt it was my duty to challenge him. All Elaine and I had intended by accepting the invitation to this couple's home was to have a nice, cordial get-to-know-you conversation; we hadn't bargained on leaving with such a bad taste in our mouths, which had nothing to do with the food on the menu.

As my visit with the church dragged on into its fifth and last day, I realized that the more I scratched away at some of the spiritual perspectives and ministry philosophies of the upper echelon at the church, the more I wondered if I was a compatible leader for them.

After my lunch engagement that day, I felt like the number of people who would decide against my candidacy was about to take a huge spike. Despite that possibility, there was enough sense left in me not to call the whole thing off. Overall, Elaine and I still liked the ministry.

Chapter 49
Sliding Doors

After preaching my "call" sermon at The Believers' Church, I thought my delivery and overall performance in the pulpit was adequate, leaving the church the job of judging whether or not they desired for me to become their next pastor. I did my homework with the church. From my past experiences, I had learned the hard way that every ministry setting, no matter how healthy a face they put on, has hereditary sicknesses. Seeing symptoms are one thing, but knowing what the sickness is and how it might be treated is vital for the incoming shepherd.

Realistically, churches are dysfunctional families with crosses on the tops of their houses. Unlike the families we are born into, however, we get to choose whether or not we're going to take on certain churches.

One day I contacted the former pastor of The Believers' Church. I was a bit nervous at first, but it turned out to be beneficial. Though he seemed surprised to hear from me, the pastor was willing enough to give me his recollections of the good and the bad in his time at the church. The conversation acted as a valuable guide for me to assess how I saw the personalities and powers lining up within the church hierarchy. The former pastor gave me a head's up in naming three people who could present trouble for me if I were to take on the church. Predictably, I had already experienced some form of difficulty with two of the three people he named. Most churches have such names, don't they? I have known of several in my time; no doubt we all have. It's hard to think of fellow Christians in that light—after all, they possess the same Holy Spirit we do and love the same Jesus we do. That said, good reputations are like money; here today, and too easily gone the next. Some of God's people, for whatever reason, habitually make ministering at their churches a chore, no matter who the leader is. As Christians, it is as unfortunate as it is mysterious.

Whether we like to face the fact or not, even believers like to have their egos stroked from time to time. There are those Christians who like to be an upfront presence, who don't mind nonverbally giving the impression that they like the spotlight being put on them. Others are pastor-wannabes, people who have a knack for telling the minister how things should be done. There are those well-intentioned Christians who act as gatekeepers to the institution of the church, as well as others who have to be "in the know" or need to feel important. This shouldn't surprise us, however. The gospels reveal that the very followers of Christ jockeyed and jousted for titles and positions in the Kingdom of God. The Believers' Church, in this way, was a church no different from any other.

The day they voted on my candidacy, those who could flex their disgust and distrust in me had the voting power to do so. And they did. I needed a minimum of 85% of the people to vote in my favour in order to become the new pastor. On the very morning of the vote, I recall being restless as to what I wanted more: to keep searching for an even better situation for Elaine and I, or to get settled in at The Believers' Church, its ostensive challenges aside. The church had a good emphasis on outreach. There was a history of good, solid Bible teaching. There was a core of young families, as well as an up-and-coming youth ministry. In addition to all that, I really liked a few of the leaders, and I relished the opportunity to minister alongside them.

Elaine's and my trusted circle of friends simply prayed that God's will be done for us in the final outcome. If the result was a "no," we would have to see it as God's roadblock; if it was a "yes," we would see it as God's permissive voice for us to take on a church whose leaders were genuinely hooked with my gifts, strengths, and abilities as a pastor.

The night before the vote, I asked to meet with the elder who I had become quasi best friends with. Over coffee, we discussed an array of topics, including our individual passions for ministry and our love for our families. However, my main concern was in reference to a couple of the leaders at Believers who I had observed were suddenly not as positive about my candidacy as they had once appeared to be. Whether it was a case of cold feet or not, I couldn't have been faulted for fearing that I might run into another crisis. After some of my

My Fanatical, Regrettable Tour of Ministry

prior hurts in ministry, I couldn't possibly relive those kinds of agonizing hurts again—or so I thought. This elder calmed me by making an observation that he felt would make an immediate, lasting impression upon the people at the church, and in time win over even those who might not vote for me.

As if with x-ray vision, he told me that he could tell that I had a big-time pastor's heart, and that he and his wife really hoped I would come to The Believers' Church. I felt better about things after our talk, yet this man represented only one vote, and I was certain that the two fellows I had disagreements with hadn't kept their views about me to themselves.

The call announcing the results of the vote came in much later in the day than I had expected it to. It was too easy to speculate that something had gone wrong, a hunch which would turn out to be right. The sombre and shaky voice of the caring, friendly elder was on the other end of the phone. The inflection and tone of his words communicated to me that he was fighting back a good cry.

"It was a no vote, Ron," he quietly lamented. "I don't know what happened. I'm really sorry." The problem, I was told, was not the result of the vote as much as it was what they had discovered as the ballots were being counted.

Four different types of ballots came back to the scrutineers: those with "yes" on them, those marked by a "no," some disqualified ballots reflecting a "yes" as well as a "no" vote, as well as some with no preference mark at all. The elder was so distraught that it felt like I was the one who had to do the consoling. The final tally reflected a bizarre 84. 2% vote in favour of me coming on as their pastor, a result that might have been good enough for some churches, but not good enough at Believers'.

I was stupefied at how close I had come from an affirmative result. At first, I thought it was a joke, but the elder wasn't letting on that he was kidding around. The result of the vote, however, wasn't anything near being funny. If the vote would have fallen decisively short, I would have felt a lot more clarity. I could have chalked it up to a total misreading of the people at the church. The elder expressed that according to their constitution, the vote could not be graciously accepted as being "close enough."

Though I was .6% off from being voted in, the suspicious activity that surrounded the vote invariably showed that some of the people at The Believers' Church were not in my corner, and had made that known. Even though it amounted to 15% of the naysayers telling 85% of the rest what was best for the church, they had just enough pull to be *heard*, and just enough numbers to keep me out.

Ron Mahler

The real kicker was when I became aware of the fact that two people (who would have voted in my favour), had forgotten to get their ballots in to the church while they were away on holidays; no proxy votes were allowed to be accepted. Those two votes would have obviously catapulted me over the top. It all seemed too weird, but also too easy to believe that something demonic had taken place the night of the vote. Then again, we all know what happened to the poll results in the state of Florida during the 2000 U.S. presidential election. Though casting ballots should be an exact science, human error and a malfunctioning system of counting votes can factor in. However, the results at The Believers' Church could only be blamed on the people themselves.

I was subsequently asked by the chairman of the search committee if I wanted the church to take another vote. In hindsight, I should have gone by the rule that Elaine and I established before the first vote, that a "no" vote was a "no"—from *God*. Period! However, after a period of two weeks, in which both ourselves and the leaders at The Believers' Church prayed intensely for God's guidance, Elaine and I came to the conclusion that due to the odd turn of events during the voting, perhaps another kick at the cat was warranted. One can interpret silence from God one way or another, yet either way, a perceived non-response from Him is the hardest response for anyone to take. Feeling as if it was our choice to make, Elaine and I resolved that we owed it to ourselves, as well as to those at the church who had thrown their support behind us, to permit the leaders to hold another congregational vote.

We also figured that once again we could count on God's sovereignty to rule the day (and the vote), no matter the result. As much as I was willing to concede that God's providence may have played a part in my missing a "yes" vote, by the slimmest of margins, I couldn't discount that the Devil had worked his way into the situation as well. It was close to Christmas time at that point, so a second vote wouldn't take place until the new year (January 2004), which was roughly seven weeks after the first one.

The second congregational vote at The Believers' Church, free from any observable shenanigans on the part of God's people, yielded an almost identical result to the first one: I received an 84% vote. God had spoken, and the door into the church I had once thought myself a shoe-in for was slid shut. It was only then that I turned my heart towards the one door I had already walked through. My only other viable option was Northern Bible, and they weren't even supposed to hire me.

Difficult Decisions

As a pastor who's endured multiple painful ministries, I'm thankful for those churches that God kept me away from taking on. Though no pastor likes to be rejected, any given church's decision to turn them down shouldn't be viewed as a personal failure, as a rejection of their giftedness. Rather, sometimes, closed ministry doors should be seen as acts of God's mercy. As my own experience attests, though God doesn't always divert us from walking into difficult situations, He knows which ones He wants us to take on, and which ones He doesn't.

Five years ago, I preached for another call at a church that had a much lower vote threshold for a pastor to be extended an invitation. This particular church held to a 70% bar, but after I preached what I thought was a fairly well-crafted and well-received message, I only received a 65% vote. That experience devastated me, for more reasons than the results.

The leading deacon of this church, who was designated to give me the bad news, astonishingly rubbed the proverbial salt in my wound, telling me how he thought that I had looked "all nervous and uptight" that morning. For lack of a better term, the deacon went on to tell me that I was the one who had basically "blown it." I knew that the deacon was partly speaking through his frustrations of having to conduct more interviews, and that he was upset over the fact that their church had already been without a pastor for a lengthy period. Still, I can tell you that to this very day, I get down on my knees and thank God for slamming the door shut on that ministry. When a pastor is handed the blame for something that went wrong in the church before they even get there, *they shouldn't go there.*

My candidacy experience at The Believers' Church managed to push me closer to the people and ministry at Northern Bible Church. Most of those who had some knowledge of my candidacy at another church felt bad for Elaine and me, for the expenditure of time and emotion we had invested.

As the number of suitable resumes coming in to the search committee's mailbox began to dwindle, they inevitably began to look more in my direction as their permanent pastor. That occurrence also lit a fire under my already pumped and vocal fan club, who were more than a little motivated, now that I was an eligible candidate, to coronate me as the next pastor of Northern Bible.

I was touched and inspired by their rallying around me, yet it created an unforeseen scenario for Elaine and me. The million-dollar question burning within us was whether Northern Bible Church was the right ministry for us, even if there were no other ministry prospects open to us. We coveted the luxury we'd enjoyed only a few months earlier, of not thinking we'd have to make such a choice. Now, with every congregational criteria aligning in our favour at Northern, we needed to make a decision. Once again, we had come face to face with potentially the biggest ministry decision we had yet to make. In light of the rough rides we'd had in our two previous ministries, which had hurt us both, we knew we couldn't afford another ministry disaster.

At face value, and from what I could determine, Northern Bible Church didn't have that much in the way of possible trouble spots, if certain parts of the ministry weren't tinkered with. I wasn't enthralled with the tinge of country gospel that their worship music came across as sounding like. Elaine and I weren't altogether comfortable with how the majority of the people looked so well put-together—men in suits women in nice pantsuits or dresses. For me, the congregation almost appeared too prim and polished at times. We were more accustomed to ministries where the attire one wore to church didn't exactly represent their "Sunday best," but instead represented who they were—and where they were—as people. I also wasn't too crazy about the fact that the church was situated next to a cemetery. If stereotypes tell us that a lot of unchurched people view the atmosphere of most church services as resembling "funerals," then having a graveyard out front wouldn't provide a lot of incentive to enter the church.

Even though the believers in those graves were a part of the great cloud of witnesses overlooking Northern Bible Church, walking by gravestones has always depressed me, wondering whether or not that person was in God's eternal presence or not. On another level, cemeteries tend to remind most people of their own mortality, which can either be seen as the rock that gets them back to church or the monument that keeps them focussed on their fear of death. Taking those factors into serious consideration, my peremptory response to those in the church who wanted me to consider replacing my interim status with a *permanent* one should have remained a categorical "no."

At the time, our family was living in a cabin some thirty kilometres away. The drive to the church was lengthy, and a bit burdensome to us who were not used to the types of winter conditions and steep inclines, that characterized the roads in the region, even if it was a creative masterpiece to behold.

Elaine and I desperately wanted to know God's will for us, and we intensely feared landing in another church where we would later regret being. On top of receiving bundles of sage advice from mature Christians, Elaine and I weighed out, on paper, all the pros and cons of taking on the ministry at Northern on a more permanent basis. We also balanced the risks and rewards of saying yes or no; it goes without saying that pouring over God's Word and waiting upon Him in prayer was paramount in our hour of decision. After being at the church for five months, the deacons at Northern Bible Church approached me to consider preaching for a call. I would also be granted a two-week period in which to accept their call, in the event that the vote went in my favour, as was expected by the majority.

I consulted about the opportunity with a friend, who reminded me that sometimes timing was a good indicator of God's will. The church seemed to have come along at a desperate time for Elaine and me, something that had become a recurring theme in our marriage. Besides, the last time we had made a ministry decision out of somewhat desperate circumstances, it hadn't exactly worked out well for us. However, with Elaine home with our two young children—one of them not even a year old—and no other ministries on the horizon, we felt pressed up against the something-has-to-give glass.

We were also nearing the point where we needed to find a more permanent place to move to (déjà vu all over again), for the cabin we were renting was part of a camping resort, and we needed to free up the living space. Important questions about our situation flooded our hearts and minds. Was the timing of Northern Bible Church and *their* lack of any other suitable ministry candidates a sure-fire clue that God was calling us there? Or was His will for us as simple as our common sense, in that we remained too unsure as to whether we and the church were a match made in Heaven?

Ron Mahler

We still harboured some thorny reservations about the complexion of the ministry at Northern. However, I scrambled to accept that perhaps the kind of church *I* wanted wasn't the kind that God desired for me to have. Maybe it was me who needed to learn a new trick, and not the church I was sent to. Perhaps I needed to learn something in the way of a leadership lesson, a lesson I hadn't learned from my time at Faith Church.

At this point, we had roughly two months to find another place to live, in a town where vacancies were as sparse as they were impractical and unsuitable. Nothing about the decision we had to make appeared straightforward. Once again, we were in the unenviable position of having to choose a ministry, more out of a hope that we would adapt to it than out of a deep conviction that it was where we belonged.

We all fail spiritually at times in our lives, but the failures in my Christian life—my failure to trust God more so, my failure to decline ministries I didn't feel a healthy tug towards— have come with a hefty price tag. I reasoned that if I turned Northern Bible Church down, I would probably not get another ministry opportunity anytime soon. God had put Elaine and me in a corner, where we simply had to exercise faith in Him. No matter what choice we made, we had to remember the fact that He was still in control.

We continued to lack clarity about our place at the church, yet in the end it was the people at Northern Bible who factored hugely in our eventual decision to accept a permanent call. What was interesting, as the months went on and the spiritual condition of the church began to take a bad turn, was the advantage we had to begin with to be able to make a truly informed decision, for we had already been at the church for nearly half a year. One would have thought that by that point in our lives, we should have been the consummate decision makers.

If it was possible, this latest decision was the worst yet.

Blind Acceptance?

I informed the deacons at Northern Bible that I would accept the call to be their new permanent pastor, if voted in as such. After the formality of preaching for the call was completed one sunny but brisk February morning, the congregation gave me a convincing 100% vote. I had easily cleared the 75% hurdle required by their constitution!

One member of the church, a tall, imposing man, came lumbering out of the church and walked right up into my personal space. He stated that if anyone had voted against me, they'd have to be shot. The comment came across as brazen and odd, almost as much as I considered it a hearty endorsement in its own way. Such personalities formed the make-up of the church at Northern Bible. There were those who had an obtrusive slang that they weren't afraid to use, even if it sounded uncouth or didn't quite square with biblical expectations.

By far, Northern Bible was an assembly of predominantly middle-to-older-aged people. Many of them were accustomed to rural living and retired. They just seemed glad and relieved to have a leader—locked, stocked, and barrelled. Elaine and I resigned ourselves to believing that the church would grow on us, as many of its people already had.

There was something awkwardly underwhelming about the day I was crowned Northern's new pastor. I didn't in any way feel that a round of celebratory cartwheels was in order, or even a party. It was "just alright," as the saying goes. At the most, I felt a tempered joy that at the very least it was good to still be in ministry. At the age of thirty-six, I had become one realistic, if not pessimistic, pastor. The unsettling experiences of past ministries had naturally begun to colour my perceptions of every church I came into contact with.

Not that I felt every church after Faith was out to get me. I promised myself that I would no longer allow any church to captivate me to the extent that I blindly adopted the "things are going to be different here" mindset. The ministries at Grace and Faith had taught me something; I was becoming more astute at pinpointing potential hot buttons in ministries. Though it's advised that pastors not hold the unfortunate experiences of prior ministries against their present ones, past hardships can provide them with a valuable litmus test by which to guard them as they move forward. That's why, to this day, I still experience waves of regret over accepting the permanent pastor's position at Northern Bible Church. I should have known better.

In hindsight, I consider it one of my worst ministry decisions ever. Exactly eight months after a promising statement was made (the congregation's unanimous vote), unpredictable events would culminate in our leaving. Incredibly, though the previous hurts Elaine and I had endured might have been more than enough for other pastoral couples, Northern Bible would prove to be our saddest blow yet. Did we ask for it? Certainly not! Could it have been avoided? Absolutely! I have always rejected the temptation to believe that Elaine and I have some kind of invisible magnet stuck to us, courtesy of the pit of Hell, that orchestrates attacks and abuse from the very people we have tried ministering to. Though Satan would dearly love for nothing better than to take down as many church leaders as he can, perpetual behaviours in ministry usually lead to predictable consequences and results as well.

Life in general is like that. If we make a habit of eating a bag of Dorito's at 11:00 p.m. at night, we better believe that our stomach will consistently let us know that it doesn't appreciate it the next morning. There are cause-and-effect patterns built into every facet of our lives. They exist in the life of the church, as well. Christians who constantly undermine the authority of godly pastors and leaders, and who refuse to follow their lead, will drain the leader's joy and resolve, weakening the unity in the Body of Christ. Pastors, by the same token, who exhibit poor leadership ability will alienate themselves from those they are endeavouring to lead. As it is in life, it is in ministry; destructive habits or lessons unlearned always lead to the same ugly, hurtful results. Upon my commencing the ministry at Northern Bible Church, I sincerely believed that I had made a clean break from some of my more ill-advised and inexperienced decisions from past ministries.

My Fanatical, Regrettable Tour of Ministry

Not that I'm willing to acknowledge all the blame for what I'm about to recount from my brief time at Northern Bible, but I should have been slightly wiser than to have believed I could once again venture into the one area long known for its contention and potential to divide a church: worship. All the components of a ministry disaster in the making were textbook at Northern Bible Church, and should have made for a quick-and-easy reading of them. Once again, in my zeal to see change in the church, I neglected to read between some cautionary lines. In some ways, I just never thought things could get any worse from the way they had already been for me.

The older a church gets, the more bogged down with sacred cows it becomes. These sacred cows are the mainstays of its ministry: the cross behind the sanctuary, the pews, the organ, the hymnal vs. the screen, the order of service, the dress code, women's roles, etc. The more I ministered at Northern Bible Church, the more I uncovered such sacred cows. Merely recognizing these landmines is not nearly enough for a leader, however; being able to navigate safely around them is essential. Leaders are never the same after they've tripped landmines in the church! Though the church feels the explosion, and though some outside the pastor's office get injured in the process, it's usually the pastor himself and his ministry that gets the brunt of the blast.

I perceived the sacred cows at Northern Bible Church in a way that many, perhaps, couldn't. To me, they were cement shoes that kept the church's ministry not only sedentary on the inside, but practically immovable. In contrast to many of the more long-standing members, the sacred cows were objects of tradition and memories, which deemed them "untouchable."

Some churches may as well have their own Ten Commandments posted for every pastoral candidate to read. Commands such as: "Thou shall not move the pulpit to the left part of stage (it's been there for over fifty years, and so it shall remain until our Lord returns)." Maybe another command might read: "Thou shall not preach for more than twenty-five minutes (any pastor who has tried came in one door and we escorted him out the other)." This command is already in use in some churches: "Thou shall not use the Powerpoint when reading the scripture."

You name the "cow," every church has some that they hold sacred. It was obvious that Northern Bible Church had one in the form of, you guessed it, the music ministry. Looking back, it was definitely one of the so-called "untouchable" areas in the church that bordered on being venerated. Sadly, some at the church would literally go to war with me in order to protect their stake and claim in the music ministry.

Ron Mahler

Their attitudes and actions unveiled a type of unbridled pride and self-righteousness the likes of which I had never before witnessed in any church. This issue would not only bring an end to my brief term there, but would unnecessarily damage the vitality of the church for some years after. If it is true, as one pastor estimated to me after the fact, that it takes twenty-five years for a ministry to recover from the kind of church-quake that hit Northern, I wonder how long it should take those who had a hand in the event to get over it. In the first few years following our exit from the church, the kinds of emotions that would well up in Elaine and me, at the very mention of its name, were so raw in us that Northern Bible Church became known in our household as "the church that shall be referred to solely by its initials: N.B.C."

Digging Deeper

THE FIRST IMPRESSION ELAINE HAD OF ME WHEN SHE MET ME WAS THAT I WAS shy and quiet. In fact, a lot of people have that impression of me, even to this day. These are people, however, who have obviously never heard me preach, have never seen me watch my favourite sports teams during the playoff season, or seen how I can wail on my electric guitar! During our very first date, however, Elaine saw a different side of me; I was quite talkative, deep, and seemingly fun to be around, even though I tried to play hard to get by making her pay for her own desert!

When it came to our first encounter with Northern Bible Church, however, our first impressions should have made us wonder whether a second date was necessary. That very first day, when as the guest speaker we arrived at the church late, we were greeted to the sounds of music that was well-suited for a barn dance. In other words, the music was not an element of the ministry that would naturally attract us to it.

As we looked around, we noticed very little in the way of young people. *Here we go again,* we thought. We wondered why we kept meeting up with churches of this nature, where the younger generation was absent and the average age of the church was too high to attract them. This is one of the reasons why we initially resolved that Northern Bible couldn't possibly be the type of church we would go to after my interim role was over. We had a very young family and a serious burden to see young people present, serving, and growing in the local church.

Ron Mahler

Our background in youth ministry, not to mention our preference for contemporary expressions of Christian music, caused us to feel a bit restless and out of place from the Sunday morning atmosphere at Northern Bible. Though many Christians don't care what kind of music is played at church, there are those, like myself, who have always purported that the type of music a church plays on Sunday is important, on various experiential levels.

Most notably, worship music sets the tone for the rest of the service. It injects energy and a celebratory mindset, and can prime an increasingly distracted culture to stay "logged" in, focused, and more expectant as the service moves on. The worship music also communicates a philosophy of church ministry, in that it shapes an atmosphere of praise. Most importantly, our worship music can clearly communicate the ever-relevant, theological truth that God wills to put a new song in our mouths (see Psalm 40:3).

Even after subsequent visits to Northern Bible, we found the worship ministry to be reflective of a church that was in an obvious state of stagnant, fragmented decline. There were those at the church who represented some hope for change, yet they seemed reluctant to press too hard for it. Then there were those who were great servants and supporters of the ministry, who appeared indifferent to any direction it should take. There were also those individuals who unfortunately felt entitled to stand guard over the status quo, who felt responsible to batten down the hatches of their traditions. I would refer to these individuals as the "sheriffs" of the church; I may have been the pastor, but *they* were wearing the badges. They thought it was their God-given responsibility to ensure that nothing out of the ordinary happened under their jurisdiction.

For the better part of the year, I played it cool, both as the interim pastor, and then as the permanent pastor. I didn't tip my hand either way as to what kind of music I preferred, or even that I wouldn't have minded joining the worship team now and again. I concentrated on building up the Body of Christ by instituting some concert of prayers, by formulating some ministry training and suggesting that the church put on a talent show to allow for the display of any hidden abilities. I used the evening to invite some of the young people who were associated with the church, young people who hadn't been around for a time. While those efforts were appreciated, I still felt burdened for what I was experiencing on Sunday mornings. Whenever the time came for me to get up to preach, I felt a type of malaise emanating from a lot of the people on a weekly basis. I decided to tell jokes before I preached, to loosen up the people I was about to talk to for half an hour.

Lacking, however, was an atmosphere of anticipation and expectation. The excitement level in the services, most Sundays, was near comatose. The congregation seemed to be lulled into the same countenance week after week. In saying this, I realize that the spiritual temperature of the people had a lot to do with the culture.

I was relieved to eventually hear that I was not the only one who felt the way I did about the services. Even a couple of the members on the worship team were looking for something new to take place with the mode of the music, something that would bring more variety. I noticed that a drum kit sat vacant on the platform most of the time. Knowing that I could play, I thought I would enlist myself, if they were willing. I was trying to be cautious to a fault, thinking that if I were to effect any change in the music ministry, the team needed to see me as one of them. For a time, my involvement with the worship team was a complete success. Adding drums to music often completes the sound, and for sure it keeps the other instruments (including the vocals), in time. They communicated that I added a component to the worship that was missing. In part, I agreed.

The problem was not necessarily having a full band as it was the predominant style of music and their predictable choice of songs. Though there wasn't the typical hymn vs. chorus, tug of war going on, the choruses they did play, if I had been blindfolded and didn't know any better, would have convinced me that Johnny Cash was the band leader. That may sound neat to some, even attractive to others, but after receiving a steady diet of it for over six months, the wear and tear on my resolve to remain cautious and patient about the music broke down.

I began to discuss my feelings on a deeper level with one of the deacons, and took to prayerfully considering a certain proposal for the leadership. I knew I was in the minority of those in the church who thought the Sunday morning worship could use a bit of a facelift. By communicating this, I knew of two particular leaders (who themselves were members of the worship team) who would likely take offense. I was right. The stony looks on their faces when I discussed my idea with them told the story!

Nonetheless, that didn't dissuade me from suggesting that we needed to generate a little more enthusiasm in the services, to shake people out of their comfort zones. I asked them to consider having an alternative worship team take the service once a month. This would not have been an altogether foreign thought to them, for Northern Bible at one point in its history had multiple worship teams. This second worship team, I proposed, would introduce some newer worship songs and play in a more contemporary style. I felt at the time that it was a positive step forward, and one that might even persuade some of their absent youth to come back to church. Being at the church for roughly seven months at that point may not have been long enough for me to have amassed the trust and respect I needed to earn as their leader

However, if I was truly their leader and they were looking for me to lead, I reckoned that they needed to at least hear what I had to say. Like them, I knew full well of how many families would drive by Northern Bible Church on their way to the larger, more attractive contemporary church in the next town. They were growing; we were clearly not.

Some of the leaders on the board didn't seem as concerned as I was about our inability to lure families to church. I, as well as a few other leaders on the board, didn't share their indifference. Predictably, my suggestion was met with some opposition, even prejudice. Select members of the worship team each took turns expressing their concerns about having two separate worship teams. One felt that employing two teams would only set up competition in the eyes of the people. Another went as far as to state that it would make the church appear like it was trying to compete with the other, larger churches, and that basically there wasn't enough talent in the church to support two teams, anyway.

I thought the comment about the lack of talent was a bit odd, considering that there were obviously some great musical abilities scattered in and amongst the congregation; either they were unaware of them, or they were ignoring them. But I was becoming increasingly aware of something far more spiritually alarming: the air of superiority coming from members of the worship team was not only unacceptable, but worrisome. Though I tried to understand the perspectives of some of the existing worship team members, I couldn't help but feel that they were biased opinions, to say the least. To me, they were not good enough reasons, in and of themselves, to totally waylay the idea of creating and implementing an alternative worship team. It wasn't something that had to take form overnight, or even in the immediate future. If the plan to create another worship team didn't work, I agreed that it should be scraped and revisited at a later time.

However, I couldn't help but sense that there were some on the worship team who perhaps wanted the whole thing to fail before it ever had a chance to succeed. The idea was never to take anything away from the appreciation of the first worship team; rather, my hope was to complement them. I had already discerned from observing the two leaders on the worship team that they were more than comfortable with presiding over and directing the worship ministry. It's always safer for a pastor to embrace a good ministry initiative that they didn't

My Fanatical, Regrettable Tour of Ministry

generate on their own. It would have been far easier for me if the idea of forming an alternative worship team had come from one of the existing worship team members. However, from what I had gathered, there was a better chance of selling an Eskimo a refrigerator than that happening. Yet something in me, foolish or not, was unwilling to back down.

That decision thrust me into a divisive and highly injurious battle with most of the existing worship team members. They used their leverage of seniority, and their popularity with some in the church, to put an eventual end to my hopes of having multiple worship teams at Northern. I fully understood that the territorial attitudes of some on the worship team were indicative of the reality that the music ministry was *their* area, and had been that way for many years before I came along. I was also aware that their previous pastor and his wife not only had held a significant role in the Sunday morning worship, but had been allowed to influence its direction.

Given the pounding I had received over the changes in worship music at Faith Church, I probably needed my head examined for even attempting to tamper with the music at Northern Bible. Far from my being a glutton for punishment, I genuinely believed I had learned enough from my last experience to effectively spearhead a transition in this church from a one-style/one-worship team model to a multi-styled/multi-worship team music ministry. I might have attempted to do so too soon, yet a second worship team might not ever have worked at Northern.

In ministry, reading people and political situations, is an invaluable leadership tool to possess. I do that much better now than I ever have before. Incoming pastors and other church leaders are usually more adept at being able to be objective about a given ministry than the existing members are. Even though I have made my mistakes in ministry, it might just be that I actually had my leadership finger on the "pulse" of the problem. At least half the people at Northern Bible recognized that to be true of my assessment. Consequently, they willingly got behind me, supporting any efforts on my part to challenge the deeply-static mentality that had bored down into the core of parts of its leadership. I wasn't alone in my discontentedness over where Northern's ministry was going.

One person from the church called me one day and communicated their frustration with the lack of vision at Northern Bible. He asked me for assurance that I had a plan. Though I felt rather insecure and miniscule in offering an answer, I alleviated his concerns by expressing my desire to see the church move ahead in its ministry. However, I cautioned him that it would not only take time, but also much prayer to see change take root and blossom. As with my concern with Faith Church, the task facing the leadership at Northern was that it desperately needed to consider why it wasn't growing numerically, and why its influence in a town it had been in for nearly a century was almost non-existent. Though I realize numerical growth is not always an accurate indicator of true, spiritual growth in the Body of Christ, Northern (like Faith Church) had been on a steady decline, attendance wise, for some years. For me, that reality spoke of the church's inability to inspire its community to identify with the church. As I have stated earlier, spiritual apathy and the darkness of people's lives can only account for so much of their absence in the church.

If anything, I determined that the tradition-huggers at Northern Bible were out of step, and out of touch, with many of the restless people within their own ranks. The problem for any church (irrespective of its size, style, or age) in reaching its community is not that the Word of God is irrelevant; it's that there's an unspoken motto in some churches that any attempts to adapt to the ever-changing culture they are endeavouring to evangelize, shall not be tolerated. Northern Bible had become one of those churches; consequently, I spent time submersing myself in trying to turn that mindset around. Despite the odds facing me, I was up for the task. Unfortunately, so was my bitter enemy, Satan, who can never resist getting involved in a good church spat.

CHAPTER 53

Worship

I CAN RECALL A CONVERSATION ABOUT CHURCH POLITICS I HAD ONE EVENING with one of my professors while I was studying in my seminary's library. While in class, he would candidly share from time to time about his own unfortunate experiences as a pastor. I chose that moment in the library to lament openly about some of my own trials at Grace Church, which at the time I was only one year removed from. It was then that my professor, with an intentionally hushed voice, bent down as if to issue me a classified tip. He expressed his sentiment that sometimes the church can be profoundly mean. Sitting there, I felt like I had "been there, done that," and even got the t-shirt. Then came Faith Church, and the t-shirt I got there for my troubles. Unimaginably, there was yet another t-shirt awaiting me at Northern Bible Church, the events of which even now are difficult to relive. The first Sunday featuring the alternative worship team came and went with a rather average, if not unspectacular, review.

It had been a couple of years since I'd been on a platform with my guitar, leading worship. I couldn't believe how nervous I was the night before. My hands were shaking so much as I strummed the guitar that it was hard for me to keep the pick between my thumb and forefinger. As we were worshipping, I couldn't help but notice how half the crowd (the more mature in age) barely made an effort to mouth the words. Given the fact that they were probably unfamiliar with some of our song choices, it was to be expected.

The real test of how well our worship had gone over happened after the service, when our performance was gauged by the leader of the other worship team.

Ron Mahler

He was less than encouraging in his appraisal of our musical abilities, and was also quick to point out some things that we apparently didn't get right. Initially, I shrugged the comments off, chalking them up to someone who was too used to making his opinions known about how music should be played. I tried not to take the criticisms too seriously, even though the person had obviously meant for them to be taken that way.

Though I was affirmed by the smiling faces of my supporters interspersed in the crowd that morning, it was the defiant-like countenance of the older crowd that stood out the most after the opening prayer. Having to entertain the critique of the other worship team leader on top of that made the experience that Sunday a bit of a downer.

I thought the poor assessment we had received that Sunday morning would get old and that in time, the deliverer would lay aside his opinions. That wasn't to be the case. This particular leader prepared quite scrupulously for Sunday morning worship. Having sat under his leadership as a drummer on the main worship team, I saw firsthand how he would repeatedly rehearse portions of songs with irritating and nauseating frequency. In my opinion, the worship practices weren't fun to attend, and from my observations they lacked the spirit of volunteerism.

I was happy to be free from that sort of atmosphere at the worship team practices, in which every missed chord or vocal assignment was seemingly pointed out. After a few more Sundays, the same worship leader couldn't help from insisting that he attend the worship practices of the alternative worship team, in order to "correct" a few things. I hadn't expected to inherit an adjudicator for the new worship team I had formed. However, his request turned into "Let me come and join you guys a few times, to help you get better. Then you're on your own."

At that moment, I knew I had a potential conflict on my hands. It's not that I didn't appreciate the leader's offer to be of assistance to the new worship team; I was more concerned about his approach to rehearsals. He could be a little overbearing at times. Moreover, I had an opinion of my own about the style in which *he* played his instruments for some of the praise songs. However, I didn't feel it was important to voice any such opinions. For me, it has always been more about where a person's heart is *while* they worship than how well they play or sing. Pride was another obstacle for me, for I was not exactly a novice at my instrument, nor was I a rookie at being on a worship team.

I often struggled with my own motives for keeping this persistently aggravating worship leader at arm's length. Was it a case of me just not liking the way he carried himself? Was it the sense I got that he had obviously elevated his ability to play music over and above what it meant to simply engage in the spirit of worshipping? Would I be more teachable and open to receiving criticism from him if I had a greater respect for how *he* played? Was I upset that I could teach him a few things about music, but didn't feel it was my place to do so?

Whenever I caught myself entertaining such thoughts, I became angry. To me, it was about worshipping God, not about turning practices into a music school. It wasn't about who was a better musician. I resolved to cheer the main worship team on when they were leading the church, just as I hoped that they would return the favour when the new, alternative team was on the platform.

The alternative worship team gained more confidence every Sunday morning we led the worship music, and we began to receive positive feedback on more of a consistent basis. In my mind, there was no need for any more talk on the issue. I was trying to prevent a potential clash over creative differences, which I could see happening if the other worship team leader was encouraged to attend our practices. He had the type of personality that didn't like cheering from the sidelines! If he was given even an inch, I felt he would turn it into a mile overnight. In a way, I was trying to train him to see that he didn't have to be in control of everything all the time. I was hoping that we would reach the point of a mutual understanding. The main, underlying complication, however, was how we differed from each other in personality; this proved to be a huge issue to overcome. Since I had arrived on the scene, I'd quietly put up with some of his comments over certain issues, never once voicing how incredibly bothersome he could be to me. Perhaps I should have.

Both of us could have used a little dose of selflessness, no doubt. I communicated to him that his approach (even if his musical expertise was superior to mine) wouldn't go over well with the personalities on the alternative worship team. As it was, some of its members already had to strum up enough confidence just to come out of their shyness.

Finally, I had to tell this leader straight out: "You lead your team, and I will lead mine." I offered him an opportunity to write down his suggestions on paper, and that I would discuss them at our worship team practices. I also thought it would be beneficial for both teams to get together every so often, for encouragement and prayer. That way, if there were any concerns, they could be voiced there in a constructive manner. However, my inability to get on the same wavelength with the other worship leader was more serious an issue than I had first calculated.

Call it naiveté, but I thought the issue would die down, that the other worship leader and I could move forward despite our differences. Yet the sparks of our conflict eventually spread throughout the church like a prairie fire. The hot winds of rumour seemed to affect everyone in their path. When word got out that I had rejected his help, those whose loyalties swung in his favour made sure I heard about it. Those who were encouraged to see their pastor exhibit some fortitude and stand up to this leader stood with me all the more.

Before too long, the divisive undercurrents heating up in the congregation travelled all the way up the leadership hierarchy of Northern Bible Church. Soon after, battle lines were drawn between the camps; neither the board nor the congregation as a whole were immune from the ever-growing dissension. A church split was well underway, over an issue that should never have gotten so out of hand.

I knew God was grieved; for that, I was very sad. I remember telling someone at the time, "It's just a worship team!" If only it was, though. As I would find out in the ensuing months, the conflict was really about something far more spiritually embedded in the DNA of the church. Sometimes certain issues have to be tapped in order for the real, underlying problem to come flying out. Once the worship issue was peeled back, other realities were revealed. There were deeply engrained power struggles, old rivalries, and unresolved conflicts that had been stewing for a few years. Now, they were all boiling over as a result of people taking sides over the worship. The result was nothing short of spiritual chaos. As I sat in my office at the church one morning, at wits end, sickened by the buzz of Sunday morning congregational murmurings, I received a call from the church's denominational representative mediator.

He had been made aware of the situation between myself and the worship leader, and had been asked by the church's board to intervene by mediating the dispute. After sitting down with us individually and making a batch of notes on what looked like reams of paper, the mediator rendered a lopsided verdict. After asking to meet Elaine and me for dinner, he concluded that by forming another worship team, I had violated the other team's territory. I was incredulous. Everything in me wanted to respect this individual's decision, but I could not. It was obvious to both Elaine and me that our side of the story hadn't registered that significantly in this person's deliberations. Then we learned that this same mediator was good friends with certain members of the other worship team.

So much for retaining neutrality when mediating between feuding parties! I was upset over the fact that I felt he had an obvious conflict of interest in the matter, compromising his ability to be truly objective. I fired off an email to him, expressing how alone I had felt in my struggles at the church and how nothing in the process of his troubleshooting gave me any confidence that I could gain a

My Fanatical, Regrettable Tour of Ministry

fair hearing. I made my sentiments clear; from my perspective, I was sorely at a disadvantage. To my satisfaction, two other members of the board came to the same conclusion. However, even after these two leaders met with the mediator to share their thoughts and concerns, they had a feeling that their words had fallen on deaf ears. The message must have gotten through on some point, however, for the mediator asked if he could visit with me again. Things didn't go well. All that the encounter accomplished was to cause a further divide between us. The meeting left me believing that I was at a dead-end.

Then, after informing him that I would not meet with him again alone, he showed up at my office a week later. It turned out to be another meeting that went nowhere in a hurry. It ended with my walking out on him.

By that point, not only was my relationship with the contentious worship leader becoming increasingly strained, but my relations with the other members of their team were breaking down as well. I did everything I could to keep that from happening. I tried to see things their way, but when spouses and personal agendas factor into the picture, there was little I could do, outside of prayer and exhibiting humility, to prevent further fragmentation of fellowship and unity. The church's board was showing real signs of irreparable division—those aligned with the mediator and the first worship team were on one side, while those aligned with me and my worship team were on the other.

The business of the church still needed to be attended to. The reality was that, whether the six of us on the board were happy campers or not, we still needed to work together. For most of these business meetings, it took all I could muster not only to show up, but to be able to make it through. More than a few of the meetings resulted in some eruption over the worship issue; quite often with me being on the receiving end of some board member's negativism. One meeting between the board and the two worship teams (a meeting I was dead-set against) seemed like a setup, and a one-sided one at that. For almost two hours, without break, I endured an onslaught of some of the most spiritually careless and mean-spirited statements that had ever been directed my way. Admittedly, out of a defensive posture, I was probably less than diplomatic in the meeting myself. Derogatory comments were also tossed at some of the other members of the alternative worship team (and two of them were present to hear it). I spoke up at one point and challenged them that if we, the alternative worship team, were so inadequate, why were they acting and sounding like they were threatened by us?

One leader, who tried hard to stay judicious, called for some sanity, reminding us that we were all servants, that none of us were professional musicians. The emotions of some of the people were definitely getting the best of them, and when that happens people can say things they may regret later. The first worship team, I was told, was *the* talent in the church, and apparently I needed to go back to doing what I had been hired to do in the first place: preach! One person even had the gall to offer me consolation, by stating, "Refuse to be offended, pastor."

The vitriol of the first worship team's comments seemed almost comical to me. By how they spoke, it sounded like they, as well as their backers on the church board, were convinced that *I* was the enemy. If they could have only heard their own words and the way I was receiving them! Such meetings made those days the worst I have ever had to endure in ministry.

Not only was the task of still having to preach close to being unbearable, some of my content was conveniently dissected out of context and later used against me by some of the same characters in the aforementioned meeting. It's hard enough as a pastor to have the energy to study for and write sermons during seasons of intense, heart-wrenching conflict, hard enough to get your legs and breath when you're mired in anxiety over having to face your detractors from behind the pulpit (knowing they think you're a hypocrite). Preaching is even more daunting a task when you know the people are hanging on your every word for all the wrong reasons.

Oftentimes, Sunday mornings would find Elaine not even wanting to go to church with me. Her mounting despondence worried me, turning me into a defensive and distant pastor. As a leader, I felt the furthest thing from a loving, caring, and long-suffering shepherd. I was ashamed of what I had become, and madder still at many of God's people who were hurting me.

A parade of phone calls came flowing into our home during those days, most of which were from supporters who promised their prayers. I felt horrible inside that I had become the stimulus for them to turn away from their fellow brothers and sisters in Christ. I felt I didn't have the pastoral integrity, or the will, to ask my supporters to keep loving those who were making my life miserable. Jesus may have said that the world would know the church by their love for one another, but I had more than a few doubts that many of us had any right to identify ourselves as "little Christs" (Christians). I even thought of taking a ladder from the church's basement, climbing up, and rubbing out the word "church" on our outdoor sign.

Statements

People, by nature, like to make statements. However, statements don't always have to be given *orally* in order to be voiced. We see this in the realm of celebrities; iconic and enigmatic figures make a living by standing out from the crowd, by how they promote their lifestyles, their social views, and even their own physical appearances. Many people want to be known in life; they want to have their say, their day in court, as it were. Many people just want to be heard, even when they best be advised to remain *silent*. People, some famous and others not so famous, love to be quoted. Oftentimes, they use a Twitter account just to be able to make their statements. Some statements are made for good and valid reasons, for noble causes; some, on the other hand, are not.

The statements we really need to be careful of, however, are the ones that we make as God's people. Some are made to glorify and honour God, like Daniel's insistence on defying the Babylonian king, Nebuchadnezzar, when the pagan monarch issued a decree that no one in his kingdom was to bow and pray to anyone but him. I have always found it heart-warming to read of what the king's cronies found Daniel doing fresh off the king's threats. Did they find Daniel reading the Old Testament for loopholes? Not a chance! They found him on his knees, in plain view, doing the exact opposite of what the brooding king had commanded him not to do—praying to his God! Daniel, by defying the king's wicked decree, was making a statement. Don't you wish sometimes that all of

God's people would act like Daniel did in the face of trials—just pray? Many of the members at Northern Bible Church, during its darkest moments, chose to embrace ungodly hysteria instead of sitting at the feet of Jesus, at the foot of His cross—and staying there.

A number of them defied the best of the Bible's instructions on how to chop down the monster of interpersonal conflict. God's people at Northern Bible forgot to bear with one another, neglecting to rid themselves of such sinful vices as anger, malice, and slander, ignoring the need to clothe themselves with compassion, kindness, and humility (see Colossians 3). Instead, they opted to make a few statements of their own. For one, the entire first worship team stepped down, citing their decision as a sign of loyalty to their leader. It was a nice attempt on their part at looking compassionate, selfless, and noble for a change, but I couldn't help feeling that their decision to step away from the platform had more to do with their displeasure of me than it did with their absolute allegiance to their leader.

The move, however, put me on the spot. If I continued on with the alternative worship team, I would look insensitive, and come across as being opportunistic. If I backed away, on the other hand, I would somehow be conceding that our presence on the platform was inappropriate.

I didn't need to read a few good books or whip through my pastoral theology notes from seminary to be cognizant of the fact that I was in a no-win situation. One of the board members, an obvious detractor of mine, came into my office and told me that I should back away from the area of worship. I told him that in some regard that the first worship team had probably already decided that one for me. Despite that, I made it clear that I wouldn't be intimidated off the platform by people who used ungodly means to make their point. I told this leader that I didn't feel that stepping down would be the best way for me to lead as a pastor, and that it might set a negative precedent for our people. The leadership of a church, I told him, is to set an example for what is acceptable conduct from its members, and for how its concerns are to be handled. The board member scowled as he lifted himself from his chair, leaving my office more miffed than ever. Then came a letter campaign, which was designed, in the spirit of Nehemiah's enemies, to send me a message.

When Nehemiah returned from exile in Persia with a number of other Jews, they purposed to rebuild the wall around the city of Jerusalem. The Bible tells us that they faced an onslaught of threatening messages from individuals like Sanballat, Tobiah, and Geshem, whose band of errand boys and muscle men aimed to accomplish one purpose: weaken the resolve of the Jewish repairmen. Behind the scenes of the reconstruction of Jerusalem's tattered wall were shadowy characters who, for their own selfish, political reasons, opposed Nehemiah. Though they were relatively few in number, their intimidating comments made it sound like an army was waiting over the hills to come and waylay their rebuilding efforts. However, their talents at barking were far worse than their ability to bite. In the end, their fear tactics didn't work. Nehemiah's faith in the sovereign power of His God to see the reconstruction project through won the battle. The walls were rebuilt!

It became an almost daily occurrence for me to receive a new letter from one of my detractors, which was always copied to the church board, as well as to the person I have referred to as the mediator. At first, I tried to ignore them. However, when my detractors felt that Elaine was fair game, and rudely implicated her in some of their letters, I'd had enough. Not even my supporters in the church who backed me were spared from criticism.

The whole ordeal had gone too far. Some church members showed their displeasure by sending a twisted email to the denomination. They sent them to me as well, just to brighten my day! Incredibly, it is possible for a Christian to grow in their knowledge of God's Word, but flunk in their ability to grow in grace and wisdom! It was a longshot for me to accept, even on my worst, self-critical days, that all the animosity being hurled at me, had come about as a byproduct of my conflict with the other worship team leader.

Another pastor in the community, who I had spoken to on occasion and who had good knowledge of Northern Bible's history, told me that the church should have been working on certain relationships long ago. The whole worship controversy wasn't the foundational disease that caused the uproar; it was only a symptom of a greater, carnal sickness. The worship issue acted as a tornado that moved across the landscape of long-standing dissension, whipping up other, uglier debris that had been lying dormant. In the eye of the storm sat the Devil himself, sowing lies and discord amongst God's people.

There were some progressives in the church who were fighting amongst each other for the right to see change happen, on their terms. There was the old guard, who had an over-my-dead-body attitude towards anything that differed from their traditional way of doing things. There were also those in the church who were hurting for their own reasons. There were families who were not on speaking terms with others, and leaders who had issues with certain people in the church. Old disputes were being rekindled, misunderstandings being warmed over, dirty laundry being aired, all of which originated long before I ever stepped foot in the pastor's office.

The letters kept coming, but one in particular saddened me the most. One of the most respected board members and leaders in the church finally had enough. In his resignation, he mentioned that in all of his thirty-five years in the church, he had never seen a pastor spoken to with such disrespect as he heard some speak to me. This same leader revealed to me that for weeks they had felt sick to their stomach over the whole affair, and that it was time to leave. The church lost a wonderful, grounded, and godly voice of reason that day; I lost a person I greatly respected, and someone who had my ear. More devastating to me, personally, was the fact that I had just lost a friend among many adversaries, and a key supporter at that.

I had a couple of subsequent meetings with the worship leader I had disagreements with, but they failed to resolve the deeper issues of the conflict. Therefore, the governing board decided to look at clarifying what my role as the pastor should be. To do that, they consulted the church's constitution in the hopes of finding something they may have overlooked. They found what they were looking for. In a section tucked away under the pastor's duties was a line that stipulated that the pastor was to conduct the worship of the church. It was a hollow, moral victory of sorts for me, but it didn't matter anymore. It wasn't about who was right; what mattered was that all hopes for unity were ebbing away.

One of the church's annual business meetings turned out to be a convenient forum for some who were now in full, combative opposition to my presence at Northern Bible Church. They used the church-wide meeting to put even more provocative words to their agenda. The evening got off to an auspicious start, when one of my detractors used a time of prayer as a divisive weapon instead of as a soothing balm. There aren't many more spiritually deplorable things we can do to the Body of Christ than to manipulate people in corporate prayer.

Another equally despicable practice is to offer a fellow Christian support with one hand, then do something far worse to them with the other when the opportunity arises. There was one person in the church who had greeted me every morning since my first week at Northern Bible by saying, "Good morning Pastor!" They would consistently follow this up with, "I have prayed for you." As a pastor, I'd received similar encouragements from God's people in times past, but not quite with the amount of repetition this person offered them to me. However, when the worship war set in and threatened to cut the church in half, this person's weekly greeting was conspicuously absent. I read between the lines

My Fanatical, Regrettable Tour of Ministry

and determined that this person, along with his spouse, had most likely aligned himself against me.

I was bang-on. A regrettable moment arose during one service, just before I was about to preach. It was the International Day of Prayer for the Persecuted Church, and I had planned to show a brief video which offered challenging visuals and testimonials of some of the sufferings our brothers and sisters were going through in other parts of the world on account of their faith. My hope was that such a video would convict the church, just as it had convicted me when I first saw it.

Whether it was God's providence, the Devil's influence, or just some coincidental, technological glitch, for some reason our sound person could not get the video player to work properly that morning. If it had, I would not have done what I did. Out of frustration that nothing was working out for me, I proceeded to explain to the church (which, oddly, was filled to the brim that morning) some of the video's contents. As I was speaking, I could feel the anger brewing from some of those present who had only days earlier eaten me up and spat me out behind the closed doors of the board room.

Then a thought occurred to me. After carefully panning the crowd to make sure there weren't any visitors, I rolled into a rant of—serious proportions. I yelled at the top of my voice for a few seconds, not quite bloodcurdling, but enough to provide an example of what tortured Christians must have sounded like at the hands of their persecutors. I told the church that even though their cries were unlike our worship, God must have honoured it as worship and received it all the same. My point was that here we were, in the safe confines of the western church, fighting over how we sound as worship teams, when all that some of our brothers and sisters in other countries have to offer are horrifying screams that, even then, are acceptable to God as forms of worship. If that was good enough for God, I reasoned, then shame on us for this controversy over worship teams.

I'd never heard a sanctuary so silent. As I looked at the people, I saw a mixture of reactions—some with petrified countenances, some with tears streaming down their cheeks, and others still with a "What's happened to you, pastor?" look. Incredibly, I even saw a spattering of people nodding in agreement with what they had just witnessed. Some of the people reacted by popping up from their seats and tearing out of the place. A few of my detractors sat quietly, while some of the others heckled me all the more, with one individual postulating that I was the *real* problem and calling for me to leave. My outburst temporarily relieved some of my pent-up frustrations, and may have even convicted a few people, but in the end all it accomplished was further hardship.

It was never my intention to dishonour the Lord's Day. Unfortunately, it just happened to be Sunday when my fuse reached the blowing point. I was angry and appalled at all the self-affirming pettiness that had infected the church, and I was tired from all the abuse I'd taken over the previous few months, abuse I'd never thought I would have to endure ever again.

As I walked out from behind the pulpit, I suddenly noticed my whole body shaking, and I felt physically drained. In a much softer tone, I then asked that those still in the sanctuary who wanted to stay and join with me at the altar should feel free to do so in seeking God's forgiveness and mercy. As I thought would happen, my detractors vacated the building in a hurry. Immediately, I got down on my knees and faced the platform in a posture of prayer. To my surprise, I found that not only did tears come easily, but an all-out, cathartic weep freely flowed out of me. As I went in and out of crying spurts, mixed with words of prayer, I felt an arm gently slide up and over me from behind, covering my back. It was a person I never would have expected to stay behind, to pledge their support for me. It was the best part of a very bad day.

After a half-hour of prayer, I left the church with Elaine. Fortunately, she had been in the basement with our kids for the morning and heard nothing of the ruckus. As I opened the front doors of the church, there in front of me, out in the parking lot, was a crowd of detractors who, for all I knew, may have been plotting something. As I walked towards them to get to my car, they dispersed faster than a family of deer at the sound of a gunshot. The church had finally collapsed into three groups: those who were supporters, those who were vehement in their opposition of me, and those who still had no inclination of what the whole brouhaha was about.

After that Sunday morning, I had no idea whether I would have a job by Monday morning, or if I would even have many friends left in the church. Amazingly, on both counts, I would be pleasantly surprised. I received a call from someone in the church the Monday morning after the service. It wasn't the call I thought would come, announcing the termination of my employment. However, it was still an unfortunate call. I was informed that a certain person's spouse had suffered a mild stroke and had been taken to the hospital as a result of my actions on the platform the previous morning. At first, I thought it was some sort of cruel, sick joke being played on me by the people I was suspicious of. But I felt mortified as the possibility of it really having happened began to sink in. I was wary, however, of the source of the information, and doubly so with the party who was said to have experienced the stroke, leading me to wonder if it were indeed true at all. To this day, I still don't know.

What I can say for sure is that this couple was amongst the disgruntled group, the group who had been in the parking lot as I left the church the Sunday morning of my infamous scream.

Chapter 55
Hello, Goodbye

Elaine and I had already been through a few long goodbyes in our short ministry life, but our exit from Northern Bible Church would come suddenly and without a chance to say a proper goodbye. Both of us felt we could no longer be at a ministry where our dignity had been stripped from us, where questions about my competence to lead had become open season, where godliness was as rare as water in the desert, and where all that remained was contempt and resentment.

A few weeks prior to the service in which I produced a wake-up scream of epic proportions, I resolved to have nothing further to do with any aspect of the worship ministry. However, that move was exacerbated by the fact that no one else would willingly spearhead the effort of putting together songs and leading them in the service. A short time after, the worship leader I'd had run-ins with resigned his position. By that point, all the remaining alternative worship team members expressed that they wanted out as well; I was the sole one left. I hardly resembled a king in his worship castle. I looked more like the dirty rascal, like someone who was desperately trying to look as if they were "in the right." That didn't sit well with me; in fact, I hated what it had all become.

On the first Sunday where there was no worship team at all, I came off the platform and gathered as many willing singers as possible to join me on the floor of the sanctuary. It felt strange and awkward to lead worship this way, yet it was also a liberating exercise in trying to worship a different way, with different faces upfront—other than mine, of course!

My Fanatical, Regrettable Tour of Ministry

One Saturday morning, I was at the church preparing for the next day's worship service when I was interrupted by a board member. This person had the unfortunate responsibility of delivering me a message. I was told that it wouldn't "go well" for me if I didn't step back and cease from any involvement with the worship ministry. I chuckled at what had come across as a blatant threat. It wasn't, of course, a threat in the physical sense. Pursuing the matter a bit further, I pressed for him to divulge who was behind the message. When I was informed who it was, I wasn't surprised.

The warning was passed along from another dissenting member of the board, who was a big-time sympathizer of the former worship leader. This person also stood in solidarity with those who were opposing me through ungodly means. I took his advice to heart, that maybe I should heed the message. I did. Though I didn't appreciate the underlying spirit of it, I'd finally had enough of the stupid power plays and silly bickering. By that time, the church's main governing board was lacking a few leaders; a few of them had either stepped back for a time or resigned outright. The only individual who was left to lead the Sunday morning worship was an older, long-attending gentleman who had to make do without any instrumentation. Consequently, the following few Sundays featured this sole person leading the congregation in song with the use of a simple hymnbook. It was different, yet peaceful.

Two Sundays later was the infamous "scream" service, which would set the wheels in motion for the merciful end of my short, obtusely chaotic term at the church. The Sunday following that service seemed to arrive with lightning speed. As Elaine and I awoke that morning, apprehension hovered over the breakfast table. We were both suffering from sleep deprivation, and it had more than a little to do with us also becoming somewhat overly sensitive with one another. If she'd had it her way, Elaine would have preferred to stay home that morning, and most Sundays prior to that one. This was hard for me to take, and not merely because I was the pastor; I wanted to worship and fellowship with my wife alongside me. However, it was near impossible to be at the church anymore without feeling grossly unhappy and spiritually weighed down. The very sight of the church building became more a focal point of strife and hardship for us than a location of worship and a symbol of God's presence. Besides, Elaine and I had both come to the conclusion that perhaps God had already plugged His ears and was no longer listening to His embarrassingly divided children.

Like many people at the church, we had absorbed more than enough junk from some of God's people over the past half-year. Quite literally, our constitutions could no longer withstand the contention. Psychologically, we were already removed from the situation; all that remained was to pursue peace and to explore a way to leave the church on some good note, if possible. That would prove difficult. With the cool November winds flapping around us, and with the onset of winter making its presence prematurely known, we buckled our kids into a warm car and headed towards an uncertain reception at the church. It had just been seven days since I'd walked off the platform in ignominious fashion. Our week had been burdened with thoughts of how the people at the church would react to seeing us again.

As we drove to church, I was looking forward to a couple of things. After such a difficult few months, I was determined to get our family out of the church, as soon as possible. Since Christmas was coming, I mulled over in my mind that I would leave in the New Year, with or without another job waiting in the wings. In my heart, I achingly wished I had never come to Northern Bible in the first place. Even if my detractors left, the damage done to my ability, my zeal to lead, and my influence were wholesale. I couldn't even fathom seeking another ministry, but worrying about that wasn't a priority to Elaine and me at that point. She had revealed to me, months earlier, that she was ready to make the move any time, even if that once again put us in dire financial straits. The move was mine to make, and Elaine was looking for me to take the lead.

As our car pulled into the church's parking lot, one thing struck me as strange. There were fewer cars than usual, so I assumed that people were either away or had decided not to come out that morning. When we opened the double doors that led into the foyer, the place seemed even more vacant. Since the previous Sunday, I recalled throughout the week that there had been no office visits, no calls, no complaints—other than the one informing me of someone's perhaps phantom stroke. There hadn't even been a single threat or letter. It had been surprisingly refreshing, though odd. All was quiet. Almost too quiet.

When Elaine and I got to the doors of the sanctuary, a certain board member was standing there, wearing a smile from ear to ear. That, too, was odd. This was the same leader who had issued me the message that I had to back away from the area of music ministry. This person gave my wife a hug, and whispered "Love ya," which was often his custom.

On this morning, though, Elaine couldn't help but cringe a bit while receiving his embrace. I was cordial but reserved in my greeting. As he handed us a bulletin, I absentmindedly tucked it away in my Bible and headed for the platform to put some items behind the pulpit. It was then, out of the corner of my eye,

My Fanatical, Regrettable Tour of Ministry

that I noticed something alarming: Elaine was crying. I rushed down and asked her what had happened, and became absolutely livid at her revelation.

She pulled out the morning bulletin, which contained a letter asserting that a congregational vote would be taken to have myself and Elaine removed from any involvement on an independent worship team. Elaine, who is a solid vocalist and had from time to time been a helpful presence on the alternative worship team, was no longer involved. At that moment, I had to sit down and gather my anxious thoughts. Without praying (I should have), I began to tremble within.

Then I tried to locate the other remaining board member to ask about the letter, but I couldn't find him around. Nor could I, all of sudden, locate many of my detractors at all. Seeing red, as it were, I charged right up to the board member and pulled him by the edge of his suit into a corner.

"Why are you doing this, now?" I demanded. "What is this garbage you're handing out?"

He defiantly shrugged off every question I had, asserting his agenda all the more. The vote *was* going to take place, I was told. It was bad enough that he had chosen to do this on the heels of what had happened the previous Sunday morning. It was bad enough that he had greeted us so warmly, knowing what we were about to read, bad enough that he had already tried to strong-arm me off the platform. Now, as I found out later, he had acted unilaterally, without a consensus from the board, to devise a purely political plan that humiliated the pastor and his wife. While I was going on with this leader, a few women who had been sitting with Elaine took her into my office to pray with her.

Looking the divisive board member square in the eye, I told him that he'd gone too far this time, and that his irresponsible actions might very well lead to an unstoppable split in the church. Sadly, that was the case. Finally, running into the other board member (a supporter), I told him that I couldn't preach that morning, and that I was probably finished at the church. I grabbed Elaine and we exited the building for what would prove to be our last time.

It was finally over—the games, the innuendo, the cutting remarks, and the threats. Everything would stop.

My time at Northern Bible had to end sometime, but it didn't have to end the way it did. Officially, my status reflected that I was on a "stress-related" leave. No one, however, had any illusions that I would return. This leave simply allowed me to collect a few paycheques for a brief period of time, not to mention that I *really* needed the rest.

Ron Mahler

What I could not have foreseen, though, was that a continuation of the trials would come, in another form, from an all too predictable source.

A couple of months after that last, excruciatingly painful Sunday, and just after my final resignation from the church, I began to explore other pastoral positions at random. My motives and emotions in doing so were mixed. Though my confidence level as a man and leader was at an all-time low, and my trust in the church almost non-existent, and even though it felt like this time it was all over for me—for good—something in me needed to keep a flicker of hope alive. I wanted to be told by someone that I was *not* the single worst pastor of all time, to ever be in ministry. I was hoping that my time in vocational ministry would not have to end on such a terrible note. If they were to ask me about it later in life, I wanted to be able to share with my children good experiences about pastoral ministry. I also needed whatever monies I could gain from offering to at least be a guest speaker in churches.

Part of me applied to other churches just to see if they would respond. If churches didn't respond to my resume, it would only confirm my feelings that I was completely done for in ministry. However, not one but two churches responded with invitations for me to come and preach, just three or so months after I left Northern Bible Church. I visited these two churches, weeks apart from each other. It amazed me how therapeutic I found preaching to be. In my sinful nature, though, I periodically felt like I wanted to keep preaching in order to inwardly say to my detractors, "Take that!" I had become accustomed to preaching while under duress, so I was up for preaching to people whom I had no ties with, and who at the very least were willing to compensate me for it. However, after both preaching engagements, I was alerted by a certain insider at one of those churches to a very troubling development.

The letter campaign that had been used against me at Northern Bible Church was once again being utilized. What seemed to me like a possible attempt to sabotage any efforts on my part to pursue any further ministry opportunities, someone associated with Northern Bible—without the church's knowledge—had written discriminatory letters (two that I was aware of) to people who I was told could have been associated with the churches I went to preach at. I highly doubted that it was a coincidence. It might have been by chance if only one of the churches I preached at received a letter, but surely not if both of them did. I also assumed that the person who had penned the letters did so because she felt she had a responsibility to caution, or even protect, the churches I went to in the future.

My Fanatical, Regrettable Tour of Ministry

Unfortunately, she should have considered my reputation in writing the letters. Whether or not it was directly related to any letters they may have received about me, I wasn't surprised when neither church I preached at desired to go no further with me. Frankly, their decisions didn't bother me.

For the next three years, I stayed in the same community as this individual. Amazingly, not once during that time did I ever meet up with her. The last time I spoke to her was when I called her directly, after I found out what she was up to. In retrospect, I probably should have let someone else handle it. I asked her why she had written those letters. After giving me the silent treatment, I promised to have her held accountable at the board level of Northern Bible Church, and perhaps even at the church's denominational level, whether I returned to the church or not (even though I already knew I wasn't going to).

She most likely misconstrued that conversation on purpose, interpreting it as if I had threatened her. Panicking over what she was doing to my reputation, I ended up exacerbating the matter by opening the door for her to possibly harm my character even further. Though I didn't call her any names or act in an ungodly manner, I should have known much better than to react the way I did. I should have left my reputation to Jesus; He, after all, is greater than our reputations and better able to vindicate us than *we* are.

One night, about four years later, my phone rang. It was this same woman who had written the letters. I stood, with phone to ear, absolutely speechless. She was the last person in the world I'd thought I would ever hear from. I was convinced she would forever remain angry at me. After having a few years to dwell on the matter, she sounded quite contrite. She shared how she had been convicted after hearing a certain sermon, and felt she had to call me to ask for my forgiveness.

By that chapter in my life, I was much calmer, for the passage of time had allowed me to prayerfully move on and forgive her. I communicated those sentiments to her, and sincerely thanked her for her admissions, and willingness to put the past to rest. Unbelievably, after her phone call, I began to see her, in increasing fashion, wherever I went around town. Without exception, every subsequent encounter I had with her led to a handshake, a brief, polite conversation, and even a lighthearted laugh and embrace. Only God could have brought about such a wonderful end to a story that had such a gruesome beginning. That is to His glory!

Reconciliation is the spiritual herald of the Kingdom of God. Trust in others may need to be re-earned, but we don't have to hold grudges against our brothers

Ron Mahler

and sisters in Christ. In a world ripe with division, it is always for God's greater witness that His children reconcile with one another and patch up their wounds of conflict, for we know that He desires for His will to be done on earth as it is in Heaven.

Chapter 56

Ministry Perspectives

Some shoe advertisements emphasize that in order for marathon runners to have a successful run, they need a good fit. Analogously, most leadership gurus say that in order for a pastor to have a lengthy tenure at one church, they need to be able to continuously adapt to its culture. In other words, a good ministry fit should naturally equal longevity of service at a church.

However, should we take a pastor's lengthy tenure at one church as an automatic guarantee that it is a healthy ministry? Not too long ago, I was at a seminar for ministry couples where one pastor shared how he had been ministering at the same church for over twenty-seven years. As I listened to him, I kept shifting around in my seat. Most likely, it was out of sheer insecurity *and* inferiority over my seeming inability to stick it out in one ministry long enough to look older by the time I left that ministry.

I couldn't help but interrupt him by asking, "What's your secret, my friend?"

Oddly enough, this same minister went on to admit that, even though God had blessed him with good people to work with over the years, he still felt that the number one problem pastors face is the conflict that arises over their relationship with church leadership. It took everything in me to keep myself from popping up from my seat and interrupting him a second time with shouts of, "Amen, brother. You can say that again!"

Ron Mahler

When I go to ministry conferences, I tend to feel a bit like an outcast. As much as I can relate to most pastors in terms of the pain they've endured in their ministries, it's been my experience that the average pastor is seldom able to really relate with my own. I'm sure they're out there, but I haven't met them. You can find out a lot about the state of a church just by listening to its leaders and hearing the stories they share.

There are times, however, when I'm amazed by what some pastors classify as an "issue" or "concern" to them. Sometimes I'm tempted to utter, "Man, you call *that* a problem?!" Oftentimes, I've been too fearful of being judged by other, more established and successful pastors to share my own disappointments and failures. "Who wants to sound like a three-time failure with a chip on his shoulder?" I've often griped to Elaine.

The truth is, the gaping and oozing ministry wounds of pastors fresh off a battle, or mired in one, litter the ballrooms and backrooms of every conference they attend. More than just being a place for networking, strategic planning, and vision casting, pastors' conferences can take on the look of military triage, where combat-weary and reeling shepherds lean on another and help to bind up each other's hurts and wounds.

True community in the church is supposed to be authentic. Pastors should feel the safety and freedom that comes with the kinship they share with other pastors to voice their pain and concerns. In reality, though, the experts will tell you that a lot of pastors are actually reluctant (each for his or her own reasons) to let their guards down, to openly communicate that they're either hurting and feeling inadequate or just downright angry. In general, it's difficult for anyone to ask for help (counselling), so it shouldn't surprise us if even pastors are reluctant to seek the professional counsel they need. Many leaders don't want the people they're in charge of to have any knowledge that they're weary and worn out, let alone suffering emotionally and psychologically. After all, what parishioner would be fully willing to place his or her confidence in such a leader? I know that I've felt like that. We're so convinced as pastors that our people are counting on us to be models of spiritual consistency and strength that we feel we cannot divulge our deepest fears and angst.

It's a nightmarish thought for us to reveal anything other than the type of exterior that communicates spiritual maturity, trust, and which gains the admiration of our people. That's why the pastoral persona you see at most seminars or conferences is the strong, silent type. In other words, we try to look like we've got it all together, even if we feel like we're falling apart. Sometimes I think pastors could use a support forum, in the vein of Alcoholics Anonymous. Instead of trying so hard to be strong and silent, maybe pastors should just remain anonymous, yet feel like they can air out their thoughts and feelings about where they're at in ministry and in their lives, in an environment where others will best be able to understand and relate to them. Imagine a pastor sitting before their peers at a PA (Pastors Anonymous) meeting, freely admitting, "I acknowledge Jesus Christ as my higher power and I'm recovering from the effects of a church split."

That would have been me—a beat-up and broken man—after dragging myself out of Northern Bible Church. In the end, I stayed at the church one day *too* long. It was extremely difficult for me to come away from what remained of the splintered church feeling good about myself as a leader, especially since I'd inherited it in one piece, though not in great shape. Leaving the contentious environment of Northern Bible may have taken me out of the firing lane, but it didn't prevent me from taking shots at myself. Admittedly, I spent too many days and nights second-guessing myself, bemoaning decisions I had made, and feeling enormously guilty—long after Elaine and I walked away.

One of the contributing spiritual factors (outside of God's healing presence in my life) that assisted me personally in eradicating the intensity of my guilt were the many endearing friendships Elaine and I preserved with people from Northern Bible Church. These were people who had left either before or after we eventually departed from the church. The depth and substance of those relationships were helpful in getting us through some of the early days after leaving the church, when our pain was still so grave.

I reckon that all the selling of homes and physical moves we've had to make in the name of ministry has cost Elaine and me more than the salary I've garnered. I've had to keep in mind that God hasn't promised us, as His people, monetary riches, only His ability to meet our needs.

As we approached Christmas a month after our departure from Northern Bible, predictably we found ourselves in dire financial straits. The paycheques I was still receiving were coming to an end. Having some knowledge of our circumstances, our friends who subsequently left the church after we did coordinated a "money tree" party, which brought us over $700. Without that kind gesture, the holidays that year would have been very lean and bleak!

In the ensuing year, these same friends would periodically pop up on our doorstep with gifts in hand. Others would show up and just listen to me vent, while offering encouragement and prayer. The people I had ministered to and

Ron Mahler

fed, as a pastor, for a year at Northern Bible were now standing with Elaine and me, ministering to and feeding us. This turnabout was new for us.

At the end of our previous two ministries, Elaine and I had left the churches feeling largely isolated, even ostracized. This time around, though some members of the leadership at Northern failed to care, those who came out from under them picked up the slack. If it wasn't for the mercy, kindness, and generosity of some of these church "refugees," I probably would have resolved never to minister ever again. Not many people would have blamed me if I'd come to that decision. Thankfully, God didn't permit me to choose that option.

As you will see, there was more in store for me.

Learning Curves

LEARNING TO BE A GOOD PASTOR AND LEADER IS A LOT LIKE LEARNING TO BE A good parent. We can't parent our kids when they're thirteen like we parented them when they were five. We have to grow and adjust in our parental skills to be able to apply them appropriately as our children progress in life and meet the challenges inherent in becoming men and women in the world.

In the same way, leaders, whether they are in the church or not, must evolve in their leadership abilities in order to effectively lead others who depend on them to be their guiding influence. Just as there are different seasons in our children's lives, there are different seasons in the church and ministry. Church leaders need to know how to appropriately weather all the seasons that will come upon them in ministry. Though I'm not through with my education as a leader, not by any stretch, in the following paragraphs I have listed the imperative learning curves that I have experienced in the church. The points I make, though they aren't an exhaustive list, are foundational for undertaking key leadership roles in the church—especially the pastoral role.

1. Don't take yourself too seriously.

As pastors and leaders in the church, we can sometimes wonder whether we're really necessary for the Kingdom of God to advance. It is possible for shepherds of God to be deceived into thinking they (in their giftedness, education, and popularity) could be even bigger than their ministries. "Sadly, walk-on-the-water syndrome triggers in a few pastors an obnoxious, pseudo-holy, prideful opinion of themselves."[7]

This is the extreme antithesis of bearing an inferiority complex in ministry, which is arguably the predominant default character of most pastors who live and serve by biblically-grounded self-awareness. Obviously, reaching the danger zone then means venturing into that area of our minds where we can put more stock in ourselves and our ministries than we ought to. The sobering truth about our service to God, and His Church, is this: though God chooses to use us individually, He doesn't *need* us as much as we might think.

Though every Christian is expected by God to serve Him with their spiritual gifts, every one of us is expendable in doing so. Though the people of the Church require us, as pastors, to shepherd them, there will always be a graduating seminary class, loaded with prospective pastors, to take our place. There will always be someone coming after us who can take up the mantle.

Moses is a great example of this. After all that the patriarch did for the nation of Israel—leading them out of Egypt and into the Sinai regions, putting up with their rebellion, etc.—he was actually deemed expendable enough to be kept from entering the Promised Land. God granted that privilege to another leader: Joshua! Every leader has a successor, and though the new leader may not be able to fill the exact size of shoe of the previous leader, they will follow in their predecessor's footsteps. So as leaders in the church, let's get over ourselves.

God certainly honours and rewards our service to His people, and our part in advancing the Gospel, but there comes a point when He will do without us. Often the best medicine for our self-inflicted "what would the church do without me" complex is to simply learn to laugh at ourselves more. At appropriate times and intervals, a little self-deprecating humour would do us some good. People appreciate leaders who can poke fun at themselves. I try to do this on occasion. It's not that we're endeavouring to exhibit false humility, but we should try to keep ourselves as "real" as possible.

2. Lower your expectations of others—and yourself!

I've been in various leadership situations in the church where I have failed to lower my expectations—and it's come at a cost. Every pastor struggles with disappointments. It's okay for pastors to want their people to be all that God wants them to be, but we run into difficulty when we expect them to be as committed to the ministry as we feel we are. The problem is that sometimes we may want more out of our people than even God can get out of them!

The reality is that we're dealing with people who, like ourselves, are short on time, long on excuses, and are distracted by the priorities of their lives. But there may be times when it's natural to have certain expectations. If people in our church have responsibilities on a Sunday morning that they frequently shirk, if they make a habit of not following through on their promises, or if they consistently fail to call you when they can't make their appointments, we may be justified in being a little upset.

It's not too much to ask your elders to be supportive of your church's outreach events by being present at them every once in a while, but when our expectations of people (especially fellow leaders) rise to dizzying levels, we are setting them—and ourselves—up for failure and disappointment. We need to know a person well enough to gauge how much we can reasonably expect from them while resisting the urge to press them too much, too often. Feelings of resentment and inadequacy often manifest in those upon whom we place unrealistic expectations.

Every search committee is looking for a Jesus-type minister. Let's face it: He's the ultimate model for assessing one's pastoral ability. It may not be spoken, and churches may not even realize it, but our Saviour is the standard by which most pastors are measured. It also helps to be able to "scale tall buildings in a single bound," as one church I applied to jokingly put on their job description. A pastor has to be a good Bible teacher, even effective and proven. They have to be there for the hurts and pains of the congregation. They must be able to attract people to the church, be desirable and effective in counselling, be the consummate evangelist, love everybody, keep good schedules, and be able to take whatever criticism is thrown at them in a godly manner, despite the motives and spirit in which it may come at them or whether the criticism is fair.

Churches that hope they'll find the diamond of a Jesus replica in the rough of their resumes build expectations that pastors simply cannot meet. The disparity between our finite ability to serve God and the Lord's sinless ministry is staggering. We cannot be compared to Jesus, and pastors should know this more than most people in the church. So if we don't want it done to us, we must refrain from turning the tables on others. We can love people like Jesus, and we may even be able to emulate Him effectively in our ministry, but none of us can get things as right as our Lord did. So even though we should attempt to pastor and lead *like* Jesus (in principle), we can't expect our service to the Church to be anything more than what it is: administered via redeemed, albeit sinful and finite vessels.

In terms of leadership expectations, pastors and their churches should keep the Apostle Paul's words to the Corinthian church constantly in mind: *"Therefore judge nothing before the appointed time"* (1 Corinthians 4:5). As leaders in the church, it's not the people who have the best perspective on the quality of our ministry. In fact, it's not even us; it's God! There is a time to serve God, and there is a time to have our service for Him fairly and finally weighed.

3. The importance of maintaining relationships.

I cannot emphasize this point enough. In ministry, the consensus is that success is defined by those pastors and leaders who are able to *influence* those whom they lead. As much as fostering healthy relationships is a vital aspect of ministry, it can also be the most difficult to cultivate and maintain. Ask a handful of pastors what one of their greatest frustrations in the ministry is, and they will probably be tempted to list off a few things. However, I believe a good number of them might answer, "The relationship I have with the leaders in my church."

This has been a challenge area for me, personally. Contrary to what some Christians may think, we will not be able to get along with all the people all the time, nor will we be able to work out every conflict. For the ultimate proof, we need look no further than the gospels, which show us that not even a sinless Jesus could always come to terms with His detractors! Some conflicts in the church are so sharp and polarizing that they result in irrevocable chasms.

Not all squabbles will be resolved this side of eternity. We will not be able to work with everyone whom God puts in our path. It's not a sin to have differences with our brothers and sisters in Christ. Having different points of view is not the same thing as having discord, just as refusing to talk to someone in the church isn't the same thing as fostering peace and unity. However, there may come a time when we're at such loggerheads with others that it warrants a separation from them, for the good of the ministry and for God's greater glory.

Paul and Barnabas came to that conclusion over their colleague, Mark, in terms of his place in their apostolic ministry (see Acts 15:39). The Church of Jesus Christ, whether the thought sits well with us or not, is stockpiled with abrasive, obstinate, and even ego-driven Christians. Sometimes these people are pastors; other times they're those who hurt pastors and their families, as well as other Christians.

My Fanatical, Regrettable Tour of Ministry

God may love them, but we'll find ourselves scrounging to even *like* them and digging really deep to even remain civil. Though the best resolution is always reconciliation, sometimes it's better for our spiritual health to break away from the Christians we have discord with, even if just for a time. It's a good thing that on Heaven's streets of gold, even our most defiant detractor will be perfect. Is that wonderful or what?

The harsh reality, however, is that we're not there yet. When fellowship between parties breaks down, as much as we long to cauterize the damage and keep it from infecting the greater Body of Christ, more than likely it will spread and spell a divided church. In the same way, a divided leadership can have such a trickle-down effect that it can part a congregation into camps like a comb divides hairs.

I once knew a guy who played house-league hockey. He told me that when he snapped on his helmet and pulled the visor shield down to go out on the ice, it was almost as if his mentality changed. His adrenaline began to flow, his heart pumped with a heightened, competitive beat, and his mindset became one of war. Likewise, entering the church boardroom with other leaders, sadly, can feel more like a battle than a peaceful business meeting. This is unfortunate. Positions of authority can bring out the best in God's people, but they can also reveal the worst. Some believers just switch into "power" mode when they're called upon to exert leadership, as if they're flicking down the shield of a helmet.

It's vital for broken relationships in the church to be mended, to the best of our abilities. As hard as it can be to see at times, relationships are always more important than being right. As Paul instructed the church in Rome, *"If it is possible, as far as it depends on you, live at peace with everyone"* (Romans 12:18). While this is God's standard for our lives, our sin can resist it and make the process difficult, if not impossible.

Wouldn't it be good for us to just admit to ourselves—and more importantly, to God—that sometimes we just don't want to make up with a certain person? Since maintaining relationships is far easier a task than mending them, it's best for us not to work too hard at fracturing to begin with. Joseph shouldn't have shared his dreams with his brothers, at least not with such zeal; Rehoboam shouldn't have treated the people who were loyal to his father's kingdom with such contempt; Peter should have been more careful with how he acted in front of the Gentile believers when he chose to exclude them.

Conflict amongst God's people is a given, but being able to patch up all dissension for the good of our testimony, in my experience, is not.

4. Keep doors of good communication open.

Broken relationships always affect the quality of our communication. That's why it's so important to work on relationships, so that we keep the lines open. However, when we're going through conflict with another person, communicating with them can be an arduous and debilitating endeavour, mentally.

I was once asked by a church leader why it was that he and I weren't communicating well. I responded to him by saying, "The door swings both ways." For any relationship to have good communication, there are no one-way attitudes allowed. My response to the leader's question acknowledged that perhaps one of us was waiting for the other to make the first move. If we're honest, though, the last thing we want when we're embattled and entrenched in personal conflict is to go out of our way to talk directly to the one we are at odds with.

Thankfully, God didn't create us with the ability to read each other's minds; that's why we need to communicate with each other! Nothing can take the place of face-to-face communication, however, especially if there are divisive issues that need to be worked out. When the person we're having discord with is sitting in front of us, we can hear their tone of voice, see their facial expressions, consider their body language, and benefit from how they immediately receive our words. We can't do those things if we try to patch up grievances via an impersonal, long-distance route. Let's not fool ourselves; firing off emails (which are too easy to hide behind), or getting a message across through a middleman, are ineffective modes of expressing one's thoughts and feelings. It may be more convenient and safe that way, but it resolves very little.

Communication is an important aspect for maintaining any relationship, for it is part and parcel of how we process life, whether that's in the context of marriage, the workplace, or leadership. If leaders and pastors expect their people to communicate effectively, they must set an example for their people to follow.

5. Shun unnecessary and demonic feelings of guilt.

Whenever I left a church feeling like I'd blown it, I could have pinpointed all the ways in which I could have handled certain situations more effectively. Pastors who take a sober view of their accountability before God care about the state of their leadership. I don't know too many pastors who wouldn't take to heart the brunt of people's criticisms towards them and their perceived failures. No pastor wants to carry the stigma of having come from a split church, but like many other pastors, it's something I have had to deal with. No pastor wants to carry a reputation for being a rogue. As pastors, we're good enough at beating ourselves up over the ministries we've had to leave under less than ideal circumstances; it's another spiritual battle altogether to have to contend with the relentless, satanic accusations that come whispering into our vulnerable minds, accusations which say, "You blew it! God's going to get you! You're so inadequate, it's not funny."

Paul gave the believers in Corinth some pointers as to how to wage war against powers that set themselves against God's truth. The apostle counselled them to *"take captive every thought to make it obedient to Christ"* (2 Corinthians 10:5). A lot of thoughts that come across our minds aren't good for us to hold on to; that's because they didn't originate from the throne of Heaven.

One of the saddest spiritual realties is when a believer suffers unnecessarily for past sins that have *already* been forgiven! When Satan accuses Christians, they tend to believe his prosecution of them more than they believe the vindicating power of God's Word to defend them. It's always God's perspective that counts, not the Devil's, or even others who think they have the goods on us. No one has more on us than the all-knowing, all-present God we worship and serve. If He can pardon us, we have no spiritual right to withhold forgiveness from ourselves. Satan doesn't want us to believe that.

Yes, we need to own up to our mistakes, but we must reject the Devil when he comes to convince us to take all the credit for the problems in our churches. We need to discipline ourselves to resist Satan's attacks. Every person, in every area of conflict, has to take a certain amount of responsibility. Rarely are any of us a hundred percent innocent in matters of personal conflict. When disputes, complaints, and political battles arise in the church, everyone—including the pastor—needs to humbly put themselves at the merciful steps of Heaven's throne. Not only do we receive mercy and find grace there in our time of need (see Hebrews 4:16), but we can also do some prayerful introspection about our motives, and what actions we should take to remedy the situation.

6. Surround yourself with caring people.

It is a good idea for pastors to have a buddy system, a support circle of trusted and experienced people who allow them to be who they are. I have appreciated having such people around me, people who let me sound off without reprimanding me or trying to convict me if my comments aren't exactly politically correct.

All leaders, no matter how many people they lead or at what level of leadership they lead from, need to keep themselves surrounded by people who lead them in return. The longer a pastor remains in ministry, the greater the chances that he or she will experience a form of burnout. Pastors enter into different phases of effectiveness which can drain their resolve. Perhaps some leaders can't detect when they move from the zealot stage, to the irritable stage, to the withdrawal stage, to the unfortunate zombie stage. Third-party observer buddies can.

Leaders will not benefit from surrounding themselves with "yes" people, but they do need people around them who love and care for them enough to covenant with them in prayer, who have enough of the pastor's ear to be able to tell them "no" if they see them going down a bad road.

7. God can still use a wounded servant.

The more we learn to see the spiritual value in the hurts God allows to flow into our lives as Christians, the more we'll be able to develop perseverance as servants of God. Our pilgrimage of faith on this earth may be a long one, and may involve us unknowingly stepping on more than a few ministry explosives, that will inevitably lead to suffering. Fair or not, there's a certain expectation placed upon pastors that calls for them to spiritually endure the harsh gales of church trials. Pastors are called to motivate their people by encouraging them to live for Christ.

Someone once said that God cannot use someone mightily unless He has hurt them greatly. A profound statement such as that really hits too close to home for me. I don't know if I've been used mightily by God yet, but I do know He has allowed me to be hurt greatly. To my own spiritual detriment, I regret that I've often permitted the echoes of my futility in pastoral ministry to bounce around in my mind.

However, there are unappreciated silver linings which come to us in the form of milestones, which God builds into our ministry missteps. I'm a far better and more effective pastor now than I was when I started out in ministry some fifteen years ago. That should be a given, yet I attribute a lot of my maturity to my failures, and to how God has taught me by them. As the saying goes, sometimes you need to learn how to lose before you can learn what it takes to win. A lot of my growth as a Christian, not to mention as a pastor in the ministry, has come via the vein of suffering I've experienced. It has taken many setbacks and heartaches for me to appreciate how I view the pastoral role today.

My Fanatical, Regrettable Tour of Ministry

Our churches are filled with ministers and other leaders who have been through the proverbial wringer. If they remain humble and godly in their ministries, despite their trials, I believe they deserve our utmost respect. Give me a pastor to lead me who has been through tough trials *any day* over the pastor who has never experienced much in the way of opposition and hardship. That's not meant to disrespect those ministers who've had relatively pain-free runs, but a wounded servant can perhaps more acutely empathize with those who intensely hurt, who seek an understanding ear when they come to their pastor for counsel.

Being able to commiserate with the desperate and depressed is almost as crucial as being able to impart to them sound biblical counsel. If we allow Him to, God can still use those of us who have been through trying and emotionally debilitating ministries. In the final analysis, God will always be greater than our mistakes and perceived failures. In God's economy, the good and the bad work *"for the good of those who love him, who have been called according to his purpose"* (Romans 8:28).

Keep in mind that the scriptures are packed with examples of those people whom God commissioned to fulfill assignments, to lead His people who flunked a ministry lesson now and again. Others may have seen them as compromised and weak, but God deemed them as Heaven's choice. We could point to embattled leaders such as Moses, who was given the leash to lead a nation that would have delighted in totally running roughshod over him. At every turn, it seemed as though the Israelites had their thumbs out for the nearest caravan to take them back to Egypt. I'm convinced that if Moses (a great but imperfect leader) had lived longer, God would have set him up for another assignment.

Then there's the prophet Jeremiah, who wasn't taken all that seriously by his own people. With all the mishaps and trials he endured in his years of ministry (some extremely detrimental), Jeremiah's prophetic ministry continued, as God enabled it to. Paul is another fine example of a leader whom God used incredibly, in spite of the brutal forms of persecution that befell him, administered by the hands of God's own people; Paul's suffering was so intense at times that the apostle even despaired of living (see 2 Corinthians 1:8).

Being hurt does not render a servant useless to God. In fact, the longer pastors lead, the more they realize that it's the heat of ministry's circumstances that acts as the anvil God uses to cool us down, to round off our rough spots, and to shape us into the instruments He desires us to be. Paul knew the simple truth that the Lord will bring to completion all the good work He began in us when He saved us and called us (see Philippians 1:6).

8. Even when you think you've prayed enough, keep praying.

This point should be academic, shouldn't it? However, how many of us really commit to praying for some significant decision or need long enough for God to grant us the direction we desire? We impatiently jump ahead in our lives, sometimes by leaping over prayers that were actually meant to hem us in and hold us back from making bad moves and ill-advised decisions. God, however, never forgets a petition.

Oftentimes, He purposes to do more *in us* by having us wait on Him. Jesus, the greatest shepherd of them all, knew this and quite literally spent *hours* in prayer. In certain life situations, such as looking for a job, we must make practical, proactive moves *even* as we pray. My first ever pastor, whom you read about earlier in this book (Pastor Andrews), used to advise me to tell God what I was planning on doing in a particular circumstance, even though He already knew about it.

Pastor Andrews' counsel was designed to help me wrap my mind around what it looked like to balance action with faith in God. There are times when leaders need to make appropriate moves simultaneous with prayer, just as there are times when nothing but total inactivity and submission is required before they act. At times in my ministry life, I would have benefitted from praying further about certain issues before taking action. I have always found John Wesley's view of prayer challenging, in that God does everything by prayer, which consequently meant for Wesley that God did nothing without it. Too often, believers view prayer as a sedentary exercise more than as a productive discipline which eventually propels us towards God's desired end for us. Prayer is qualitatively and quantifiably the absolute *best* vehicle to take us to the place where God reveals His will and His best path for us. A praying leader is a leader who really believes he or she doesn't have what it takes to lead! The problem is that our self-confidence and self-reliance can get in the way.

It not only takes faith to bring us to prayer; it takes humble self-awareness to keep us there. We have a constant, habitual need to be in God's presence. It's like the age-old question that asks, "How much Bible reading is *enough* Bible reading?" The answer, of course, is that you can never get enough of God's Word. Likewise, we can never pray enough about a given situation, unless we sense God has spoken and directed us. At the same time, that doesn't always mean that we should never make a move unless we directly "hear" from God, for oftentimes we *will* get His silence in return for our prayers. We can pray, but God may want us to make our move anyway, then trust Him with the results of our choices. There's an element of prayer, when we interface with God in that secret place and lay our lives before Him, that is a mystery.

We might even struggle so much in prayer that we come to wonder, "Does it change anything at all?" We shouldn't be surprised if God takes His good time answering our inquiries, or lets us linger long in pursuit of Him. Who can figure God out? I'll bet the Christian theologian John Chrysostom, in the fifth century, felt that same way when he said, "A comprehended God is no God."[8] Nonetheless, we are invited by God in scripture to petition Him continuously, to wait on Him and persist in that way. It may not change our circumstances, but it will change us. Perseverance, after all, should be the marquee of our faith as believers. If we falter and give up in prayer too soon, what will we gain of any lasting spiritual worth?

9. Plant a church!

My days of futilely attempting to change a church are long over. We set young pastors up to fail in their ministries if we don't adequately educate them about the inherent complexities (even spiritual dangers) in trying to manage change, especially in older, more established churches. Leaders do more harm than any lasting good if they enter the pastor's office on day one thinking they know how to get the job done, how to get a church moving. The problem with that mindset is that they're not the only ones who think that way; the people they are leading feel the same way! That's why I propose that young pastors who take on older churches, as self-professed agents of change show their church board the classic 1945 movie *Going My Way*, starring Bing Crosby. In the film, Crosby (Father O'Malley) comes to a new parish under the auspices of assisting the head priest, who was still deeply engrossed in the ministry, even though he was an aging "yesterday's man."

In reality, Father O'Malley turns out to be the desired successor for the church, the man to help turn around its dying fortunes. Crosby's character goes about changing the mindset of the church's ministry philosophy through creative, albeit controversial and provocative, means. Inevitably, a conflict of ideals arises between the two priests; one sees ministry through a more relational and religiously scaled-down lens, while the other sees it through traditional idealism. In many ways, the principles of change management interwoven in the film depict the kind of power struggles that are at the heart of a lot of church splits—the struggle between those in the church who want the "new wine" and those who prefer the comfortable confines of the "old wineskins."

Ron Mahler

It's a tricky, high-stakes venture for a pastor to attempt introducing a new vision for ministry into an existing environment where the people may think nothing is wrong. That's why we might want to consider an alternative plan: church planting! A popular and often proven theory is that the best way to do ministry in new and perceptively relevant ways is not by trying to remodel or reinvent an existing church culture, but by starting a new one. Having said that, the task of planting and growing a new church is not an easy one. Church plants are what they are; they require all the spiritual parallels of water, sun, and good soil in order to grow and develop to the point where people who don't know the Lord can come and settle on their branches (see Matthew 13:32).

Currently, I pastor a planted church, which I touch on briefly in the epilogue. Though there are days when I long to once again have the benefits of a building, and to get around the whole church-in-a-box operation, I find myself not as covetous for the perks of a well-oiled, polished ministry as I thought I might be at this stage in my life. Whether a church is old or new, it possesses its own unique strengths and advantages, no matter what the expression of worship is on Sunday morning. For those who desire to do ministry in non-traditional ways, church planting may be the right way to go.

10. Be known for forgiveness, not bitterness.

If there's a more vitally important spiritual component to an effective ministry than forgiveness, I have yet to see it. Absolutely no church will benefit from a leader's ministry if they harbour bitterness and unforgiveness in their hearts. In the wake of the Heath High School shootings in West Paducah, Kentucky some years ago, a group of Christian students offered what was interpreted as "immediate" or "automatic" forgiveness. The bodies of three teenage girls were not yet cold when the Christian students announced, "We forgive you, Mike (Michael Carneal)." However, a debate arose in some Christian circles as to whether or not it was the right way for those young believers to react to the horrendous event. Should they have so freely forgiven the gunman who had opened fire on their prayer group, killing three friends and wounding five others?

Personally, I don't know why the matter was even a debate in the first place. The Christ-like attitude of those students, whose friends' lives were snuffed out in a heartless second, was exemplary. Their attitudes were a tribute to our crucified Lord's own utterances on the cross, *"Father, forgive them…"* (Luke 23:34) The Christian students at Heath High School were merely mirroring

My Fanatical, Regrettable Tour of Ministry

the Saviour's expectations of them, to forgive those who sin against them (see Luke 11:4).

It's never too early or too late in life to do the right thing; sometimes the right thing is forgiving others for the things they've done to us, whether we feel like it or not. Whenever we read the gospels, we are hard-pressed to get very far before meeting up with someone harassing the Lord. Sure, we could attribute that to the hard-heartedness of sin in the people's unbelieving lives, but there was another factor in play: Jesus had a Devil-sized bull's eye on His back. That sums up the life and times of Jesus—despised, rejected, even vilified. However, by the same token, we can't get very far in the gospels without reading of Jesus performing some loving act. The Lord didn't allow the offenses that were inflicted upon Him to take Him off His ministry game. Though He was perfect and without sin, as the pre-incarnate Son of God, the book of Hebrews tells us that He was *"tempted in every way, just as we are"* (Hebrews 4:15).

If we think Jesus wasn't affected by the snide remarks and cutting criticism He received, we might as well believe that He was just doing theatre, as it were, that it was somehow all an act. Pain and hardship irreverently stuck to our Lord, but it was how He handled it that convicts us who have difficulty forgiving others. When Peter asked Jesus how many times he needs to forgive someone, the Lord is clear: *"I tell you, not seven times, but seventy-seven times"* (Matthew 18:22). In other words, Jesus said that we are to forgive those who have hurt us in life, as often as necessary. That goes for pastors, too!

How can we not heed such a statement, considering whose mouth spoke the words? What about those people who won't admit that they hurt us? What about those people who only offer us a shallow, token apology? I'm convinced that at some point, no matter how we have been hurt or by whom, we must put it in God's hands and move on. Even though I've had more than my desired share of contention with God's people, Jesus' command leaves me no loophole; bearing grudges or carrying unforgiveness in my heart is never an option.

Forgiving those in our churches who have wounded us greatly, as hard as that can be, doesn't render what they did to us any less significant. Though forgiveness may not come automatically or immediately, a time must come when we finally do forgive. It takes us off the hook with God, and puts the onus back on those who hurt us. It's one thing to have to lead a group of fellow believers when the leading isn't easy, but it's quite another to lead by denying others a basic tenet of our faith. If we're known for having been hurt, we will glorify God by also being known for our forgiveness.

Ron Mahler

11. Get used to a little loneliness.

My sister Linda once told me that when she was a young girl (before my birth), she sometimes got so lonely that she would wish that Snap, Crackle, and Pop on the Rice Crispies cereal box, could come to life and play with her. My sister's admission of desperate childhood loneliness has stuck with me. I've always thought that the last thing a child should ever be is lonely. There's just something not right about that, yet life can get harder in terms of loneliness as we get older.

When my kids were a bit younger, I had nicknames for them. The names I assigned applied to some aspect of their nature. Our daughter Cassidy liked playing with water, sticks, and flowers as the brightness of the summer sun bounced off her golden locks. This led me to call her "Water Willow." Our son Dakota had an iron grip as a toddler, which earned him the name, "Little Bear Claw." It was fitting for him, as he remains an outdoorsy youngster who loves to make his own fun by roaming hills and climbing trees. However, like all children, our kids periodically complain that they're bored—or even lonely.

Sure enough, boredom and loneliness can seem like they're part of the same, mundane family, yet there's something about human loneliness that sets it apart from boredom. Loneliness craves for *interaction with someone*, where boredom craves more for *something to do*. There are no socioeconomic barriers to loneliness or boredom. The rich and famous, as well as the poverty-stricken and outcast, all experience tangible feelings of loneliness and boredom.

Loneliness is a universal reality and is no respecter of persons or occupations. Even when we have something to do, we can be lonely. That's why acute loneliness often stalks those who are God's shepherds, even as they find themselves enveloped by a constant chorus of appointments, meetings, and other daily commitments that bring them into constant contact with people. Perhaps there are times when we choose to be loners. Pastoral lone rangers and hermits populate the ministry.

Despite that reality, I believe every pastor needs someone to be around them, if for no other reason than just to make them feel human. We were created by God to live in community, and so we can only fully realize the full potential of our humanness when we engage other human beings. Adam found that to be true when no animal brought before him could satisfy his longing. Adam craved the relationship of another human (Eve).

Dr. David Jeremiah, in his book *Living with Confidence in a Chaotic World*, discusses the hunger people have in our current age of radical individualism, to still experience genuine community. He writes, "It's possible to have three hundred 'connections' on Facebook, two hundred [people] 'following' you on Twitter, and still feel as if no one really knows you at all."[9] How profoundly true that can be, even in the pastoral role!

After a few years in full-time ministry, the spectre of loneliness was a bit of a phantom to me. *How can anyone be lonely in ministry?* I used to think. Then I bombed in three consecutive ministries, and only then did I fully come to appreciate how quickly the road of ministry can become riddled with potholes of loneliness. However, it doesn't just take a bad ministry experience to be awakened to the realities of loneliness in the pastorate. Who is there for the pastor when they need someone to minister to them? Who is there when they have floundered in the pulpit, when they have experienced that late-night call that a congregant has taken their own life, or when they encounter more criticism every morning than cups of hot coffee?

I used to be perplexed at why I often felt a letdown on Sunday afternoons, even after preaching a bang-up sermon. Over the years, I've found that even though I might have had plenty of interaction with people on a given Sunday morning, I would consistently arrive at a lonely place later that afternoon. Whether it's spending significant time listening to hurting people rehash their predicaments or holding the hand of the gravely ill in hospital, it has often been commonplace for me to return home in a slightly depressed haze.

Psychologists will tell you that there is such a condition as "compassion fatigue." Any pastor worth his or her salt will agree with that. The often underestimated, yet harsh reality of ministering to others, especially when the minister is already under stress, is that it takes something out of the minister, something that needs to be replenished. Being ministry-weary can lead to a loneliness which only another minister can really identify with. As pastors, we see our own images reflected upon the mirrors of each other's ministry experiences. A pastor friend of mine who is currently working on a doctorate once told me that for the first time in over twenty-five years of ministry, he can now truly sit back and be ministered to and fed.

The Bible says that the greatest pastor ever to walk the earth lived and ministered under a shroud of loneliness. That reality should tell us that we who minister in the church ought to expect some degree of loneliness. It's part and parcel of the role. The world is filled with people, yet it can be an awfully lonely place at times. Personally, I have performed many more funerals than weddings, but I've observed that genuine loneliness can affect both occasions, specifically in the secular realm, where the pastor is surrounded by the unchurched.

Ron Mahler

On such occasions, I have all too often felt segregated as the minister and denied meaningful conversation, whether it was amongst the celebrants of weddings or the mourners of funerals. Talk about feeling alone in a crowd! It's like I had a terminal case of religious cooties, that if people engaged too much with me it might spread to them. Perhaps it's just me, but there must be something about when a pastor says hello to some non-churchgoing individual that strikes a kind of heavenly horror in them. Whatever the reason for some of the peculiar reactions I have received, I've often walked away feeling diminished and discarded in my role as a pastor. In most Hollywood wedding scenes, it's uncanny how many ministers or priests are portrayed as being wimpy, dorky, old-fashioned, or relegated to resembling a kind of wallflower. In some instances, I've actually experienced people physically avoid having to walk by me in a line.

It can be humorous at times to observe how people react to the presence of a minister. On some occasions, I have gone to hospitals for visitations and had people stare warily and uncomfortably at the Bible tucked under my arms, as if it were a weapon I was going to whip out and shoot them with. Those who observe pastors, from a secular standpoint, can make us feel like we're aliens, as though we cannot see the *three eyes* bulging on our foreheads or the grotesque tentacles protruding from our heads. People outside the church want us to perform ministry tasks for them, but they sometimes act like they'd rather us not be there.

Are pastors mere figureheads who stir their conscience, reminding them of their accountability before God? Is the presence of a pastor an embodiment to them of everything they can't stand about the church? Do they think we are predictably religious—boring and too heavenly-minded? Is it the whole spiritual dynamic of light penetrating darkness? The pastoral role can conjure up feelings of tangible loneliness, and even leave the one who ministers feeling unappreciated and insignificant as a person. That's why when I'm out with Elaine at some social function, the last thing I want people I'm meeting for the first time to know about me is what I do for a living. It has been my experience that people usually change how they talk and act around me when they make the discovery that I'm a man of the cloth.

All I know is that when I'm among the unchurched, though it is good for me as a Christian to be in that spiritual dynamic, as a fisher of men and friend of sinners, I often feel loneliness set in just the same. Every seminary on God's green earth must alert aspiring pastors that the perception of occupational loneliness in the pastorate is no myth, and that they'd better get used to it.

12. At all times, keep at least one eye on the spiritually lost.

Jesus called us not to a good commission, but to a Great Commission! Pastors and other church leaders who have a real, heart-thumping burden for evangelism, though it's not solely their responsibility, must lead the church's charge into the community so that the spiritually lost, and those distant from God, can get into the church!

To me, great leaders should have Paul-like hearts. The apostle Paul had one great goal in life, and if he were still around today, he'd have it written on his shirt or plastered on his car: "To know Christ and make Him known." Many churches have a variation of that saying in their mission statements, but Paul had it first in his heart, and because of that he made it a priority in his pastoral leadership.

If we want a fish dinner, no amount of wishing will get a piece of cod or trout on our plate; we have to go buy it, or fish for it! The same goes for Christian evangelism. Pastors sometimes lead their best when they lead their churches to the markets and lakes of their communities—in pursuit of Kingdom fish.

Evangelism, whether it is employed as part of a corporate church activity (outreach) or modeled and encouraged by pastors, is the compulsory task of every church. Indeed, what kind of disciples are we if we lose sight of evangelism, which is what distinguishes the church in the first place? The problem with divisions in the church is that it causes God's people to take their eyes off their commission. Putting out fires in the church is a smoky business, which can cloud the real business that God's people need to be going about: evangelism.

EPILOGUE

Future Hope

AFTER ALMOST TWO YEARS (FROM 2005 TO EARLY 2007), THOUGH I STILL ministered in various capacities in the church, I did some soul-searching rehab, in which I exhausted every pity party God allotted me to hold for myself, He helped me to find a way to yet again embrace His call on my life to be a pastor to His people. I would learn to love the church again, and to appreciate what a privilege it is to serve the Kings of Kings and Lord of Lords. At a time when my appetite to continue in the pastorate again reached peak levels, God came calling.

In the spring of 2007, Elaine and I returned to our roots by joining a contingent of other Christians in the planting of a new church. I have had the privilege of leading Highland Lakes Community Church for more than four glorious years now. Though the ministry is still in its infant stages, and it possesses all the challenges that come with a church plant, it's been the most rewarding ministry I have ever been involved in.

I continue to learn and relearn valuable leadership lessons. Dare I say, I think I'm even getting more acclimated to this thing called pastoral ministry! In the spirit of the great protestant reformer, Martin Luther, I too resolve to admit that I am, and should be, in constant process as a Christian leader. In fact, I have resolved to give myself permission now and again to say, "I am God's gift to the church!" (see Ephesians 4:8, 11)

Medical professionals say one thing that's so surprising about the human body is not what kills us, but what we can survive. It is a strange reality at times that I am still doing the very thing that, in all honesty, has caused me the greatest heartaches over the last fifteen years. As a result of having been through more than just a few conflicts, I struggle with heightened forms of anxiety today. Why should this be a shock to anyone? If military figures come back home with post-traumatic stress disorder, it is possible that such a condition could strike anyone in any occupation, including those in ministry, who have been through a great number of trials, and who have seen, felt, and heard things that affected them emotionally and psychologically.

That's the core of some of my regrets in having served God as a pastor, even if I remain fanatical about the effects godly ministers can have on the people they minister to. The fact that Elaine and I are still trucking along in ministry, that the tour continues and we're still able and willing to endure its hiccups and disappointments, is a testament to the unfathomable grace of God. We can still function, still dream, still sacrifice, and still believe that the church is the greatest of all organizations and organisms. We really do worship a great God! For longer than I'd like to admit, much of my self-esteem and identity as a man and leader has been tied up in how I performed in ministry. I still grapple with that gorilla-sized lie from time to time. What I'm left with today, however, despite my bumpy road, is love and gratitude for the church, and an eternal burden to see its influence in society progress.

I am also thankful that God still wills to use me to shepherd His people, something that says more about Him than it will ever say about me. Ministry is a calling that has oftentimes been far from predictable, and it hasn't always led me to interpret my labours for God as having been fruitful. It's hard for pastors to sense that they're growing in their giftedness and pastoral role when one month they could be preaching a sermon to a big congregation, and the next month find themselves unemployed and willing to clean eaves troughs or shovel snow just to make some money for their family. I have been there—a few times. It's entirely possible for ministries to raise up those who minister to the spiritual thresholds of a Heaven-like euphoria as quickly as they can plunge them into the deepest spiritual regions of a desert-like wilderness.

However, if there's one thing about the ministry that I have embraced and accepted, it is that things are rarely always as bad as they seem, nor are they usually as good as they appear. Pastoral ministry is a call to live in the middle of our expectations, where realism and optimism must be balanced—not the extremes. If I hadn't already been broken in throughout my short life prior to entering the ministry, life as a pastor has definitely done the trick! All things considered, my hope is that, through all the hardships that have come to colour my ministry life, I have become more like Christ. Some days I'm convinced of it; other days I'm convicted otherwise. Experience and wisdom are wonderful things, yet the way we acquire them sets the stage for lives which we hope will glorify God.

My story may be a foreign one to many Christians, and perhaps even to some pastors. What you've read might have been hazardous to your spiritual perceptions about the church. Though I can't show you visuals of my battle scars on these pages, no doubt you have spotted them branded on my words. To me, pastoral ministry is the most complex of all occupations. Those men and women who are entrusted with caring for the souls of God's people have a higher accountability before God. When pastors are in conflict with the very people they are charged by God to shepherd, it cuts grievously deep within their heart and soul.

Some form of theological education and training are absolutely necessary to prepare one for the ministry, yet nothing can thoroughly alert a prospective pastor to the reams of challenges that await them as church leaders; if it could, I wonder whether we would have enough willing students to train for the ministry, to shepherd our churches. Whether pastors such as me like it or not, the altruistic views of the role we hold so dearly get weeded out over time in the churches we are called to.

Nonetheless, pastoral ministry is a calling that I became completely enamoured of. It is a call on my life that has taught me much about myself and the human condition. Most of all, it has taught me much about the great God we all serve as Christians.

Endnotes

1. *The Oxford Dictionary of Current English* (New York, NY: Oxford University Press, 1992), p. 660.

2. Bloesch, Donald G. *Essentials of Evangelical Theology, Volume 1: God, Authority, & Salvation* (Peabody, ME: Prince Press, 1998), p. 150.

3. John T. McNeill, ed, Ford Lewis Battles, trans. *Institutes of the Christian Religion* (Philadelphia, Westminster: Library of Christian Classics, 1960), IV.xvii.2. Originally published in 1559.

4. Prime, Derek & Alistair Begg. *On Being a Pastor: Understanding Our Calling and Work* (Chicago, IL: Moody Publishers, 2004), p. 19. From the revised and expanded edition.

5. London, Jr., H.B. & Neil B. Wiseman. *They Call Me Pastor: How To Love The Ones You Lead* (Ventura, CA: Regal Books, 2000), pp. 21, 24.

6. Stanley, Andy & Reggie Joiner & Lane Jones. *Seven Practices of Effective Ministry* (Sisters, OR: Multnomah Publishers, 2004), pp. 104–105.

7. London, Jr., H.B. and Neil B. Wiseman. *Pastors at Greater Risk* (Ventura, CA: Regal Books, 2003), p. 38.

8. Ross, David. *1001 Pearls of Wisdom, Wit, and Insight to Enlighten and Inspire* (London, UK: Duncan Baird, 2006), quote 151.

9. Jeremiah, Dr. David. *Living with Confidence in a Chaotic World: What on Earth Should We Do Now?* (Nashville, TN: Thomas Nelson, 2009), p. 54.

www.ingramcontent.com/pod-product-compliance
Lightning Source LLC
Chambersburg PA
CBHW050553170426
43201CB00011B/1680